12

Bibliography of United States Government Bibliographies 1968-1973

A Bibliography of United States Government Bibliographies 1968-1973

by

Roberta A. Scull

Assistant Librarian
Louisiana State University

Pierian Press
ANN ARBOR, MICHIGAN
1975

International Standard Book Number 0-87650-055-6
Library of Congress Catalog Card Number 75-4281

Pierian Press, P.O. Box 1808, Ann Arbor, Michigan 48106
Printed in the United States of America

PURCHASE & AVAILABILITY CODES

*	U.S. Government Printing Office
**	Limited use. Not generally available
****	Available from issuing agency
NTIS	National Technical Information Service

For further information see Appendix A

Contents

Introduction

As the world's largest publisher, the United States government annually produces hundreds of bibliographies which are considered vital to the needs of the many and varied federal agencies and offices or the public they serve. *Bibliography of United States Government Bibliographies 1968--1973* contains approximately 1250 of these federally produced bibliographies.

These bibliographies cover a wide range of topics, include government and non--government publications, and may be of interest to almost anyone from an astronomer to a woodsman.

Until the last few years very little had been done to coordinate and relate to the public the vast amount of reference and research material compiled, written, published, and distributed by the federal government. In the late sixties and early seventies the library world was awakened to the worth of United States government publications through such works as:

> Body, Alexander C. *Annotated Bibliography of Biblio--graphies on Selected Government Publications and Supplementary Guides to the Superintendent of Documents System.* Kalamazoo, Michigan: Western Michigan University, 1967; Suppl. 1, 1968; Suppl. 2, 1970; Supp. 3, 1973.

> Hoover, Jimmie H. "Government Reference Publications," *Reference Services Review.* Quarterly review column since Vol. 1, no. 4 (Oct.--Dec. 1973--).

> Morehead, Joe H. "U.S. Government Documents: A Maze--way Miscellany," *RQ.* Quarterly review column since Spring 1968.

> O'Hara, Frederick J. "Selected Government Publications," *Wilson Library Bulletin.* Monthly review column from March 1969--December 1973.

> O'Hara, Frederick J. "Government Serials and Services," *Reference Services Review.* Quarterly review column since Vol. 2, no. 1 (Jan.--March 1974--).

Pohle, L. *A Guide to Popular Government Publications: For Libraries and Home Reference.* Littleton, Colo.: Libraries Unlimited, 1972.

White, A.S. *Thirty Million Books in Stock: Everyone's Guide to U.S. Government Publications.* Allenhurst, N.J.: Aurea, 1969.

Wynkoop, Sally. *Government Reference Books 68/69: A Biennial Guide to U.S. Government Publications.* Littleton, Colo.: Libraries Unlimited, 1970.

Wynkoop, Sally. *Government Reference Books 70/71: A Biennial Guide to U.S. Government Publications.* Littleton, Colo.: Libraries Unlimited, 1972.

Alexander Body's work, mentioned above, and its three sup--plements cover from 1956 through 1971. Because of their highly selective nature these bibliographies provide only a representative sampling of the many federally published bibliographies. Hence, has come the need for a much more comprehensive listing of federal bibliographies.

This particular work was begun in 1971 as an annual informational publication primarily intended for Louisiana State University faculty. It was subsequently distributed to public, college and university, and special libraries served by the Louisiana State University Regional Depository for Government Publications. After the listing of "Bibliography of United States Government Publications, 1971" in the *Monthly Checklist of State Publications,* it was requested nationally, and the need was seen for a cumulative edition of United States government bibliographies. 1968 was selected as the beginning date because publications older than that would be hard to purchase or maybe even borrow, the relevancy of the material covered might be too dated, and a period of more than six years was just too much for one person to assimilate in as comprehensive a form as is attempted in this bibliography.

The *Monthly Catalog of Government Publications* was the primary index searched in identifying and locating the bibliographies included in this work. Other sources searched were the *Congressional Information Service Annuals, Government Reference Books 68/69* and *70/71* edited by Sally Wynkoop, *Government Reports Announcements, Nuclear Science Abstracts,* and *Scientific and Technical Aerospace Reports.* While an attempt was made at complete coverage of bibliographies mentioned in the *Monthly Catalog* from 1968 through May 1974, no effort was made to include all bibliographies listed in *Government Reports Announcements, Nuclear Science Abstracts,* or *Scientific and Technical Aerospace Reports* because comprehensive coverage of these three indexes could not be undertaken short of a computer search.

The entries, most of which are annotated, are listed according to primary subject and thereafter arranged alphabetically by corporate author. Full bibliographic information is given for each entry as well as Library of Congress card number, Superintendent of Documents Classification number, and price and availability, when known. Because of the completeness of information provided, it should be possible to borrow or photocopy through interlibrary loan from a cooperating Regional Depository most of the bibliographies listed. (All Regional Depositories for U.S. Government Publications should have all of the bibliographies which are indicated as being available from the Government Printing Office.)

A comprehensive index directs the user to specific bibliographies. Titles are included in the index only if they are distinctive or can be used in place of a subject.

I would like to express my deep appreciation to my friend and colleague Jimmie H. Hoover for encouraging me to compile this bibliography and to my husband "Bo" for bearing with me during its many long months of preparation.

AGRICULTURAL SCIENCES

General

1. U.S. Dept. of Agriculture. *Color Filmstrips and Slide Sets of the United States Department of Agriculture.* Revised. 1970. 13pp. $.20*** (USDA Miscellaneous Publication 1107).
   Filmstrips and slides listed are available on loan from the USDA.

2. U.S. Dept. of Agriculture. Information Office. *Bimonthly list of Publications and Visuals.* Free*** L.C. card Agr 9--1414.
   A21.6/5:date

3. U.S. Dept. of Agriculture. Information Office. *List of Available Publications of the United States Department of Agriculture;* compiled by Mattie W. Johnson. 1971. ii + 87pp. $.45*. S/N 0103--0002.
   This list gives the publications of the USDA available as of July 1971. Publications cover all aspects of agriculture from agricultural economics and engineering to forestry and fire pre-vention. Information is provided on how to obtain free and purchase publications.
   A21.9/8:11/8

4. U.S. Economic Research Service. *Checklist of Reports Issued by the Economic Research Service and Statistical Reporting Service.* *** Monthly. (AE--CL series).
   A1.97:nos

5. U.S. Economic Research Service. *Economics of Agriculture, Reports and Publications Issued or Sponsored by USDA's Economic Research Service, Supp. 3, July 1970 – June 1971.* 1971. vi + 19***. (ERS no. 368).
   Listed are citations to all published material of more than temporary interest which were done by the ERS. Publications are grouped by subject areas and by ERS divisions responsible for research in such areas.
   A93.21:368

6. U.S. Government Printing Office. *Farm Management, Foreign Agriculture, Rural Electrification, Agricultural Marketing.* Free* (Price List no. 68).
   Listed are free and for sale publications dealing with the topics mentioned in the title. This list is revised frequently, and all publications listed are supposedly available.

GP3.9:68

7. U.S. Government Printing Office. *Home Economics: Foods and Cooking.* Free* (Price List no. 11).
Listed are selected for sale and free publications on home economics, food, and cooking. This list is revised frequently, prices are updated, and all publications listed are currently available from the GPO.
GP3.9:11

8. U.S. National Agricultural Library. *Available Bibliographies and Lists.* Revised edition. 1968. 2pp. Free*** (Library List no. 25). L.C. card AGR46--109.
Listed are bibliographies and lists of publications which are currently available from the USDA Library.
A17.17:25/13

9. U.S. National Agricultural Library. *Bibliography of Agriculture.* Monthly. Vol. 1 --. 1942 --.
Published commercially since 1970, this former government publication is the foremost index in the agricultural sciences. It is international in scope and covers virtually every agricultural topic conceivable, whether political, popular, or scientific.
A17.18:Vol./no.

10. U.S. National Agricultural Library. *Drainage of Agricultural Land, Annotated Bibliography of Selected References, 1956–1964.* 1968. 524pp.*** (Library List no. 91). L.C. card Agr68--287.
Over 2800 references up–date USDA Miscellaneous Publication no. 713, *Drainage of Agricultural Land,* published in 1956. This should prove to be a useful source book for "those interested in drainage and its many aspects such as history, economics, needs, designs, applications, use, and problems." A subject index facilitates its use.
A17.17:91

11. U.S. National Agricultural Library. *Serial Publications Indexed in the Bibliography of Agriculture.* Revised edition. 1968. [1] + 94pp. Free*** (Library List no. 75). L.C. card Agr63–209.
This is an alphabetical listing of the serials, foreign and domestic, indexed by the *Bibliography of Agriculture.*
A17.17:75/4

12. U.S. Rural Electrification Administration. *Current REA Publications*

in the Rural Electrification Program, Additions, Index, Numerical List, etc., as of Dec. 31, 1968. 1969. 36pp***.
A68.3:Ind/969--2

Diet, Food, and Nutrition

13. U.S. Agricultural Research Service. *Bibliography and Abstracts on Poultry and Egg Research in Western Marketing and Nutrition Research Division, 1950--1970.* [2] + 50 pp.*** (ARS 74--59).
   Entries are listed according to the following classifications: Poultry Tenderness; Poultry Flavor; Poultry Processing and Storage; Byproducts; Egg Processing; Egg Composition; Prepared Products; and Microbiology. An author index follows.
   A77.15:74--59

13a. U.S. Agricultural Research Service. *Bibliography of Research on the Utilization of Rice in the Western Marketing and Nutrition Research Division, 1957--70;* by D.F. Houston. 1971. 29pp.*** (ARS series, no. 74--58).
   Entries are listed chronologically within subject groups which cover various aspects of rice utilization from rice byproducts to the storage, drying and milling of rice. Patent--abstracts on the processing and preparation of rice are listed.
   A77.15:74--58

14. U.S. Agricultural Research Service. *Food Makes the Difference, List of References.* 1969. 7pp. $.10*.
   This is a selected list of free and inexpensive publications, slide sets, and other information which would be helpful to those working for better nutrition in people with limited incomes.
   A77.714:F73

15. U.S. Agricultural Research Service. *Selected References on Cereal Grains in Protein Nutrition: Human and Experimental Animal Studies of Major and Minor Cereals, 1910--66;* by Callie Mae Coons. [1968.] [2] + 150pp. Free*** (ARS Series no. 61--5).
   Approximately 1500 references give the results of human and animal studies conducted to determine the nutritional value of cereal grains.
   A77.15:61--5

16. U.S. Atomic Energy Commission. *Bibliography on Centralized Processing of Fresh Meat and Poultry, Including Radiation Pasteurization (updated);* prepared by W.M. Urbain and others. 1972. v + 72pp. NTIS. (TID--25998).
   Y3.At7:22/TID--25998

3

17. U.S. Economic Research Service. *Economics of Sweetner Marketing; an Annotated Bibliography of Selected References;* compiled by L.C. Larkin. 1972. vi + 72pp.*** (ERS--474).

The articles and books listed cover all aspects of sugar and the sugar industry. Information is general as well as specific and concentrates on such topics as: Sugar History; Types of Sugar; Honey and Syrups; and Non--caloric Sweetners.

A93.21:474

18. U.S. National Agricultural Library. *Catalog: Food and Nutrition Information and Educational Materials Center.* 1973. 286pp. Free*** L.C. Card 73–602294.

"Documents, articles, and audiovisual aids of substantial interest to the school food service and nutrition education community are selected for inclusion into the *Catalog.* To further aid the user in selecting materials of interest, each document selected for inclusion . . . has been indexed using a specialized vocabulary specifically developed for this collection." An informative abstract, extract, or annotation is also included. Users of the Food and Nutrition Information Center have full access to contents listed in this *Catalog.*

A17.18/3:973

19. U.S. National Agricultural Library. *School Lunches and Other School Feeding Programs, 1962--July 1967, List of Selected References;* compiled by Betty B. Baxtresser. 1968. [iv] & 28pp.*** (Library List no. 88). L.C. Card Agr68--161.

Four hundred and sixty--three citations cover lunches served by the school at school, "special schhol breakfasts, special summer lunch programs, Project Head Start feeding program, and diaster feeding in which school lunch facilities were used." Arrangement is alphabetical within subject groups. Author and Subject indices follow.

A17.17:88

20. U.S. National Institute of Arthritis, Metabolism, and Digestive Diseases. *A Select Bibliography of East/Asian Food and Nutrition Arranged According to Subject Matter and Area.* 1972. (Pub. in 1973). vii + 296pp. Free***.

The material presented in this bibliography is a result of references collected in the preparation of a "Food Composition Table for Use in East Asia." Most references cover the 1940–1972 period. Publications are first classified by one on the fourteen Asian areas and then are further sub--divided by subjects such as: Food Resources; Food Composition; Food

4

Supplement; Food Technology; Food Habits; Nutrition and Dietary Surveys; etc.
HE20.3316:Ea7a

21. U.S. Tennessee Valley Authority. National Fertilizer Development Center. *Nutrition of Rice.* 1971. 94pp. Free*** (Bulletin Y--36) L.C. Card 78--614870.
Contained are many of the most important articles about rice written during the previous five years. Entries, usually with short abstracts, are arranged by continent and country. Author and subject indices aid the user.
Y3.T25:3--2/Y--36

Farming

22. U.S. Agricultural Research Service. *Publications List on Tillage and Traction.* 1969. 16pp. (Free from National Tillage Machinery Laboratory, P.O. Box 792, Auburn, Al. 36830). (ARS 42--40--3).
Contained are 158 entries for articles and papers listed chronologically.
A77.15:42--40--3

23. U.S. Department of Agriculture. *Financial Management Research in Farming in the United States, Annotated Bibliography of Recent Publications and Current Work;* by Virden L. Harrison. 1971. v + 78 pp. Free*** (Miscellaneous Publication no. 1222). L.C. Card 79–616240.
"This annotated bibliography describes the contents of 300 recent publications and 50 current research projects relating to financial management of agricultural firms. A topic index groups the publications and current projects into subject matter areas with financial management. Also included are lists of teachers of graduate level courses in farm management and agricultural finance in State Universities."
A1.38:1222

24. U.S. Farmer Cooperative Service. *List of Publications;* compiled by Marjorie B. Christie. 1971. 58pp. Free*** (Information Series, no. 4).
A89.15:4/8

25. U.S. Government Printing Office. *Animal Industry, Farm Animals, Poultry, and Dairying.* Free* (Price List no. 38).
Listed are free and for sale publications on raising, utilizing, and selling farm animals. This list is revised frequently; prices are updated; and all publications are supposedly available from the

5

Forests and Forestry

26. U.S. Forest Service. *Forest Service Films Available on Loan for Educational Purposes to School, Civic Groups, Churches and Television.* 1969. 32pp. Free***.
Films are described in some detail, and an indication is given as to which age groups they would pertain.
A13.55:969

27. U.S. Forest Service. *List of Publications by Subject.* 1970. iv + 85 + [1]pp. Free*** L.C. Card 79--608188
Several hundred Forest Service publications dealing with all aspects of forestry from Smokey the Bear to technical marketing research reports are listed. Order information is provided.
A13.11/2:P96/970

28. U.S. Forest Service. *Materials to Help Teach Forest Conservation.* Revised 1971. 8pp. Free***.
A13.11/2:T22/971

29. U.S. Forest Service. Forest Products Laboratory. *Literature Survey of Populus Species with Emphasis on P. Tremuloides;* by Dimitri Pronin and Coleman L. Baughan. Rev. [1968]. 67 + [1]pp. Free*** (FPL Research Note no. 180).
The growth, development, management, and marketing of aspens is covered by this bibliography. Publications are arranged alphabetically by author under broad subject headings.
A13.79:FPL--180

30. U.S. Forest Service. Intermountain Forest and Range Experiment Station. *Publications (date) Intermountain Forest and Range Experiment Station, Ogden, Utah.* (Annual). Free***.
Publications are grouped according to twelve broad subjects such as: Forest Disease; Forest Engineering; Forest Genetics; Range and Wildlife Habitat; Recreation; and Watershed Management. Not indexed.
A13.65/14:yr.

31. U.S. Forest Service. North Central Forest Experiment Station. *Annotated Bibliography of Walnut, Supp. 1;* by Martha K. Dillow and Norman L. Hawker. [1971]. 23pp. Free*** (NC Research

Paper no. 70).

"A supplement to Research Paper NC–9 published in 1966, this list covers 208 additional references dealing with the growth and production of walnut."
A13.78:NC–70

32. U.S. Forest Service. North Central Forest Experiment Station. *Forest Soils Bibliography for North–Central Region (Including Subject Matter Index through 1972);* by William H. Carmean. 1973. 68pp. Free*** (General Technical Report NC–5).
A13.88:NC–5

33. U.S. Forest Service. Northeast Forest Experiment Station. *Operations Research in Forestry: a Bibliography;* by Jeff A. Martin and Paul E. Sendak. 1973. 90pp. Free*** (General Technical Report NE–8).

"This annotated bibliography is a compilation of selected literature sources that deal with the application of operations research to forestry situations. Included among the techniques are decision theory, mathematical programming, input–output analysis, simulation, PERT, queuing models, etc. The sources are listed alphabetically by author; also included is a key–word index."
A13.88:NE–8

34. U.S. Forest Service. Northeast Forest Experiment Station. *Selected and Annotated Bibliography of Pitch Pine (Pinus Regida Mill);* by Silas Little, Jack McCormick, and John W. Andresen. 1970. [2] + 103pp. Free*** (NE Research Paper no. 164).

Five hundred and eighty–nine articles and comprehensive reviews containing significant information on the pitch pine are included in this bibliography. Publications are arranged alphabetically by author under subdivisions of the following broad subject areas: Distribution and Resource Statistics: Botanical Characteristics; Forest Ecology; Silviculture and Management; Forest Damage and Protection; and Wood Technology and Utilization. An author index further facilitates its use.
A13.78:NE–164

35. U.S. Forest Service. Pacific Northwest Forest and Range Exper Experiment Station. *Annotated List of Publications of the Pacific Northwest Forest and Range Experiment Station for the Year (date).* Annual. Free***.

Publications are grouped by twenty–four broad categories.

Among these are: Atmosphere; Chemicals; Economics in Wood Industry; Plant Ecology; Recreation; and Water Quality. Order information is provided for the publications listed.
A13.66/15:P96/yr.

36. U.S. Forest Service. Pacific Northwest Forest and Range Experiment Station. *Forest and Range Soils Research in Oregon and Washington, Bibliography with Abstracts from 1964--1968;* compiled by Glen O. Klock. 1969. [1] + 28pp. Free*** (PNW Research Paper no. 90). L.C. Card 79--607243.
The 195 annotations continue a series of bibliographies formerly published by R.F. Tarrant in 1956, 1957, 1958, 1959, and 1964. Its purpose is to reference and briefly summarize all published forest and range soils research done in Oregon and Washington from 1964--1968.
A13.78:PNW--90

37. U.S. Forest Service. Pacific Northwest Forest and Range Experiment Station. *List of Available Publications.* Quarterly. Free***.
A13.66/14: yr./no.

38. U.S. Forest Service. Pacific Northwest Forest and Range Experiment Station. *Regeneration of White Spruce with Reference to Interior Alaska, Literature Review* [with biblio--graphy; by] John C. Zasada and Robert A. Gregory. 1969. [1] + 37 + [1]pp. Free*** (PNW Research Paper no. 79).
Much of this paper discusses the results and conclusions reported by the literature. The lengthy bibliography of this literature follows.
A13.78:PNW--79

39. U.S. Forest Service. *Sitka Spruce: a Bibliography with Abstracts;* compiled by A.S. Harris and Robert H. Ruth. 1970. 251pp. Free*** (PNW Research Paper no. 105).
A13.78:PNW--105

40. U.S. Forest Service. Pacific Southwest Forest and Range Experiment Station. *List of Available Publications.* Quarterly. Free***.
A13.62/11--3:yr./no.

41. U.S. Forest Service. Rocky Mountain Forest and Range Experiment Station. *List of Publications.* Quarterly. Free***.
A13.69/10:yr./no.

42. U.S. Forest Service. Rocky Mountain Forest and Range Experiment Station. *Literature Review of Spruce, Western, and Two--Year--Cycle Budworm* [with bibliography] ; by M.E. McKnight. 1968. [2] + 35 + [1]pp. Free*** (Research Paper no. 44).
   Covered are "370 literature citations on the spruce (C. fumiferana (Clemens)), western (C. occidentalis Freeman), and 2--year--cycle (C. Bennis Freeman) budworms through November 1967. Citations are also organized in a subject index."
   A13.78:RM–44

43. U.S. Forest Service. Rocky Mountain Forest and Range Experiment Station. *The Southwestern Pinyon--Juniper Ecosystem: A Bibliography;* by Earl F. Aldon and H.W. Springfield. 1973. 20pp. Free*** (USDA Forest Service General Technical Report RM--4).
   This is a compilations and classification of the pertinent literature for the pinyon--juniper ecosystem in the Southwest through 1972.
   A13.88:RM--4

44. U.S. Forest Service. Southeastern Forest Experiment Station. *Research Information Digest: Recent Publications of the South--eastern Forest Experiment Station.* Semi--annual. Free***.
   Publications are grouped by broad subjects such as: Forest Protection; Forest Management: Forest and Water Resources; Forest Environment; and Marketing, Utilization and Housing. Not indexed.
   A13.63/13:date

45. U.S. Forest Service. Southern Forest and Range Experiment Station. *Eastern Redcedar, Annotated Bibliography;* by E.R. Ferguson. 1970. 21pp. Free*** (SO Research Paper no. 64).
   Annotated are more than 300 publications dealing with Juniperus virginiana L.
   A13.78:SO--64

46. U.S. Forest Service. Southern Forest Experiment Station. *Longleaf Pine, Annotated Bibliography, 1946--67;* by Thomas C. Croker, jr. 1968. [2] + 52pp. Free*** (SO Research Paper no. 35).
   Contained are all known publications on the longleaf pine from 1946--1967.
   A13.78:SO--35

47. U.S. Forest Service. Southern Forest Experiment Station.
*Selected Bibliography on Southern Range Management,
1962--1967;* by V.L. Duval, A.W. Johnson, L.L. Yarlett. 1968.
[1] + 34pp. Free*** (SO Research Paper no. 38).
About 650 publications are listed alphabetically by author
under minor subdivisions of the following major subjects:
Range Plants; Range Management; Range Livestock; Range
Influences; Range Resources and Economics; Wildlife
Management; Range Research; and Range Education. This
supplements a 1963 publication by the same title.
A13.78:SO–38

48. U.S. Forest Service. Southern Forest Experiment Station.
*Selected Bibliography on Southern Range Management,
1968--1972;* by H.A. Pearson and others. 1973. 50pp. Free***
(USDA Forest Service General Technical Report SO--3).
A supplement to the above (no. 47), this contains about 950
additional entries that deal with the forest ranges of the South
and with the livestock and wildlife which use this resource.
A13.88:SO--3

49. U.S. Government Printing Office. *Forestry. Managing and Using
Forest Range Land, Including Timber and Lumber, Ranges and
Grazing.* Free* (Price List no. 43).
Listed are free and for sale publications on all aspects of forestry.
This list is revised frequently. Prices are supposedly current,
and the publications included are available.

Plant Science

50. U.S. Agricultural Research Service. *Annotated Bibliography of
Nematodes of Soybeans, 1882--1968;* by J.M. Epps and others.
1973. 75pp.*** (ARS Southern Region, P.O. Box 53326, New
Orleans, La. 70153). (ARS S--10).
A77.15:S–10

51. U.S. Agricultural Research Sercice. *References on Regional
Cotton Mechanization Research Project S--2, S--69, W--24, and
W--99;* prepared by Rex. F. Colwick. 1973. 41pp. Free***
(ARS Southern Region, P.O. Box 53326, New Orleans, La.
70153). (ARS S--10).
Publications are listed by subject and cover the following
topics: Crop Residue Disposal; Seedbed Preparation;
Planting; Fertilization; Weed Control; Insect and Disease
Control Equipment; Defoliation; Harvesting; Varietal

Characteristics Affecting Mechanical Harvesting; Handling
and Storage. Availability is indicated for each publication.
A77.15:S--10

52. U.S. Department of Agriculture. *Bibliography of Potato Diseases
Through 1945;* compiled by Muriel J. O'Brien and E.L. LeClerg.
1970. [4] + 243pp. $1.25* (Miscellaneous Publication no.
1162). L.C. Card 76--608932.
This comprehensive bibliography of potato diseases is
complimented and faciliatated by subject, author, literature
citation, and general reference indices. The subject index
contains fungus names and the names of bacteria and viruses
corrected to show both old names and present synonomy.
A1.38:1162

53. U.S. Department of Agriculture. *Evapotranspiration and Water
Research as Related to Riparian and Phreatophyte Management,
Abstract Bibliography;* complied by Jerome S. Horton. 1973.
iv + 192pp. $2.00* S/N 0100--2530 (Miscellaneous Publication
no. 1234).
Abstracted are 691 publications and articles that will help land
managers and research workers to (1) evaluate relations of
vegetation to water loss and to (2) estimate the probable effect
on water yield on manipulating vegetation. Moist--site
vegetation is emphasized, but watershed and plot studies are
included if they are useful in determining the effect of
vegetation management on water yield.
A1.38:1234

54. U.S. Department of Agriculture. *Selected Bibliography of
Natural Plant Communities in Eleven Midwestern States;*
prepared by Arnold J. Heerwagen. 1971. [3] + 30pp. $.30*
S/N 0100--1436 (Miscellaneous Publication no. 1205).
Contained are 742 entries arranged by author. Described
are the natural plant communities in Illinois, Indiana, Iowa,
Kansas, Michigan, Minnesota, Missouri, Nebraska, North
Dakota, South Dakota, and Wisconsin.
A1.38:1205

55. U.S. Government Printing Office. *Plants, Culture, Grading,
Marketing, and Storage of Fruits, Vegetables, Grass, and Grain.*
Free* (Price List no. 44).
Listed are free and for sale publications on the many aspects of
growing, marketing, and storing fruits, vegetables, grass, and
grain. This list is revised frequently, and all publications listed

are supposedly available from the GPO.
GP3.9:44

56. U.S. National Agricultural Library. *Historic Books and Manu-scripts Concerning Horticulture and Forestry in the Collection of the National Agricultural Library;* compiled by Mortimer L. Naftalin. 1968. [2] + 106pp. Free*** (Library Lists no. 90). L.C. Card Agr--195.

 This is the third of a series of historical holdings of the National Agricultural Library. The others are: *Historical Books and Manuscripts Concerning General Agriculture in the Collection of the National Agricultural Library* (Library list no. 86) and *Linnea in the Collection of the National Agricultural Library* (Library List no. 89).

 Included are titles published before 1800 (European imprints) and 1830 (American imprints). A few significant historical works of a later date are included. The bibliography is divided into two sections -- Horiticulture and Forestry. In each the arrangement is alphabetical by author. Not indexed.
A17.17:90

57. U.S. National Agricultural Library. *Linnea in the Collection of the National Agricultural Library;* compiled by Mortimer L. Naftalin. 1968. [3] + 43pp. Free*** (Library Lists no. 89). L.C. Card Agr--197.

 This is the second of a series of historical holdings of the National Agricultural Library (see above, no. 56). Listed are the "monographs which were written by or about the eminent botanist, Carl von Linne." Arrangement is chronological from 1935 to 1968. Indexed by author and subject.
A17.17:89

58. U.S. National Agricultural Library. *Sunflower, Literature Survey, January 1960 – June 1967;* compiled by Merne H. Posey. 1969. ii + 133pp. Free*** (Library List no. 95). L.C. Card 70--603089.

 Included are 1846 citations to material on sunflower cultivation and utilization internationally. Arrangement is alphabetical by author with a subject index pinpointing specific areas of interest. Briefly annotated.
A17.17:95

59. U.S. Department of the Interior. *Index to Federal Aid Publications in Sport Fish and Wildlife Restoration and Selected Cooperative Research Project Reports.* 1968. 726pp.*** L.C. Card 68--62958
Complete coverage is given through March 1968 for all Pittman--Robertson and Dingell--Johnson published report literature. Over 5600 reports are listed according to broad subject categories and are indexed according to the *Thesaurus of Sport Fish and Wildlife Descriptors.* Complete bibliographic and project information is provided.
I22.9:F52

60. U.S. Fish and Wildlife Service. *Bibliography on Methods of Analyzing Bird Banding Data, with Special Reference to Estimation of Population Size and Survival* [with bibliography] ; by David R. Anderson. 1972. ii + 13pp. $.25.* (Special Scientific Reports, Wildlife, no. 156).
I49.15/3:156

61. U.S. Fish and Wildlife Service. *Bureau of Sport Fisheries and Wildlife Publications in the Calendar Year, (date).* Annual. Free*** L.C. Card 68–62318.
I49.18/6:(date)

62. U.S. Fish and Wildlife Service. *Selected List of Information Leaflets on Wildlife.* 1969. 1pp. Free*** (Wildlife Leaflets no. 485).
I49.13:485

63. U.S. Fish and Wildlife Service. *Selected References on Management of White–tailed Deer, 1910–66;* by N.W. Hosley. 1968. [2] + 46pp. $.30* (Special Scientific Reports, Wildlife, no. 112).
I49.15/3:112

64. U.S. Fish and Wildlife Service. *Wildlife Review: An Abstracting Service for Wildlife Management.* 1935--. Quarterly *** (Bureau of Sport Fisheries, U.S. Fish and Wildlife Service, Washington, D.C. 20240). L.C. Card 53–17432.
As one of the foremost abstracting services in the field of wildlife and wildlife management, this bibliography covers conservation, plant life, mammals, birds, and wildlife in general. The arrangement is by subject with an author index. Cumulative indices entitled *Wildlife Abstracts* are issued irregularly.
I49.17:Nos.

65. U.S. Forest Service. *Range and Wildlife Habitat Publications Issued in 1967 by Forest Service Personnel and Cooperators.* 1968. [1] + 10pp. Free***.
Listed, but not indexed or annotated, are 91 publications on range and wildlife habitat research.
A13.11/2:R16/3/967

Wood Technology

66. U.S. Bureau of Domestic Commerce. *Utilization of Wood Residues, Annotated Bibliography;* prepared by Adair A. Mitchell. 1968. [2] + 46pp. $.35*.
This selective annotated list of references touches many areas of the utilization of waste wood. Some of the subjects covered are: Bark, Briquettes and Charcoal; Composition Boards; Molded Products; and Wood Molasses. The majority of the items selected are technical and are research reports or articles in trade journals.
C41.12:W85

67. U.S. Forest Service. Forest Products Laboratory. *Dividends from Wood Research, Recent Publications of the Forest Products Laboratory.* Semi--annual. Free***.
Publications are listed according to subject. Availability is given. Not indexed.
A13.27/8:date

68. U.S. Forest Service. Forest Products Laboratory. *Forest Products List of Publications on the Chemistry of Wood [1945–68].* 1968. ii + 41pp. Free***.
Provided is a list of publications which gives general information and research results on the "analysis, chemical and physical properties, and conversion processes of wood and wood products."
A13.27/7:W85/3/968

69. U.S. Forest Service. Forest Products Laboratory. *Forest Products Laboratory List of Publications on Drying of Wood.* 1968. 29pp. Free***.
Included are publications on various wood drying methods and problems (moisture content, shrinkage and swelling, etc.) relating to wood, drying.
A13.27/7:W85/10/968

70. U.S. Forest Service. Forest Products Laboratory. *Forest Products*

Laboratory List of Publications on Milling and Utilization of Timber Products. 1968. 30pp. Free***.

The publications listed are concerned with "methods and practices in the lumber producing and wood–consuming industries; standard lumber grades, sizes, and nomenclature; production and use of small dimension stock; specifications for small wooden products; utilization of little--used species and commercial woods; and low–grade and residue surveys."

A13.27/7:M62/968

71. U.S. Forest Service. Forest Products Laboratory. *Forest Products Laboratory List of Publications Relating to Furniture Manu--facture and Woodworkers.* 1973. 10pp. Free***.

A good reading list is provided by this publication for furniture manufactures and woodworkers. Publications are listed by the following categories: General; Grading, Manufacturing, and Utilization; Growth, Structure and Identification of Wood; Drying of Wood; Strength Properties; and Glues and Glued Products.

A13.27/7:F98/973

72. U.S. Forest Service. Forest Products Laboratory. *Forest Products Laboratory List of Publications Relating to Wood Finishing Subjects.* 1971. 9pp. Free***.

This list includes recent publications that give general information on the techniques of finishing wood structures and other wood products.

A13.27/7:W85/971

73. U.S. Forest Service. Forest Products Laboratory. *Forest Products Laboratory, Madison, Wisconsin, in Cooperation with the University of Wisconsin, List of Publications on Drying of Wood.* 1972. 12pp. Free***.

A13.27/7:W85/10/972

74. U.S. Forest Service. Forest Products Laboratory. *Forest Products Laboratory, Madison, in Cooperation with the University of Wisconsin, List of Publications on Milling and Utilization of Timber Products.* 1973. 14pp. Free***.

Publications are listing by the following topics: Machining; Milling; Grades, Specifications, and Standardization; and Utilization.

A13.27/7:M62/973

75. U.S. Forest Service. Pacific Northwest Forest and Range Experiment Station. *Literature on Timber Measurement*

Problems in Douglas--Fir Region, Bibliography; compiled by
David Bruce. 1968. 28 + [1] pp. Free*** (PNW Research Paper
no. 67).
 The 330 items in this bibliography include publications on
 tree and log measurement and measurement systems throughout the United States and Canada. A few significant foreign
 publications are also included. Subject index.
 A13.78:PNW-67

76. U.S. Forest Service. Southern Forest Experiment Station.
 Wood Machining Abstracts, 1966 and 1967; by
 Peter Koch. 1968. ii + 38pp. Free*** (SO Research Paper
 no. 34).
 Three hundred and twenty-six abstracts of significant
 research reports are included. Publications are listed under
 such major categories as: Sawing (Specific types -- circular,
 band, etc.); Chipping, Flaking, and Grinding; Defibrating;
 Propeties of the Cutting Edge and Cutter; and Properties of
 Wood.
 A13.78:SO-34

77. U.S. Small Business Administration. *Woodworking Shops;* by
 William B. Lloyd. 1968. 11pp. Free*** (SBA Bibliography
 no. 46).
 Included are publications, trade journals and associations of
 interest to those either in or considering going into the
 woodworking business.

ANTHROPOLOGY AND ETHNOLOGY

General

78. U.S. Air Force Academy. Library. *Sociology and Anthropology.*
 1968. [7] + 25pp.*** (Special Bibliography Series, no. 41).
 Listed by specific subjects are titles representing "a selected
 portion of the holdings of the Air Force Academy Library
 in the subject areas of Sociology, Anthropology, Civilizations,
 and Ethnology."
 D305.12:41

79. U.S. National Institute of Mental Health. *Bibliography on
 Ethnicity and Ethnic Groups;* compiled and edited by Richard
 Kolm. 1973. vii + [1] + 25pp. $2.85* L.C. Card 73--601601.
 The 1,694 entries, some of which are annotated, represent a
 "first step toward the development of an ongoing compre--

hensive bibliography in the area of ethnicity." Emphasis has been placed on two major subject areas: (1) "Materials dealing with the situation of immigrant ethnic groups, their psychological adjustment and conditions affecting acculturation; and (2) Materials dealing with patterns of ethnic behavior, identity, family life, and communication structure."
HE20.2417:Et3

80. U.S. National Institute of Neurological Disease and Stroke. *Annotated Anga (Kukukuku) Bibliography;* by D. Carelton Gajdusek and others. [1] + v + 85pp. ***.
A lengthy historical and anthropological introduction a accompanies the *Anga Bibliography* which covers the following areas: Ethnology, Anthropology, History, L Linguistics, Medicine, and Physical Anthropology.
HE20.3513:An4

81. U.S. Bureau of Indian Affairs. *Economic Development of American Indians and Eskimos, 1930–1967, Bibliography;* by Majorie P. Snodgrass. 1969. [3] + 263pp. $2.00* (Interior Department Library Series no. 10).
Almost 1,600 entries dealing with the economic development of American Indians and Eskimos are combined here as a research aid. Many of the publications listed are Bureau and Agency reports and will not be listed elsewhere. Entries are grouped by subjects areas, such as: Arts and Crafts Development; Farming, Ranching, Range Resources, and Related Industries; Fish and Wildlife Development; Industrial and Commercial Development; Socio–Economic Studies and Plans; and Tourism and Recreation Development. Publications are indexed by reservation.
I20.48:Ec7/930–67

82. U.S. Bureau of Indian Affairs. *Indians, Legends and Myths, Suggested Reading List.* 1969. 4 + [1] pp.
I20.48:In2

83.–93. The following Bureau of Indian Affairs publications are memeographed or memeograph type reading lists on various Indian tribes and customs.

83. U.S. Bureau of Indian Affairs. *Indians – Music.* 1973. 3pp. Free***.
Listed are the most prominent sources on Indian music. Additionally, sources and addresses are given for obtaining

recordings of Indian songs and music.
I20.51/2:M97

84. U.S. Bureau of Indian Affairs. *Indians -- Origin.* 1973. 3pp.
Free***.
Notable publications on the origin of Indians are listed. Most
of the items listed "may be obtained from most large libraries
or borrowed through inter--library loan."
I20.51/2:Or4

85. U.S. Bureau of Indian Affairs. *Indians: the Algonquians.* 1969.
4pp. Free***.
I20.51/2:AL3

86. U.S. Bureau of Indian Affairs. *Indians: the Comanches.* 1972.
4pp. Free***.
I20.51/2:C73

87. U.S. Bureau of Indian Affairs. *Indians: the Crows.* 1972. 4pp.
Free***.
I20.51/2:C88

87a. U.S. Bureau of Indian Affairs. *Indians: the Hopis.* 1972. 4pp.
Free***.
I20.51/2:H77

88. U.S. Bureau of Indian Affairs. *Indians: the Nez Perce.* 1972.
4pp. Free***.
I20.51/2:N49

89. U.S. Bureau of Indian Affairs. *Indians: the Pueblos.* 1969. 7pp.
Free***.
I20.51/2:P96

90. U.S. Bureau of Indian Affairs. *Indians: the Seminoles.* 1972.
4pp. Free***.
I20.51/2:Se5

91. U.S. Bureau of Indian Affairs. *Indians: the Shoshoni.* 1971. 3pp.
Free***.
I20.51/2:Sh8

92. U.S. Bureau of Indian Affairs. *Indians: the Winnebagos.* 1972.
3pp. Free***.
I20.51/2:W73

93. U.S. Bureau of Indian Affairs. *Indians -- Virginia and the Potomac Area: Suggested Reading List.* 1972. 2pp. Free***. I20.51/2:V81

94. U.S. Bureau of Indian Affairs. *Witchita: a Suggested Reading List.* 1973. 2pp. Free***. I20.48:W63

95. U.S. National Archives and Records Service. *The American Indian: Select Catalog of National Archives Microfilm Publications.* 1972. *** L.C. Card 72--600070. GS4.2:In2

96. U.S. Office of Education. *American Indian Education, Selected Bibliography (with ERIC Abstracts), ERIC/CRESS Supp. 2.* 1971. viii + 286pp. $2.25* S/N 1780-0872. HE5.10:In2/2/Supp.2

97. U.S. Office of Education. *American Indian Education, Selected Bibliography (with ERIC Abstracts), ERIC/CRESS Supp. 3.* 1973. vii + 437pp. $4.25* L.C. Card no. 73--601255.
The files of the Educational Resources Information Center (ERIC) and the Clearinghouse in Rural Educations and Small Schools (CRESS) were searched to compile this bibliography. Though entitled "Selected Bibliography," this publications covers American Indian education in depth. Indexed by subject.
HE5.10:In2/2/Supp.3

Minorities

98. U.S. Cabinet Committee on Opportunity for the Spanish Speaking. *The Spanish Speaking in the United States: Guide to Materials.* 1971. iv + 175pp. Free*** L.C. 75-614612.
This is a bibliographic guide to books, periodicals, articles, government publications, serial publications, theses and dissertations, audio--visual materials, and U.S. radio and television stations with a primarily Spanish speaking audience and broadcast. Indexed by subject.

99. U.S. Department of the Air Force. Air University. *Race Relations: Selected References.* 1972. 30pp. Free*** (Air University Library Bibliography no. 200).
Though all minority groups in the United States are covered, Blacks are primarily emphasized. Publications are grouped

as follows: Attitudes, Perceptions, Behavior; Inter–group Relations and Research; Prejudice and Race Discrimination; Race; Institutional Racism; Black Biography and Personal Narratives; Black Protest and Black Nationalism; Black History and Fine Arts; Minority Psyches and Life Styles; Race Relations in the Armed Services; Minority Groups in the U.S. Today. Not indexed.
D301.26/11:200/rev. 972

100. U.S. Department of the Navy. *Indian and Mexican Americans: A Selective Annotated Bibliography.* 1972. v + [1] + 42pp.***.
This detailed bibliography is arranged chronologically according to subject and tribe.
D208.15:In2

101. U.S. Department of Housing and Urban Development. *The Mexican Americans: A Bibliography.* 1970. [1] + 11pp.**.
Included are 115 entries for books, monographs, and periodical articles which reflect urban problems of Mexican Americans. Not indexed.
HH1.23:M57

102. U.S. Inter--Agency Committee on Mexican American Affairs. *Guide to Materials Relating to Persons of Mexican Heritage in the United States.* 1969. [5] + 186pp. Free*** L.C. Card 73--601854.
References are concerned primarily with the sociological and economic aspects of the Mexican American. Materials are classed by type: Books; Reports; Hearings; Proceedings and Similar Materials; Periodical Literature; Dissertations and Other Unpublished Material; Bibliographies; and Audio--Visual Materials. Additionally, there is a list of Spanish language radio and television stations in the United States and along the Mexican border. Not indexed.
Y3.In8/23:10M41

103. U.S. Library of Congress. *The Negro in the United States: A Selected Bibliography;* compiled by Dorothy B. Porter.
1970. x + [3] + 313pp. $3.25* L.C. Card 78--606085.
This is one of the first and foremost bibliographies dealing with Black history and culture in the United States. Its purpose is to serve as a reference guide to all interested persons from the researcher to the general public. Arrangement is alphabetical by author under broad subject headings, and annotations are given if the title is not self--explanatory.

Indexed by subject and author.
LC1.12/2:N31

Race Relations

104. U.S. Interagency Racial Data Committe. *Establishing a Federal Racial/Ethnic Data System. Vol. 2, Appendix B, Annotated Bibliography of Selected Source Documents on Federal Racial/ Ethnic Data Policies.* 1972. 191pp.*** L.C. Card 73–601013.
Y3.R11:2D26/Vol.2

105. U.S. National Institute of Mental Health. *Bibliography on Racism.* 1972. 196pp. $2.75.* L.C. Card 72--603640.
Contained is a comprehensive listing of all abstracts relating to racism which were available in the files of the National Clearinghouse for Mental Health Information of the NIMH at the time the bibliography was compiled. Subject and author indices facilitate its use.
HE20.2417:R11

106. U.S. Social Security Administration. *Not Just Some of Us: A Limited Bibliography on Minority Group Relations.* 1968. [5] + 29pp.*** L.C. Card HEW68–64.
This is intended to be a source book to readings which would promote better understanding among the races. Entries, most of which are briefly annotated, are arranged by subject. Reference materials are listed separately. Not indexed.
FS3.38:M66

BUSINESS AND INDUSTRY

General

107. U.S. Bureau of Domestic Commerce. *Publications for Business.* 1971. 15pp. Free***
Contained are publications for those interested in domestic or international business. (For the most recent information concerning this publication see no. 112.)
C41.12:P96/4/971

108. U.S. Department of Commerce. *Business Service Checklist, Weekly Guide to Department of Commerce Publications, Plus Key Business Indicators.* 1946 -- . Weekly. $7.20 a yr., $1.80 add. foreign mailing. L.C. Card 52–35963

Contained are weekly announcements of Dept. of Commerce publications with annual cumulation.
C1.24:Vol./No.

109. U.S. Department of Commerce. Office of Minority Enterprise. *Minority Business Enterprise, Bibliography.* 1973. [3] + iii + 231pp.*** L.C. Card 73--602647.
The 1,413 entries are grouped according to five categories concerned with the development of minority business: (1) Relevant or Related; (2) Books and Monographs; (3) Articles, Reports, and Speeches; (4) Pertinent Directories; and (5) Periodicals Relating to Minorities and Minority Business Enterprise. Purchase and availability information are given when available. Indexed by subject.
C1.54:M66

110. U.S. Department of the Air Force. Pacific Air Forces. *Accounting, Statistical Services, Data Processing;* prepared by Harold D. Peterson. 1969. iv + 60pp. Free*** (PACAF Basic Bibliography) See below for annotation.
D301.62:Ac2/2/969

111. U.S. Department of the` Air Force. Pacific Air Forces. *Accounting, Statisitcal Services, Data Processing, Supp. 1;* prepared by Harold D. Peterson. 1970. [1] + iv + 21pp. Free*** (PACF Basic Bibliography).
This frequently revised bibliography gives lengthy annotations and purchase information for new books in the areas of a accounting, auditing, electronic data processing, finance (includes the stock market), and statistics. Not indexed.
D301.62:Ac2/2/969/supp.1

112. U.S. Domestic and International Business Administration. *Selected Publications to Aid Domestic Business and Industry.* 1973. 16pp. Free***.
Includes a few periodicals, reports, and publications beneficial to business and industry located in Department of Commerce District Office Libraries. Provides purchase information.

112a. U.S. Domestic and International Business Administration. Wholesale Data Sources for Market Analysis. 1973. 11p.***.
C57.15:M34

113. U.S. Government Printing Office. *Commerce: Business, Patents, Trademarks, and Foreign Trade.* Free* (Price List no. 62).
Frequently revised list of publications on commerce, indicating

prices and titles in stock.
GP3.9:62

114. U.S. Small Business Administration. *Automation for Small Offices;* by Frank J. Carberry. 1971. 12pp. Free*** (Small Business Bibliography, no. 58).
Listed are books and other publications, including periodicals and articles, with information on office automation. Also included is a list of national organizations and associations dealing with automation.
SBA1.3:58/3

115. U.S. Small Business Administration. *Basic Library Reference Sources;* prepared by Elizabeth G. Janezeck. 11pp. 1970. Free*** (Small Business Bibliography, no. 18).
"The purpose of this bibliography is to acquaint the small businessman with the wealth of business information available through library research." Contained are the most basic business directories, guides, and reference sources available in many libraries. Purchase information is given, when available.
SBA1.3:18/5

116. U.S. Small Business Administration. *Selling by Mail Order;* by Richard D. Millican. 1968. 12pp. Free*** (Small Business Bibliography, no. 3).
Publications, trade literature, and trade associations are listed for the person interested in or in the mail order business.
SBA1.3:3

Commerce

117. U.S. Bureau of Domestic Commerce. *Information Sources on Export Opportunities, Selections from Marketing Information Guide.* 1969. [2] + 28pp.***.
Contained are 101 annotations about export markets, procedures, and techniques. Special references are given for each major world region. Special directories and sources of trade information are provided to aid the exporter in research.
C41.12:Ex7

117a. U.S. Bureau of International Commerce. *Semi–Annual Checklist, International Business Publications.* Semi–annual***.

"The opening pages of this listing describe individual publications and provide capsule summaries of Commerce's various series of publications on world trade." This is followed by a Country List which references all publications about a particular country.
C42.15:C41/date

118. U.S. Bureau of International Commerce. *Sources of Information on American Firms for International Buyers.* 1971. [2] + 37pp. $.30* S/N 0309–0197.
As an annotated reference guide to business directories, trade and professional journals, reference books, and directories of directories on American firms, this bibliography might be used as a buying guide for a business library.
C42.2:Am3/971

119. U.S. Economic Research Service. *Agriculture in the European Economic Community, Annotated Bibliography, 1958--66;* by Brian D. Hedges and Reed E. Friend. 1968. ii + 77pp.***
(ERS--Foreign Series, no. 213).
This annotated list of over 300 publications about various aspects of the European Economic Community concentrates on studies concerning factors affecting the demand, supply, and trade of agricultural commodities. Publications are arranged alphabetically by author under subdivisions of the following major chapter headings: Methodology, Statistics, and Projections; International Trade; Agricultural Situation; and Commodity Studies.
A93.21/2:213

120. U.S. Foreign Agricultural Service. *Food and Agricultural Export Bibliography, 1970;* by Dennis White. 1970. 44pp.***
(FAS--M no. 221). L.C. Card 79--609832.
Included are references to about 1,000 books, pamphlets, and government publications which will assist exporters of food and agricultural products. Among the topics are: Export Insurance; Foreign Market Structures and Distribution Channels; Trade Regulations; and P.L. 480. Besides these, there are so many other aspects of exporting included that this bibliography should be worthwhile for exporters of any product.
A67.26:221

Consumers

121. U.S. Bureau of Domestic Commerce. *Bibliography on Marketing to Low--Income Consumers.* 1969. [4] + 49pp. $.55*
L.C. Card 72--600495
See no. 122.
C41.12:M34/4

122. U.S. Bureau of Domestic Commerce. *Marketing and the Low Income Consumer;* edited by Robert J. Holloway and Frederick J. Sturidivant. 1971. 65pp. $.65* S/N 0308--0412. L.C. Card 77--613862.
The earlier *Bibliography on Marketing to Low--Income Consumers* (see above) was such a success that this bibliography, with nearly a hundred more entries, proves even more useful in providing materials which deal with "the characteristics of the market system serving low--income consumers, with programs designed to improve the market system and problems in low income marketing." The 326 entries are briefly annotated and arranged according to subject.
C41.21:M34/4/971

123. U.S. Bureau of Domestic Commerce. *Sources of Information on Containers and Packaging;* by Charles H. Felton. 1969. 24pp. $.25*.
Included are government and non--government publications which deal with such aspects of containers and packaging as manufacturing techniques, research and development, distribution, production, and trade techniques. Additionally, there are lists of trade associations and sources of technical information.
C41.12:C76/969

124. U.S. Bureau of Domestic Commerce. *Sources of Statistical Data, Textile and Apparel with List of Reference Sources;* by Barbara A. Steinbock and Thomas F. Stein. 1968. iv + 31pp. $.40* L.C. Card 68--67283.
"Original series of statistical data on the textile and apparel industries published by U.S. Government agencies, inter--national organizations, and other sources have been included in this publication. . . . Each publication is listed by title together with the publisher, price, and short description of its contents." An alphabetical subject and title index follows the annotations.
C41.12:T31/968

125. U.S. Government Printing Office. *Consumer information.*

*Family Finances, Appliances, Recreation, Gardening, Health
and Safety, Food, House and Home, Child Care, Clothing and
Fabrics.* Free* (Price List no. 86).
Listed are free and for sale publications on all types of consumer
information. This list is revised frequently, and all prices
should be current.
GP3.9:86

126. U.S. Office of Consumer Affairs. *Consumer Education Biblio--
graphy.* 1971. vii + 192pp. $1.00* L.C. Card 77–616123.
Over 4,000 briefly annotated entries pertaining to consumer
interests and education are listed. Publications are arranged
by such subject categories as: Consumer Behavior;
Consumer Goods and Services; Agencies and Organizations
for the Consumer; and Teaching Aids -- Including Audio--
visual Materials – for the Consumer. Subject index.
PrEx16.10:Ed8

127. U.S. President. *Consumer Education, Bibliography;* prepared
for the President's Committee on Consumer Interests by Yonkers
Public Library. 1969. x + 170 pp. $.65* L.C. Card 77–601488.
Revised by no. 126.
Pr36.8:C76/B47

Equal Employment Opportunity

128. U.S. Civil Service Commission. *Equal Opportunity in Employ--
ment.* 1971. [2] + 135pp. $1.25* S/N 0600–0614.
(Personnel Bibliography Series, no. 38). L.C. Card 72--600588.
Included are publications received by the Civil Service
Commission Library during 1969--1970 on the employment
of minorities, handicapped workers (mentally retarded,
alcoholics, rehabilitated offenders, and drug abusers),
the older workers, and women. Subject arrangement. Not
indexed.
CS1.61/3:38

129. U.S. Civil Service Commission. *Equal Opportunity in Employ--
ment.* 1973. [3] + 170pp. $1.75* S/N 0600--0745.
(Personnel Bibliography Series, no. 49). L.C. Card 73–603543.
Included are publications received by the Civil Service
Commission Library during 1971--72. (See no. 128 for
complete notation).
CS1.61/3:49

130. U.S. Federal Aviation Administration. *Equal Employment Opportunity, Selected References;* compiled by Dorothy J. Poehlman. 1968. [1] + 7pp. NTIS. TD4.17/3:16

131. U.S. Veterans Administration. *We Hold These Truths;* prepared by Rosemary D. Reid. 1969. 31pp.*** (Bibliographies, no. 10--7). L.C. Card 70--603223.
    Listed are books, pamphlets, and other material dealing with equality of opportunity in employment. Entries are alphabetical by author in the following subject areas: Prejudice; Minorities; Employment; The Negro; Questions Concerning Equal Rights; and Answers to the Equal Rights Problem.
    VA1.20/3:10--7

Finance and Accounting

132. U.S. Department of the Air Force. *Personal Finance and Investment;* prepared by Stella K. Watanabe. 1968.*** (PACAF Basic Bibliographies).
    See no. 133 for notation.
    D301.62:F49/968

133. U.S. Department of the Air Force. *Personal Finance and Investment, Supp. 1;* prepared by Stella K. Watanabe. 1969. iv + 39pp.***.
    Annotated references lead one to proper sources for infor-mation on (1) Earning a Living; (2) Consumer Education; (3) Personal Finance; (4) Insurance; (5) Investment and Savings; (6) Taxes; and (7) Retirement. Annotations are lengthy and critical. Indexed by author and title.
    D301.62:F49/968/supp.1

134. U.S. Department of Housing and Urban Development. *Biblio--graphy on Mortgage Finance.* 1972. 3pp. Free***.
    "This list was prepared by the Office of International Affairs" and includes periodicals and books detailing how a borrower can obtain financing, the public and private institutions which are involved, and the procedures followed by borrower and lender in processing a loan request or servicing a loan after approval.
    HH1.40/4:M84

135. U.S. Government Printing Office. *Finance. National Economy, Accounting, Insurance, Securities.* Free* (Price List no. 28).
    Listed are for sale and free publications on the multiple

aspects of finance. This list is revised frequently; prices
are kept current; and all publications are supposedly
available from the GPO.
GP3.9:28

136. U.S. Small Business Administration. *Distribution Cost Analysis;*
prepared by Gorden Brunhild and Charles Sevin. 1968 revision.
1969. 8pp. Free*** (Small Business Bibliography, no. 34).
L.C. Card 70--600055
Numerous government, non--government, and professional
association publications and periodicals are listed to assist
the businessman in investigating cost planning and analysis.
SBA1.3:34

137. U.S. Small Business Administration. *Retail Credit and Collection;*
by William Henry Blake. 1970. 11pp. Free*** (Small
Business Bibliography, no. 31).
Contained are books and other publications, including
periodicals and periodical articles, which provide information
on retail credit and collection and consumer finance. An
address list of trade associations is an accompanying feature.
SBA1.2:31/5

Jobs, Occupations, and Manpower

138. U.S. Bureau of Employment Security. *Manpower and Operating
Research Studies of U.S. Employment Service and State
Employment Services 1958–67, Selective Bibliography;* prepared
by Julia Mash, Jeremiah Jenkins, and Carolyn Broome under the
direction of Harold Kuptzin. 1968. [2] leaves + v + 145pp.***
(BES series, E261). L.C. Card 68--62863.
Designed to "acquaint researchers in the employment
security system and in other groups with the full scope of its
studies, the Employment Service has prepared the following
bibliography" which includes reports and study guides
prepared by federal, state, local, and private employment
agencies and groups.
L7.61:E261

139. U.S. Bureau of Health Manpower Education. *Minority Groups
in Medicine, Selected Bibliography.* 1972. [3] + 15pp. $.20*
L.C. Card 72--603081.
HE20.3113:M66

140. U.S. Bureau of Labor Statistics. *Bibliography of Manpower*

Projections for North Central Region. 1968. 3 leaves + vii + 55pp. Free***.
The studies listed are primarily from 1962–1967 and give ten to fifteen years manpower projections for the North Central states – Illinois, Indiana, Kentucky, Michigan, Minnesota, Ohio, and Wisconsin. Publications are grouped according to state. Additionally, the following appendices provide valuable information: (1) Sources of Current Manpower Projects Made by the U.S. Bureau of Labor Statistics; (2) Selected Sources of Federal Government and Other Manpower and Population Projections; (3) Sources of Methodology for Making Man-- power Projections, (4) Addresses of Organizations; and (5) Area Index.
L2.71/4:5

141. U.S. Bureau of Labor Statistics. *Counselor's Guide to Manpower Information, Annotated Bibliography of Government Publi-- cations.* 1968. vi + 101pp. $1.00* (BLS Bulletin no. 1598).
This selective bibliography of Federal and State materials is designed to help inform counselors about the current areas of manpower needs and to provide counselors and counselees with adequate material to enable a proper decision concerning education or occupation and training. Publications are grouped by such subjects as: Occupational Outlook Service Information; Occupational and Industry Manpower Studies; Manpower Problems and Issues; and Special Groups in the Labor Groups. Purchase and availability information is provided for the items listed.
L2.3:1598

142. U.S. Bureau of Labor Statistics. *Manpower and Employment Statistics Publications of the Bureau of Labor Statistics, Selected Bibliography;* prepared by Owen E. Delap. 1969. iv + 32pp.** L.C. Card 79–601763.
L2.34/2:M31

143. U.S. Civil Service Commission. *Guide to Federal Career Literature.* 1969. 32pp. $.55*.
Briefly described are 246 publications from a number of federal agencies and departments. These publications are used in recruiting for federal positions and are listed here to give a broad overview of the career opportunities available in the Federal government.
CS1.61:C18

144. U.S. Civil Service Commission. *Manpower Planning and Utilization.* 1971. [1972.] [2] + 58pp. $.60* S/N 0600--0615. (Personnel Bibliography, no. 39).
Emphasized in this bibliography are publications on manpower forecasting, planning, utilization, and shortages. The material included supplements *Personnel Bibliography no. 11* and covers the years 1968–1970. Entries are annotated.
CS1.61/3:39

145. U.S. Civil Service Commission. *Scientists and Engineers in the Federal Government.* 1970. [2] + 93pp. $1.00* (Personnel Bibliography , no. 30). L.C. Card 74--607712.
The title incorrectly indicates that scientists and engineers in the employee of the Federal government are the sole subjects treated by this bibliography. At least one fifth of the publication is concerned with the various aspects of recruiting, training, and pay practices of these professions in private industry.
Other topics, such as personality and professional character-istics of scientists and engineers, apply to private industry as well as to the Federal government. Entries are annotated.
CS1.61/3:30

146. U.S. Department of Defense. *College Graduate and National Security: Utilization of Manpower by the Armed Services, Bibliographic Survey;* prepared by Harry Moskowitz and Jack Roberts. 1968. viii + 74pp. $.75*.
Over 300 annotated references provide insight to (1) man-power trends in the United States; (2) American educational patterns and national needs for manpower; and (3) U.S. defense and manpower. Indexed by author.
D1.33:C68

147. U.S. Government Printing Office. *Professions and Job Descriptions.* Free* (Price List, no. 33A).
Listed are for sale and free publications. This list is revised frequently; prices are kept current; and all publications are supposedly available from the GPO.
GP3.9:33A

148. U.S. Public Health Service. Division of Manpower Intelligence. *Medical Specialties: Annotated Bibliography and Selected Ongoing Studies.* 1973. 30pp.***.
Annotated are recent publications on manpower studies in the major medical specialties. This is follwed by a list of selected

on--going medical manpower studies. The listing of publications
and studies are grouped by the name of the medical specialty:
General Practice and Family Practice; Dermatology; Internal
Medicine; Pediatrics; Surgery; Neurosurgery; Obstetrics and
Gynecology; Ophthalmology; Orthopedic Surgery; Urology;
Anesthesiology; Neurology; Pathology; Physical Medicine
and Rehabilitation; Psychiatry; and Radiology and
Therapeutic Radiology. Not indexed.
HE20.6109:M46

Labor and Industry

149. U.S. Bureau of Labor Statistics. *BLS Publications on Productivity
and Technology.* 1972. iv + 16pp.***.
Chronologically listed within major subject groups are the
publications issued by the Bureau of Labor Statistics Office
of Productivity and Technology since 1960 which deal
specifically with productivity and technology in the U.S.
and foreign countries.
L2.34/2:P94/6

150. U.S. Bureau of Labor Statistics. *Bureau of Labor Statistics
Catalog of Publications, Periodicals, Bulletins, Reports, and
Releases.* Semi--annual. Free***.
Supplements *Publications of the Bureau of Labor Statistics,
1886--1971* (no. 155).
L2.34:date

151. U.S. Bureau of Labor Statistics. *Directory of BLS Studies in
Industrial Relations, 1954--69.* 1969. 26pp. Free***
L.C. Card L58--55.
L2.34/2:In2/2/954--69 ·

152. U.S. Bureau of Labor Statistics. *Directory of BLS Studies in
Industrial Relations, 1960--71.* 1972. ii + 13pp. Free***.
Most of the publications listed in these directories were
prepared by the BLS Division of Industrial Relations. Major
subject headings are: Collective Bargaining Agreements,
Employee Benefit Plans; Union Activities; Work Stoppages;
Technical; and For Overseas Use Only.
L2.34/2:In2/2/960--71

153. U.S. Bureau of Labor Statistics. *Directory of Publications for
the North Central Region;* prepared by Maureen C. Glebes, David
J. Haster and Richard Hellman. 1969. [5] + 47pp.**.

154. U.S. Bureau of Labor Statistics. *Productivity, Selected Annotated Bibliography, 1965--71;* by Andrea Mooney Sweeny. 1973. iv + 107pp. $1.25* (BLS Bulletin 1776).

Annotated references for nearly 800 publications deal with the following aspects of productivity: concepts and methods; measurement of levels and trends; sources of productivity change (such as technology and economic growth); and the relation of productivity to the economy as a whole and to economic variables such as wages and prices. Author and subject indices make this a useful bibliography.
L2.3:1776

155. U.S. Bureau of Labor Statistics. *Publications of the Bureau of Labor Statistics, 1886–1971.* 1972. 184pp. $1.50* S/N 2901--0931. (BLS Bulletin 1749).

Listed by series and indexed by subject are the many and varied publications of the Bureau of Labor Statistics from 1886--1971. The Bureau's periodicals are not included in this list, but prefatory information provides access to them.
L2.3:1749

156. U.S. Bureau of Labor Statistics. *Sources of Information on Labor in Japan;* prepared by Theodore Bleecker. 1968. iii + 15pp.*** (BLS Reports, no. 351). L.C. Card 79--600707.

English language publications from 1960--1968 dealing with the labor situation in Japan are listed. Subject arrangement. Not indexed.
L2.71:351

157. U.S. Department of Commerce. *Industrial Processes, Selected Bibliographic Citations Announced in U.S. Government Re--search and Development Reports, 1966.* 1968. iii + 48pp.***.
C1.54:In2

158. U.S. Department of Labor. *Construction Industry Selected References, 1960–69.* 1970. [1] + 13pp.*** (Current Bibliographies, no. 2). L.C. Card 73--607062.
L1.34/4:2

159. U.S. Department of Labor. *Labor Mobility, Selected References.* 1969. 12pp.***

This alphabetical listing of books and periodicals on labor mobility supplements the original 1967 title. Not indexed.

L1.34:L11/6/supp.

160. U.S. Department of Labor. *Selected List of Recent Additions to the Library.* (3rd series). Weekly. ***.
L1.19:3d/no.

161. U.S. Government Printing Office. *Labor. Safety for Workers and Workmen's Compensation.* Free* (Price List no. 33).
Listed are for sale and free publications. This list is revised frequently; prices are kept current; and the publications listed are supposedly available from the GPO.
GP3.9:33

Management

161a. U.S. Bureau of Domestic Commerce. *Information Sources on Sales Management and Training, Selections from Marketing Information Guide.* 1970. [2] + 25pp.***.
Selected are 84 annotations on selling techniques, sales management and training, and compensation and incentives for salesmen. References are from 1965–1969.
C41.12:Sa3

162. U.S. Civil Service Commission. *Administration of Training.* 1973. [3] + 126pp. $1.50* S/N 0600–0754. (Personnel Bibliography Series, no. 51).
As a supplement to previous bibliographies in this series, the entries annotated here cover only 1971 and 1972. Materials listed focus primarily on the planning and administration of various training programs and methods. The section on supervisory development has been enlarged to include entries on supervisory methods which were formerly listed in *Supervisory Selection and Evaluation* (Personnel Bibliography Series, no. 26).
CS1.61/3:51

163. U.S. Civil Service Commission. *Employee--Management Relations in Public Service.* 1970. [2] + 62pp. $.60* (Personnel Bibliography Series, no. 36). L.C. Card 74--610105.
Specific attention is paid to (1) grievances and appeals in Federal, private, and public employment; (2) strikes in the public service; (3) employee participation in management; and (4) issues, practices and current developments in the Federal and public services. This updates *Personnel Bibliography Series, no. 7* and covers the period 1967–1969.

CS1.61/3:36

164. U.S. Civil Service Commission. *Executive Manpower Management.*
1971. 1972. [2] + 113pp. $1.00* S/N 0600–0616. (Personnel
Bibliography Series, no. 40).
The executives in federal, public, and private business or service
are the subjects of this bibliography. Various aspects of
executives are covered from their characteristics and re--
sponsibilities to their medical and health care. Entries are
annotated. Subject index.
CS1.61/3:40

165. U.S. Civil Service Commission. *Improving Employee Performance.*
1972. [2] + 95pp. $1.00* (Personnel Bibliography Series,
no. 45). L.C. Card 72–602873.
Supplementing no. 16 and 35 in this series, this bibliography
annotates materials received in the Civil Service Commission
Library during 1970 and 1971. References are primarily
concerned with the following: job enlargement as a motivating
device; fostering creativity and innovative behavior; use of
incentive awards; improving motivation and productivity; and
improving morale and job satisfaction.
CS1.61/3:45

166. U.S. Civil Service Commission. *Labor Management Relations
in the Public Service.* 1972. 2 + 74pp. $.70* (Personnel
Bibliography Series, no. 44). L.C. Card 72--602877.
References are to practices, current developments, grievances
and appeals in federal, public, and private employment.
CS1.61/3:44

167. U.S. Civil Service Commission. *Managing Human Behavior.*
1970. [3] + 177pp. $1.50* (Personnel Bibliography Series,
no. 35). L.C. Card 71–610115.
Motivation and maintaining morale seem to be the primary
subjects contained in this bibliography. Entries are
annotated.
CS1.61/3:35

168. U.S. Civil Service Commission. *Managing Overseas Personnel.*
1970. [2] + 86pp. $.75* (Personnel Bibliography Series, no.
37). L.C. Card 78–610106.
Various aspects of overseas employment in private business
and industry are presented by this bibliography. Some of the
specific topics under which the entries appear are: Cultural

Differences; Employment of Foreign Nationals; Overseas
Personnel Policies and Practices; and Foreign Visitors and
Students. Entries are annotated.
CS1.61/3:37

168a. U.S. Civil Service Commission. *Personnel Literature.* (Monthly
with separate volume index). $11.00* a year, $2.75 additional
foreign mailing. Index issue $2.25*.
Included are "selected books, pamphlets, and other publications
received in the library of the Civil Service Commission.
Periodical articles, unpublished dissertations, and microforms
are also listed." The arrangement is by subject.
CS1.62:Vol./no.

169. U.S. Civil Service Commission. *The Personnel Management
Function – Organization, Staffing, and Evaluation.* 1971. [1972].
[2] + 55pp. $.60* S/N 0600–0618. (Personnel Bibliography
Series, no. 42). L.C. Card 72–600693.
This bibliography updates Personnel Bibliography Series nos.
2, 27, and 28. Entries are primarily for 1969 and 1970.
Subject arrangement.
CS1.61/3:42

170. U.S. Civil Service Commission. *Personnel Policies and Practices.*
1970. [2] + 106pp. $1.00* (Personnel Bibliography Series,
no. 32). L.C. Card 73–609016.
Annotated references to the literature cover all aspects of
personnel management techniques and problems from
psychological testing and promotion to absenteeism and
dismissal.
CS1.61/3:32

171. U.S. Civil Service Commission. *Personnel Policies and Practices.*
1972. [5] + 69pp. $1.25* (Personnel Bibliography Series,
no. 46).
Updated by this bibliography are number 32 and 3 of this
series, which are respectively entitled *Personnel Policies and
Practices (1970)* and *Recruitment for the Public Service
(1968).*
Entries have lengthy annotations and are arranged by author
whithin the following major subject categories: Federal
Government and Public Service Examining Programs;
Recruitment; Selection and Placement; Performance Evalu--
ation and Appraisal Interviews; Promotion; Removal

Reinstatement; and Personnel Practices.
CS1.61/3:46

172. U.S. Civil Service Commission. *Planning, Organizing and Evaluating Training Programs.* [1971.] 1972. $1.25*
S/N 0600--0617. (Personnel Bibliography Series, no. 41)
Updates previous bibliographies in this series for the period 1968--70. Annotated, it treats the planning and administration of various training programs and methods.
CS1.61/3:41

173. U.S. Civil Service Commission. *Self--Development Aids for Supervisors and Middle Managers.* 1970. 208pp. $1.75*
(Personnel Bibliography Series, no. 34). L.C. Card 74--610050.
An annotated bibliography guiding management to various self--improvement aids in such areas as human relations, leadership, communicating, and decision--making.
CS1.61/3:34

174. U.S. Civil Service Commission. *State, County and Municipal Personnel Publications.* 1973. [5] + 79pp. $1.00*
S/N 0600--00704. (Personnel Bibliography Series, no. 48).
Concerned primarily with the recruitment, training, and treatment of public employees. Annotated entries grouped by subject.
CS1.61/3:48

175. U.S. Department of the Air Force. *Management, (Excluding Personnel);* prepared by Susan McEnally. 1969. [1] + v + 51pp.**
(PACAF Basic Bibliographies) L.C. Card 58--61790.
D301.62:M31/1/969

176. U.S. Department of the Air Force. *Personnel Management;* prepared by Mary Louise Sauer. 1970. [i] + iv + 71pp.**
(PACAF Basic Bibliographies). L.C. Card 58--61777.
See no. 178.
D301.62:P43/970

177. U.S. Department of the Air Force. *Personnel Management; Supp. 1.* 1971. [1] + iv + 52pp.**.
See no. 178.
D301.62:P43/970/Supp.1

178. U.S. Dpartment of the Air Force. *Personnel Management, Supp. 2.* 1972. [1] + v + 60pp.**.
Continuing, annotated bibliography of reference and general works on personnel administration, with purchase information.
D301.62:P43/970/Supp.2

179. U.S. Department of the Air Force. *Retention, Officers and Airmen, Selected References.* Supp. 4. 1969. 5pp.**
(Maxwell Air Force Base, Alabama, Air Univeristy Bibliography no. 147).
D301.26/11:147/supp.4

180. U.S. Department of the Army. *Planning and Evaluation of Personnel Management Programs, Bibliographic Survey.* 1969. ix + 73pp.** (DA Pam 600--9).
The 282 thoroughly annotated entries presented in this bibliography are intended to assist personnel managers in evaluating and planning their programs. Annotations are so complete that one should be able to determine easily which sources would help him most. The biliography is arranged by subsections of the following main sections: (1) Planning, Evaluation, and Controls in Contemporary Management; (2) Personnel Management in Theory and Practice; (3) Contemporary Manpower Problems; and (4) Selected Bibliographies and Guides for the Profession. Author index.
D101.22:600--9

181. U.S. Department of the Navy. Bureau of Naval Personnel. *Bibliography for Advancement Study.* 1971. 129pp.**
(NAVPERS 10052--S).
This is a revision of the 1969 edition of *Training Publications for Advancement.* Included is a tabular listing of "enlisted training manuals (Navy Training Courses) and other publications prescribed for use by all personnel concerned with advancement in rating training and examinations."
D208.15:Ad9

182. U.S. Department of Health, Education and Welfare. *Career Development, Selected References;* compiled by Dorothy M. Jones and Laura A. Miles. 2d edition, Rev. August 1968. 1968. [6] + 34pp.**.
"The purpose of this bibliography is to bring to the attention of line and personnel managers at least part of the materials available in the general field of career development." Entries cover all phases of employee development, including education and training. The lack of an index is a slight drawback in trying to use this bibliography.
FS1.18:C18/968

183. U.S. National Aeronautics and Space Administration. *Management: Continuing Literature Survey, with Indexes; Selection*

of Annotated References to Unclassified Reports and Journal Articles Entering the NASA Information System. 1968–. Irregular. NTIS. (NASA SP--7500) L.C. Card 68--61755. To date, the most current bibliography (no. 7) listed 389 reports, articles, and documents, mostly from the 1971--72 literature, on management. All entries, most of which have abstracts, are indexed by subject, author, and corporate source.
NAS1 21 7500(nos.)

183a. U.S. National Aeronautics and Space Administration. *Systems Approach to Management, an Annotated Bibliography, with Indexes.* 1969. vi + 62pp. NTIS. (NASA SP--7501). L.C. Card 75–603148.
NAS1.21:7501

184. U.S. National Labor Relations Board. *Bibliography, Labor Management Relations Act, 1947, as Amended by Labor--Management Reporting and Disclosure Act, 1959, Supplement 1, 1967;* compiled by Sylvia H. Washington. 1968. 64pp.**.
See no. 186.
LR1.3:L11/959--66/supp. 1

185. U.S. National Labor Relations Board. *Bibliography, Labor Management Relations Act, 1947, as Amended by Labor–Management Reporting and Disclosure Act, 1959, Supplement 2, 1970.* 1970. [1] + 16 + 37 + 8pp.**.
See no. 186.
LR1.3:L11/959–66/supp. 2

186. U.S. National Labor Relations Board. *Bibliography, Labor Management Relations Act, 1947, as Amended by Labor–Management Reporting and Disclosure Act, 1959, Supplement 3, 1973.* 1973. [1] + xii + 48pp.**.
These supplements update the original bibliography which covered labor and management relations from 1959–1966. Entries are arranged by type of publication: (1) Government Publications; (2) Books and Pamphlets; (3) General and Trade Periodicals; and (4) Legal Periodical Articles. Indexed by subject.
LR1.3:L11/959--66/supp.3

187. U.S. Public Health Service. *Training Methodology, Part I: Back--ground Theory and Research, an Annotated Bibliography;* compiled by NIMH and the NCDC of the Health Service and Mental Health Administration. 1969. vii + 90pp. $1.00*
L.C. Card 70--60177.

As the first of four bibliographies on "training methodology," this bibliography contains 310 annotated entries concerned with background theory and research in group and individual training. Entries are grouped by the following categories: Human Factors Engineering; Human Behavior and Behavioral Change (General); Perception; Motivation; Communication; Sociology of Education and Training; The Adult Learner – Socio–Psychological Factors; Learning Theory and Research (General); Learning Theory and Research (Specific Types and Aspects); Programmed Learning Theory and Research; Systems Theory and Applications; Role Theory; Groups – Dynamics, Process, Structure; Organizations and Organizational Change; Educational and Training Philosophies. Indexed by subject.
FS2.24:T68/pt.1

188. U.S. Public Health Service. *Training Methodology, Part II: Planning and Administration, an Annotated Bibliography.* 1969. vii + 119pp. $1.00*. L.C. 70--60177.
This second bibliography contains 447 annotated entries which deal primarily with the development and administration of training courses. Entries are grouped by the following categories: Learning Theory Applied to Instruction; Planning; Course Management; and Program Administration. Indexed by subject.
FS2.24:T68/pt.2

189. U.S. Public Health Service. *Training Methodology, Part III: Instructional Methods and Techniques, an Annotated Bibliography.* 1969. vii + 100pp. $1.00* L.C. 70–60177.
Contained are 330 annotated entries which pertain to specific instruction methods and techniques for both individuals and groups. Entries are grouped by twenty--five headings, among which are: Methods and Techniques; Job Instruction; Apprenticeship; Coaching; Internship, Field Work, Super--vised Professional Practice; Correspondence Study; Group Meetings; Case Method; Simulation and Gaming in Education (and Business); and Team Training and Organization Development. Indexed by subject.
FS2.24:T68/pt.3

190. U.S. Public Health Service. *Training Methodology, Part IV: Audiovisual Theory, Aids, and Equipment, an annotated Bibliography.* 1969. vii + 80pp. $.75* L.C. Card 70--601777.
Contained are 332 annotated entries concerned with the media

aspects of training, including audiovisual theory and methods, aids, facilities and equipment. Entries are grouped by subject categories, among which are: Audiovisual Theory and Research; Audiovisual Methods; Audiovisual Equipment; Television Instruction; Radio Instruction; Telephone Instruction; Visual Aids – Design and Use; Dial Access Retrieval Systems; and Guides, Other Sources. Indexed by subject.

Entries in each of these four bibliographies are generally post--1960.

FS2.24:T68/pt4

191. U.S. Small Business Administration. *Personnel Management;* by Raymond O. Loen. 1969. 12pp. Free*** (Small Business Bibliography, no. 72). L.C. Card 74–605718.

Listed are books and other publications, including business and professional magazines, which provide information on subjects related to personnel management. Not indexed.

SBA1.3:72/2

192. U.S. Small Business Administration. *Training Commercial Salesmen;* by Leonard J. Smith. Rev. 1972. 7pp. Free*** (Small Business Bibliography no. 56).

Listed are books and other publications, including periodicals and their articles, and audiovisual sales training materials concerned with the education and training of sales personnel. Prices, publishers, and a description of the publication are also given.

SBA1.3:56/3

193. U.S. Small Business Administration. *Training Retail Sales-people;* by William B. Logan. 1968. 8pp. Free*** (Small Business Bibliographies, no. 23). L.C. Card 70--600055.

See no. 192.

SBA1.3:23

194. U.S. Veterans Administration. *Executive Leadership in Public Service; Annotated List of Selected Monographs.* 1972. ii + 46pp.*** (Information Bulletin 11--17).

A revision of a 1970 publication by the same title, this bibliography contains 327 briefly annotated entries dealing with various aspects of executive creativity, decisionmaking, leadership, management, and administration. Subject arrangement. Author index. (This title was originally classed VA1.20/3:10--no.)

Marketing

195. U.S. Agricultural Marketing Service. *Available Publications of USDA's Agricultural Marketing Service.* 1973. 14pp. Free*** (AMS--546).
Publications are listed numerically by series according to subject matter. Subjects cover virtually all agricultural products (Ex. Fruit and Vegetables; Cotton; Tobacco). Most publications listed are free on request.
A88.40:546

196. U.S. Bureau of Domestic Commerce. *Information Sources on Marketing New Products, Selections from Marketing Information Guide.* [1969.] [2] + 24pp.***.
For those interested in marketing new products, this handy little guide lists and annotates publications under the headings of: Research; Planning and Production; Patents and Trademarks; Marketing Techniques; and General Information. All entries were formerly included in *Marketing Information Guide.*
C41.12:M34/5

197. U.S. Bureau of Domestic Commerce. *Information Sources on Marketing Research, Selections from Marketing Information Guide.* [1969.] [2] + 26pp.***.
One hundred selected annotations are listed under the follow--ing categories: Marketing Research; Applications to Special Markets; Advertising; Cost and Price Determinations; Data Processing; Location Research; Management Decision Making; Research Information Sources; Sales Forecasting; and Test Marketing and Surveys. Publications are dated from 1965 through 1969.
C41.12:M34/6

198. U.S. Bureau of Domestic Commerce. *Information Sources on Packaging, Selections from Marketing Information Guide.* [1969.] [2] + 26pp.***.
One hundred and five selected annotations on packaging are listed under the following headings: General Information; Directories; Economic Data; Management; Package Design; Regulation; and Research and Development. Purchase and availability information are provided.
C41.12:P12

199.   U.S. Bureau of Domestic Commerce. *Information Sources on the Youth Market, Selections from Marketing Information Guide.* 1969. [2] + 13pp.***.
Forty--five annotated references to the youth market are listed under the following headings: General; Children; Teenage; College; and Young Married. Full bibliographic and purchase information are provided.
C41.12:Y8

200.   U.S. Bureau of Domestic Commerce. *Marketing Information Guide. Annotated Bibliography.* Monthly. Vol. 1–18. 1954--1971. L.C. Card 59--30923.
This publication, which is no longer being published by the government, was arranged by: Marketing Functions, Policy, Methodology, and Operations; Areas and Markets; Industries and Commodities. Entries included were annotated, and complete bibliographic information was provided. Indexed with quarterly and annual cumulative indexes.
C41.11:Vol/no.

201.   U.S. Department of Agriculture. *A Bibliography of Marketing Research on Commercial Floriculture and Ornamental Horti-culture, 1965–1971;* compiled by Dorothy M. Lundquist. 1972. [2] + ii + 24pp.*** (USDA Miscellaneous Publication no. 1235).
Three hundred and forty--eight entries cover the production, wholesaling, retailing, and foreign marketing aspects of commercial floriculture and ornamental horticulture. Not indexed.
A1.38:1235

202.   U.S. Department of Agriculture. *A Bibliography of Tree Nut Production and Marketing Research, 1965--1971;* compiled by Dorothy M. Lundquist. 1972. vi + 37pp.*** (USDA Miscellaneous Publication no. 1255).
"This bibliography lists tree nut production and marketing research reports published during 1965--971. There is a section for each tree nut that is important in domestic trade channels."
A1.38:1255

203.   U.S. Department of Agriculture. Economic Research Service. *Marketing Economics Research Publications, a Reference List.* 1973. iii + 34pp.*** (ERS--205).

Publications and their availability are listed for all areas
of agricultural marketing and economics. Entries are
divided into four main categories and further subdivided into
more definitive subject areas. The main headings are:
Animal Products; Crops; Fibers and Textiles; and General--
Multiple Products. Not indexed or annotated. This
revises a 1968 publication by the same title.
A93.21:205(Rev.)

204. U.S. Department of Agriculture. Economic Research Service.
*Research Publications on Dairy Marketing Economics, an
Annotated Bibliography.* Rev. 1969. [2] + 33pp.***
(ERS--406).
A93.21:406

204a. U.S. National Agricultural Library. *Marketing of Livestock,
Meat and Meat Products, 1962--June 1967, List of Selected
References;* compiled by Minnie N. Fuller and Betty B.
Baxtress. 1968. [1] + iv + 73pp.*** (Library List no. 92).
L.C. Card Agr69--290.
Over 1000 entries comprise this bibliography which is
concerned with the economics of meat marketing.
Arrangement is alphabetical under broad subject
classifications such as: Auctions; Terminal Markets; Trans--
portation -- Shrinkage, Injury and Damage; Grading and
Quality -- Lamb; and Pricing and Market Organizations.
Subject and author indices.
A17.17:92

205. U.S. Small Business Administration. *Statistics and Maps for
National Market Analysis;* by Thomas T. Semon. 1968.
8pp. Free*** (Small Business Bibliography, no. 12).
L.C. Card 70--605898.
Listed are guides to statistics and maps for analyzing
market prospects.
SBA1.3:12

Small Business

206. U.S. Small Business Administration. *Apparel and Accessories
for Women, Misses, and Children;* by Karen R. Gillespie.
1971. 23pp. Free*** (Small Business Bibliography, no.
50).
Included are government, non--government, and trade
association publications for those interested in managing

a girls' and ladies' apparel shop. Not indexed.
SBA1.3:50/3

207. U.S. Small Business Administration. *Bookstores;* by Max L.
Williamson. 1968. 8pp. Free*** (Small Business Biblio--
graphy, no. 42/3). L.C. Card 68--62718.
For one interested or involved in a retail bookstore, this
bibliography could prove quite useful. Buying guides,
journals, publishers, and trade associations combine to form
a useful bookman's bibliography. (This could also prove
useful to beginning librarians or one involved in setting
up a library.)
SBA1.3:42/3

208. U.S. Small Business Administration. *Discount Retailing;*
by H. Nicholas Windeshausen. 1970. 7pp. Free*** (SBA
Bibliography, no. 68).
"This bibliography lists books and other publications, in--
cluding periodicals, which should provide information on
discount retailing. Also listed are some trade associations
that promote the low--margin retailing practices." Not
indexed.
SBA1.3:68/4

209. U.S. Small Business Administration. *Drugstores;* by Joseph
D. McEvilla. 1970. 8pp. Free*** (Small Business Biblio--
graphy, no. 33).
Listed are publications, including periodicals, which provide
information on retail drugstore management. A list of
professional and trade associations follow the biblio--
graphy.
SBA1.3:33/3

210. U.S. Small Business Administration. *Hardware Retailing.*
Rev. 1968. 4pp. Free*** (Small Business Bibliographies,
no. 35). L.C. Card 72--600190.
Listed are books, periodicals, and pamphlets of interest
to the hardware retailer. Trade associations and their
addresses are also listed.
SBA1.3:35

211. U.S. Small Business Administration. *Inventory Management;*
by Donald F. Mulvihill. 1969. 8pp. Free*** (Small
Business Bibliography, no. 75). L.C. Card 77--606965.
Besides books and periodicals on the subject, some of the

professional and trade associations active in the field of
inventory management are also listed.
SBA1.3:75/2

212. U.S. Small Business Administration. *Machine Shops – Job
Type;* by B.W. Niebel. 1968. 10pp. Free*** (Small
Business Bibliography, no. 69). L.C. Card 68–62868.
The publications listed include all basic information
needed in establishing and managing a machine shop.
SBA1.3:69/2

213. U.S. Small Business Administration. *Manufacturers' Sales
Representative;* by John C. Warren. 1970. 11pp. (Small
Business Bibliography, no. 67). L.C. Card 75--609500.
Besides the listing of books, articles, periodicals, and
associations and consultants, there is information on the
actual purpose and function a manufactures' agent.
SBA1.3:67/3

214. U.S. Small Business Administration. *Men's and Boys' Wear
Stores;* by Don DeBolt. 1968. 8pp. Free***. (Small
Business Bibliography no. 45). L.C. 68--62871.
"This bibliography provides a list of publications and trade
associations which should be helpful to persons interested
in establishing and promoting a profitable men's and boys'
wear store." Publications are so specific that they deal with
how to select shirts, underwear, etc.
SBA1.3:45/3

215. U.S. Small Business Administration. *Mobile Homes and
Parks;* by John M. Martin. 1969. 11pp. Free*** (Small
Business Bibliography, no. 41).
"This bibliography lists publications, including books,
directories, and magazines, which provide information
relating to mobile homes and recreational vehicles and their
park facilities requirements." National, regional, and
state trade associations and their addresses are listed.
SBA1.3:41/5

216. U.S. Small Business Administration. *Motels;* by Albert E.
Kudrle. 1970. 11pp. Free*** (Small Business Biblio--
graphy, no. 66).
Books, pamphlets, periodicals, and trade associations that
would prove beneficial to the prospective and active
owner--managers of motels are listed.

SBA1.3:66/3

217. U.S. Small Business Administration. *Nursery Business;* by John J. Pinney. 1971. 12pp. Free*** (Small Business Bibliography, no. 14).

Listed are books and other publications, including periodicals, which provide information to help prospective and current owner--managers develop their small nursery and landscaping business. Included is a list of trade associations.

SBA1.3:14

218. U.S. Small Business Administration. *Painting and Wall Decorating;* by J. Wade Rice. 1968. 8pp. Free*** (Small Business Bibliography, no. 60). L.C. Card 68--61397.

SBA1.3:60/2

219. U.S. Small Business Administration. *Photographic Dealers and Studios;* by William G. McClanahan. 1968. 8pp. Free*** (Small Business Bibliography, no. 64). L.C. Card 78--600432.

Listed are books and other publications, including periodicals, which provide information of interest to photographic dealers and owners of studios. Also listed are some of the mailing addresses of professional and trade associations.

SBA1.3:64/3

220. U.S. Small Business Administration. *Real Estate Business;* by Karl G. Pearson. 1968. [Published 1969]. 11pp. Free*** (Small Business Bibliography, no. 65).

Selected books, periodicals, and other publications con--taining information about the real estate business are listed.

SBA1.3:65/3

221. U.S. Small Business Administration. *Restaurants and Catering.* 1968. 18 + [1]pp. Free*** (Small Business Bibliography, no. 17).

SBA1.3:17

222. U.S. Small Business Administration. *Retailing;* by William R. Davidson, et al. 1969. 15pp. Free*** (Small Business Bibliography, no. 10). L.C. Card 76--602809.

Listed are "publications, including books, monographs, and special studies issued by governmental and private

publishers. The list of citations provide information on retailing which can be used by owner–managers of existing retail stores and prospective owner–managers."
SBA1.2:10

223.   U.S. Small Business Administration. *Small Business Administration Publications: For--Sale Booklets.* Irregular.***.
This is a checklist of currently available publications.
Not indexed.
SBA1.18:date

224.   U.S. Small Business Administration. *Small Frozen Dessert Stands;* by Karl Kern. 1971. 11pp. Free*** (Small Business Bibliography, no. 47).
"Included are books, articles, and periodicals which provide information of interest to prospective and active owner–managers of soft--frozen dessert stands."
SBA1.3:47/2

225.   U.S. Small Business Administration. *Suburban Shopping Centers;* by Robert H. Myers. 1971. 11 + [1]pp. Free*** (Small Business Bibliography, no. 27).
The small businessman who is considering locating in a suburban shopping center would find the publications listed here of great value in making a decision. Trade associations are listed.
SBA1.3:27/3

226.   U.S. Small Business Administration. *Survey of Federal Government Publications of Interest to Small Business;* compiled by Elizabeth G. Janazeck. 3d ed. 1969. ix + 85pp. $.45* L.C. Card 74--604710.
SBA1.18/2:G74/969

227.   U.S. Small Business Administration. *Variety Stores;* by Sidney Hollander, jr. 1969. 8pp. Free*** (Small Business Bibliography, no. 21). L.C. Card 77--603667.
Listed are publications and trade associations which provide information on variety stores and related fields of retailing.
SBA1.3:21/4

228.   U.S. Small Business Administration. *Wholesaling;* by Theodore N. Beckman, Alton F. Doody & Daniel J. Sweeney. 1971. 23pp. Free*** (Small Business Bibliography, no. 55).

Though intended for the small wholesaler, the basic sources of information listed here will prove useful to career students and prospective wholesalers.
SBA1.3:55/5

Wages, Earnings, and Benefits

229. U.S. Bureau of Labor Statistics. *A Directory of Area Wage Surveys, July 1965–June 1967.* (Revised) 1968. i + 24pp.***.
L2.34/2:W12/4/965--967

230. U.S. Bureau of Labor Statistics. *A Directory of Area Wage Surveys, July 1969--June 1971.* 1972. iii + 40pp.***.
L2.34/2:W12/4/969--971

231. U.S. Bureau of Labor Statistics. *A Directory of Area Wage Surveys, July 1970–December 1972.* 1973. iii + 41pp.***.
Listed by state are Bureau of Labor Statistics area wage surveys. Also included is a list of bulletins and articles issued from 1959 through 1972 which summarize area wage surveys.
L2.34/2:W12/4/970--972

232. U.S. Bureau of Labor Statistics. *A Directory of BLS Studies in Employee Compensation, 1947--71.* 1972. 20pp.***.
The studies, most of which were prepared by the Bureau of Labor Statistics Office of Wages and Industrial Relations, are listed under the following main subject headings: Em Employee Compensation and Payroll Hours; Annual Earnings and Employment Patterns; Earnings and Hour's Frequency Distributions Non--occupational Studies; Employee Benefit Plans; and Special Studies. Purchase information is provided in the bibliographic descriptions.
L2.34/2:Em7/947--71

233. U.S. Bureau of Labor Statistics. *A Directory of Industry Wage Surveys and Union Wage Rate Studies, 1960--71.* 1972. iv + 24pp.***.
Part A of the *Directory* lists wage surveys by both manufacturing and non--manufacturing industries. The entries listed in Part B "provide information on minumum wages and maximum schedules of hours at straight--time rates agreed upon through collective bargaining between trade unions and employers in selected cities. Rates over the negotiated minumum, which may be paid for special

qualifications or other reasons, are not included." Not indexed.
L2.34/2.W12/960–71

234.   U.S. Civil Service Commission. *Employee Benefits and Services.* 1970. [2] + 150pp. $1.25* (Personnel Bibliography Series, no. 33). L.C. Card 74–608657.
Extensive coverage is given for employee benefit plans such as sick leave, income loss protection, life and health insurance, retirement plans and policies, occupational health and safety, and counseling services. Entries are annotated and are grouped by subjects. Not indexed.
CS1.61/3:33

235.   U.S. Civil Service Commission. *Employee Benefits and Services.* 1972 (Published in 1973). [5] + 69pp. $.95* (Personnel Bibliography Series, no. 47).
This supplements Personnel Bibliography no. 33 (no. 234). Lengthy annotated references cover such areas as: Employee Benefit Plans; Sick Leave and Income Loss Protection; Retirement Planning; Occupational Health and Safety; Counseling Services; and Vacation Leave. Not indexed.
CS1.61/3:47

236.   U.S. Civil Service Commission. *Position Classification and Pay in the Federal Government.* 1970. [2] + 63pp. $.65* (Personnel Bibliography Series, no. 31). L.C. Card 78--608832.
As a supplement to an earlier compilation by the same title, this bibliography covers the literature received by the Civil Service Library from 1965--1969. Though most of the entries pertain to pay administration and position classification and management in the Federal Government, two full sections are devoted to similar topics in private industry and business. Entries are annotated and grouped according to topic.
CS1.61/3:31

237.   U.S. Civil Service Commission. *Position Classification and Pay in the Federal Government.* 1973. [3] + 48pp. $.90. S/N 0600--00753. (Personnel Bibliography Series, no. 50).
Covering materials received by the Civil Service Library primarily from 1970--1972, this bibliography supplements No. 31 (no. 236) of this series. (See no. 236 for

annotation.)
CS1.61/3:50

238.   U.S. Department of Labor. Unemployment Insurance
Service. *Selected Bibliography of Unemployment Insurance
Program Research Studies, 1951--1970.* 1971. ix + 163pp.***
L.C. Card 74--616109.
"This bibliography was prepared as a ready reference to
serve the needs of State employment security agencies,
other governmental and private research groups, and
students interested in research in unemployment
insurance."
L33.12:Un2/951--70

EDUCATION

General

239.   U.S. Department of the Air Force. *Television in Education:
Selected References.* 1971. 9pp. Free*** (Air University
Library, Maxwell Air Force Base, Ala. Special Bibliography
no. 18).
Contained are current references to books and articles
on television training applications, program techniques, and
technical aspects of television used for educational
purposes. Not indexed.
D301.26/11:18(rev.)

240.   U.S. Executive Office of the President. Office of Economic
Opportunity. *Selected References in the Field of Early
Childhood Education.* 1968. 5pp.***.
This is a memeographed list of books, pamphlets, and
articles on early childhood education.
PrEx10.15:C43

241.   U.S. National Institute of Education. *Research in Education.*
1966--Vol.1--. Monthly. $38.00 a yr. $9.50 add. foreign
mailing. L.C. Card 72--216727.
Known to its users as *"ERIC"*, these monthly abstracts
provide up--to--date information on all aspects of
educational research from infancy to old age. Incompassed
are the many sociological, psychological, physiological, and
ethnological studies concerning education and the physical,
mental, and social development of children, youth, and
adults. Each issue is thoroughly indexed, and each entry

has a complete bibliographic description, price and availability note, and a good annotation. Semi–annual and annual cumulative indexes may be purchased separately.
HE18.10:Vol./No.

242. U.S. Office of Education. *Aids to Media Selection for Students and Teachers;* compiled by Yvonne Carter and others. 1971. vi + 82pp. $.75. S/N 1780–810. L.C. Card 78--614373.
Describes sources (post 1965) reviewing books, audiovisuals, and multiethnic instructional materials. Gives full infor-- mation, annotation and price. Subject arrangement with author--title index.
HE5.234:34045

242a. U.S. Office of Education. *Supplement to Aids to Media Selection for Students and Teachers;* compiled by Yvonne Carter and others. 1973. iv + 67p. $.95*. L.C. Card 78-614373.
HE5.234:34045/Supp.
Lists an additional 226 entries published or revised since 1970.

243. U.S. Office of Education. *Books Related to Compensatory Education;* compiled by Lois B. Watt and others. 1969. 46pp. $.50* (OE--37045). L.C. Card 70--604358.
Books received by the OE's Educational Materials Center, including textbooks, juvenile literature, and professional resources. Includes grade level and a brief annotation.
FS5.237:37045

244. U.S. Office of Education. *ERIC Products, 1967–68, Biblio-- graphy of Information Analysis Publications of ERIC Clearinghouse, July 1967--June 1968.* 1969. iv + 18pp.***
L.C. Card 70--608002.
HE5.77/2:967--68

245. U.S. Office of Education. *Education, Literature of the Profession, Bibliography Based on Acquisitions of the Educational Materials Center from April 16, 1966–December 31, 1968;* by Eunice von Ende. [1969]. v + 34pp. $.45* (OE–10060). L.C. Card 77–602722.
See no. 245a.
FS5.210:10060

245a. U.S. Office of Education. *Education, Literature of the Profession, Bibliography Based on Acquisitions of the Educational Materials Center from January 1, 1969--June 30, 1970.* 1970. v + 41pp. $.50.*.
Entries, some of which are annotated, are listed by subjects

under two main divisions -- (1) Interpretation and Comment and (2) Bibliographies and Directories. Some of the subjects are: History, Theory, and Issues; Educational Psychology; Child Development; Curriculum Development; Higher Education; Library Service and Information Science; and Subject and Methods. Included is a list of periodicals with order information and a directory of publishers. HE5.120:10060-A

246. U.S. Office of Education. *Foreign Language, Area Studies, and Other Aspects of International Education, Completed Research and Instructional Materials Produced Under NDEA Act of 1958, Title 6, Sec. 602, Bibliography List 7;* compiled by Julia A. Petrov. 1972. v + 66pp. $.90.*.
Cumulated here are the results of all activities carried out under the research authority of Title VI, Section 602, that were completed by April 1972. Most reports have been deposited with the Educational Resources Information Center (ERIC) and bear the ERIC accession number. HE5.214:14172

247. U.S. Office of Education. *Literature for Disadvantaged Children, Bibliography from the Educational Materials Center;* compiled by Lois B. Watt. 1968. [2] + 16pp. $.20.*.
This is a reprint of "Children's Literature" from *The Education of Disadvantaged Children,* pp. 19--31 (OE–14031–38). This is a reading list arranged alpha--betically by author under subject headings. Entries are annotated and the grade level indicated. FS5.237:37019

248. U.S. Office of Education. *Mexican American Education: A Selected Bibliography (with ERIC Abstracts), ERIC/CRESS supp. 2;* compiled by Albert D. Link. 1972. 350pp. $2.50.* S/N 1780–1063.
Though the title indicates that this bibliography deals solely with Mexican American education, many entries pertain to the social, cultural, and economic characteristics of the Mexican American. Subject index. HE5.10:M57/supp.2

249. U.S. Office of Education. *Migrant Education, Selected Bibliography, Supp. 2;* compiled by David M. Altus. 1971. viii + [1] + 129pp. $1.25* S/N 1780–0850.

Entries are drawn from the *Current Index to Journals in Education* and *Research in Education.* Indexed by subject.
HE5.10:M58/supp.2

250. U.S. Office of Education. *Office of Education Publications.* Annual. * L.C. HEW64--37.
Listed are publications from the Office of Education which are currently available. Entries are annotated. Title index.
HE5.211:11000–yr.

251. U.S. Office of Education. *Outdoor Education, a Selected Bibliography, Supp. 1;* compiled by David M. Altus. 1971. viii + [1] + 254pp. $2.00* S/N1780–0832.
See no. 252.
HE5.10:Ou8/supp.1

252. U.S. Office of Education. *Outdoor Education, a Selected Bibliography, Supp. 2.* 1973. 169pp.*.
Selections in these supplements are from the Education Research Information Center (ERIC) and Clearinghouse on Rural Education and Small Schools (CRESS) files.
All phases of outdoor education, from camping to programs for retarded persons are included. A subject index facilitates its use.
HE5.10:Ou8/supp.2

253. U.S. Office of Education. *Publications of the National Center for Educational Statistics.* 1972. Fold--out. Free***.
Included are 43 publications with purchase information and order form.
HE5.10:N21/2

254. U.S. Office of Education. *Reference Tools 1968--69: a Bibliography Based on Acquisitions of the Educational Materials Center from January 1968--July 1969;* prepared by Caroline Stanley. 1969. 10pp. $.25* (OE--10063).
Arrangement is by type of reference tool – dictionaries, atlases, bibliographies, etc. – which might be of value to elementary and secondary schools. This could serve as a good basic buying guide for school libraries. Annotations are given when the title is not self--explanatory. Not indexed.
FS5.210:10063

255. U.S. Office of Education. *Selected Office of Education*

Publications and Related Information on International Education. 1973. 11pp.** (OE 73–19001).
Fifty publications are briefly abstracted. Cost and purchase information is given for each.
HE5.10:In8/3

Adult Education

256. U.S. Department of the Air Force. *Self–Education for Adults;* prepared by Louise R. Donohue. 1970.***.
See no. 257.
D301.62:Se4/970

257. U.S. Department of the Air Force. *Self–Education for Adults, Supp. 1;* prepared by Louise R. Donohue. 1971. 1 + iv + 27pp.***.
All aspects of intermediate education (and some higher education) are covered. Included are citations to selected books on such topics as public speaking, geometry, physics and philosophy.
D301.62:Se4/970/supp.1

258. U.S. Office of Education. *Adult Basic Education; Bibliography from the Educational Materials Center;* compiled by Lois B. Watt and Sidney E. Murphy. 1968. 14pp. $.30* (OE–14031–41). L.C. Card HEW68–157.
Listed with occasional annotations are the complete holdings of the Educational Materials Center for "teaching adults the first essential skills of reading, writing, arithmetic, community living, and citizenship" as of 1968.
FS5.214:14031–41

259. U.S. Office of Education. *Books Related to Adult Basic Education and Teaching English to Speakers of Other Languages, Bibliography Based on Acquisitions of Educational Materials Center, as of May 1, 1970;* compiled by Myra H. Thomas, Thelma M. Knuths, and Sidney E. Murphy. 1970. iii + [1] + 18pp. $.30*. L.C. Card 73–610058.
This is primarily a list of textbooks and professional resources. The items listed are current as of 1970. No evaluation for them is provided.
HE5.213:13039

Elementary and Secondary Education

260. U.S. Congress. House. Committee on Education and Labor.

Elementary and Secondary Education Act of 1965, as Amended; prepared by the Congressional Research Service. 1973. v + 70pp.**.

"Selected and annotated bibliography, prepared by CRS under direction of the General Subcommittee on Education, providing brief descriptions of primary aims, finding, and recommendations of the major books, articles, monographs, and Government Reports and hearings dealing with the ESEA of 1965, as amended. Includes works with a national or regional scope, omitting, with few exceptions, reports on individual States or cities.

"Organized with separate sections for the current titles of ESEA and on section on materials covering ESEA over on more than one title." (Abstract from *CIS Annual 1973*, H342–11).

260a. U.S. Office of Education. *Books Related to Social Studies in Elementary and Secondary Schools, a Bibliography Based on Acquisitions of the Educational Materials Center;* compiled by Lois B. Watt, Delia Goetz, and Caroline Stanley. 1969. iii + 27pp. $.35* (OE–31011). L.C. Card 72–605030.

The books listed here have been favorably reviewed in at least two major professional journals which cover such books or they have been reviewed favorably by group or committee action.

FS5.231:31011

261. U.S. Office of Education. *Completed Research, Studies, and Instructional Materials for Language Development Under the National Defense Education Act of 1958, Title 6, Sec. 602, Bibliography (List 6);* compiled by Julia A. Petrov. 1969. iii + 144pp. $1.25*.

The 518 entries included are reports and instructional materials completed under the NDEA of 1956, Title 6, Sec. 602 contracts before July 1, 1968. The major source(s) and publisher's or author's address is given. This sixth edition supercedes all previous editions. (See no. 246 for more recent edition).

FS5.212:12016

262. U.S. Office of Education. *Environmental--Ecological Education: a Bibliography of Fiction, Nonfiction, and Textbooks for Elementary and Secondary Schools;* compiled by Lois B. Watt and Myra H. Thomas. 1971. [3] + 34pp.

$.40* S/N 1780--0886.
The materials listed would be useful in an environmental--educational curriculum. Included are textbooks for elementary and secondary school students, juvenile literature, and professional resources for teachers.
HE5.10:En8

263.   U.S. Office of Education. *Rural Education and Small Schools, Selected Bibliography, Supplement 1;* compiled by David M. Altus. 1971. viii + [1] + 486pp. $3.50* S/N 1780--0833.
See no. 264.
HE5.10:R88/2/supp.1

264.   U.S. Office of Education. *Rural Education and Small Schools, Selected Bibliography, ERIC/CRESS Supp. 2;* compiled by Albert D. Link. 1972. 385pp. $2.75* S/N 1780--1062.
These bibliographies completely cover articles, books, and documents on small schools and rural education which were abstracted by *Research in Education* and *Current Index to Journals in Education.* A combined *RIE* and *CIJE* index assists the use in locating specific information. Purchase information is provided for the items listed.
HE5.10:R88/2/supp.2

265.   U.S. Senate. *What Should be the Policy Toward Financing Elementary and Secondary Education in the United States? A Collection of Excerpts and Bibliography Relating to the High School Debate Topic, 1972–73;* compiled by the Congressional Research Service, Library of Congress. 1972. $1.50* (Sen.Doc. 92--74).
Bibliography and excerpts are divided into three parts relating to the following debate propositions: (1) Resolved, That a voucher system should be established as the primary means of financing elementary and secondary education in the United States; (2) Resolved, That governmental financial support for all public elementary and secondary education in the United States should be provided exclusively by the federal government; (3) Resolved, That public funds should be the primary means of financing parochial and secular private elementary and secondary education in the United States. A section on "How to Get More Information on Education" is also included. Not indexed.
Sen. Doc. 92--74

266. U.S. Forest Service. *Forest Products Laboratory, List of Publications Relating to Industrial Arts and Vocational Education.* 1970. 6pp. Free***.
"This list includes recent publications that give general information and the results by the Forest Products Laboratory of interest to teachers or administrators in industrial arts and vocational education."
A13.27/7:In2/970

267. U.S. Office of Education. *Agriculture Education, Instructional Materials, Compilation of Abstracts of Instructional Materials in Vocational and Technical Education, 1967--71.* 1972. viii + 440pp. $3.25*.
Over 950 documents cover such specific areas as: Agribusiness; Agricultural Machinery; Agronomy; Animal and Plant Sciences; Farm Mechanics; Flori-- culture; Food Processing; Horticulture; Landscaping; and Off--Farm Agricultural Occupations. Subject, Author, and Contract number indexes help to make this a most useful reference sourcebook.
HE5.10:Ag8/967--71

268. U.S. Office of Education. *Business and Office Education, Instructional Materials: Compilation of Abstracts from Abstracts of Instructional Materials in Vocational and Technical Education, 1967--71.* 1972. viii + [1] + 117pp. $1.25*.
The over 200 documents abstracted here cover such specific areas as: accounting, bookkeeping, business administration, business English, clerical occupations, data processing, office management, secretarial positions, and stenography. Indexed by subject and author with ERIC descriptors.
HE5.10:B96/967--71

269. U.S. Office of Education. *Distributive Education, Instructional Materials: a Compilation of Abstracts from Abstracts of Instructional Materials in Vocational and Technical Edu-- cation, 1967--71.* viii + [1] + 140pp. $1.25*.
Over 250 documents are abstracted and cover such topics as: commercial art, food service industry, management, marketing, merchandising, retailing, sales occupations, and wholesaling. Author and Subject Indexes with ERIC

descriptors.
HE5.10:D63/967–71

270. U.S. Office of Education. *Health Occupations Education, Instructional Materials: a Compilation of Abstracts from Abstracts of Instructional Materials in Vocational and Technical Education, 1967–1971.* 1972. vii + [1] + 89pp. $1.00*.

Abstracted are over 150 documents on education for health related professions and occupations. Subject, Author and Contract Number indexes facilitate the use of this source-book.
HE5.10:H34/2/967–71

271. U.S. Office of Education. *Home Economics Education, Instructional Materials: Compilation of Abstracts from Abstracts of Instructional Materials in Vocational and Technical Education, 1967–71.* 1972. viii + [1] + 161pp. $1.50*.

Over 300 abstracts cover such specific areas of home economics education as: child care occupations, consumer education, day care programs, foods instruction, home management, homemaking education, interior design, money management, sewing instruction, and textiles instruction. Subject, Author, and Contract Number indexes make this a worthwhile reference sourcebook.
HE5.10:H75/967–71

272. U.S. Office of Education. *Trade and Industrial Education, Instructional Materials: Compilation of Abstracts from Abstracts of Instructional Materials in Vocational and Technical Education, 1967–71.* 1972. viii + [1] + 536pp.*.

The more than 1,500 documents abstracted here cover such specific areas of trade and industrial education as: apprenticeships, barbers, building design and trades, cooks, cosmetologists, electronics, industrial technology, machinists, metalworking and welders. Subject, Author, and Contract Number indexes make this a worthwhile reference sourcebook.
HE5.10:T67/967–71

273–279. The following publications consist of annotated listings of printed materials produced by Federal agencies which are relevent to a particular vocational technical education program. Theses directories list some 1,600 training and curriculum documents and provide information on materials available for use in school vocational programs. The listing for each document provides title, date published, number of pages, source and price, as well as giving relevant instructional programs and descriptive information.

273. U.S. Office of Education. *Vocational Instructional Materials for Agriculture Available from Federal Agencies.* 1971. [2] + vi + 74 + 50pp. $1.50*.
    (See note heading no. 273--279).
    HE5.10:V85ag

274. U.S. Office of Education. *Vocational Instructional Materials for Distributive Education Available from Federal Agencies.* 1971. [2] + vii + 43 + 50pp. $1.25* S/N 1780--0837.
    (See note heading no. 273--279).
    HE5.10:V85ed

275. U.S. Office of Education. *Vocational Instructional Materials for Health Occupations Education available from Federal Agencies.* 1971. [2] + vii + 26 + 50pp. $1.00* S/N 1780--0838.
    (See note heading no. 273--279).
    He5.10:V85he

276. U.S. Office of Education. *Vocational Instructional Materials for Home Economics Available from Federal Agenices.* 1971. [2] + vii + 33 + 50pp. $1.00* S/N 1780--0839.
    (See note heading no. 273--279).
    HE5.10:V85ec

277. U.S. Office of Education. *Vocational Instructional Materials for Office Occupations Available from Federal Agencies.* 1971. [2] + vii + 27 + 50pp. $1.00* S/N 1780--0840.
    (See note heading no. 273--279).
    HE5.10:V85of

278. U.S. Office of Education. *Vocational Instructional Materials for Technical Education Available from Federal Agencies.* 1971. [2] + vii + 48 + 50pp. $1.25* S/N 1780--0841.
    (See note heading no. 273--279)
    HE5.10:V85te

279. U.S. Office of Education. *Vocational Instructional Materials*

for Trade and Industrial Occupations Available from Federal Agencies. 1971. [2] + vii + 84 + 50pp. $1.50* S/N 1780--0842.
  (See note heading no. 273--279).
  HE5.10:V85tr

280--284. The following publications consist of briefly annotated listings of curriculum materials which are available from state agencies. The materials listed are designed to "apprise planners, administrators, vocational educators, and others interested in offering or involved in vocational education programs of the available curriculum materials developed by the various states. The material listed in these bibliographies is available from State education agencies and not from the Superintendent of Documents or other Federal agencies.

280. U.S. Office of Education. *Vocational Education State Instructional Materials for Agriculture Available from State Education Agencies.* 1973. iii + 73(A)pp. $1.05* S/N 1780--01169.
  (See note heading no. 280--285).
  HE5.10:V85ag/2

281. U.S. Office of Education. *Vocational Education State Instructional Materials for Distributive Education Available from State Education Agencies.* 1973. [2] + ii + 62pp. $.95*.
  (See note heading no. 280--285).
  HE5.10:V85di/2

282. U.S. Office of Education. *Vocational Education State Instructional Materials for Health Occupations Education Available from State Education Agencies.* 1973. iii + 19(H)pp. $.50*.
  (See note heading no. 280--285).
  HE5.10:V85he/2

283. U.S. Office of Education. *Vocational Education State Instructional Materials for Home Economics Available from State Education Agencies.* 1973. iii + 28(HE)pp. $.60*.
  (See note heading no. 280--285).
  HE5.10:V85ho/2

284. U.S. Office of Education. *Vocational Education State*

Instructional Materials for Office Occupations Available from State Education Agencies. 1973. iii + 25(O)pp. $.60*. (See note heading no. 280–285).
HE5.10:V85of/2

285.   U.S. Office of Education. *Vocational Education State Instructional Materials for Technical Education Available from State Education Agencies.* 1973. iii + 18(T)pp. $.50*. (See note heading no. 280–285).
HE5.10:V85te/2

ENVIRONMENTAL DESIGN AND PLANNING

General

286.   U.S. Department of Housing and Urban Development. *Equal Opportunity, Bibliography of Research on Equal Opportunity in Housing.* 1969. 24pp. $.30* (MP–86).
The 166 publications referenced in this bibliography are representative of the published studies on equal opportunity in housing. Publications are listed according to such subjects as: Settlement Patterns; Economic Aspects; Sociological Studies; Community Action Process; and Research Needs and Methodology. Indexed by author.
HH1.28:86

287.   U.S. Department of Housing and Urban Development. *Home-ownership and Resident Counseling: a Selected Bibliography.* 1972. [3] + i + 65pp.***.
"The bibliography is a selection of publications on money management, housing selection, purchase procedures, property care and maintenance, and home management." Addenda include audio–visual resources and a list of bibliographies dealing with homeownership.
HH1.23:H75

288.   U.S. National Agricultural Library. *Beauty for America, January 1966–May 1968;* compiled by Minnie L. Fuller. 1968. iii + 32pp.*** (Library List, no. 94). L.C. Card Agr68–334.
Listed are 496 references "to literature on landscape improvement, slum clearance, highway scenery enhance-ment, and related areas of conservation." Federal, State, local, and personal beautification programs are included. Entries are listed alphabetically by author and

indexed by subject.
A17.17:94

Architecture, Planning, and Design

289. U.S. Department of the Air Force. Pacific Air Forces. *Archi-- tecture, Building and Engineering;* prepared by Deloris Lawrence 1970. [1] + iv + 93pp.** (PACAF Basic Bibliographies). L.C. Card 58--61780. See no. 290. D301.62:Ar2/970

290. U.S. Department of the Air Force. Pacific Air Forces. *Architec-- ture, Building and Engineering, Supp. 1.* 1972. [1] + iv + 59pp.**. Included are references to books and articles dealing with all aspects of building from design to sanitary engineering. Supplements and revisions keep this Bibliography current. D301.62:Ar2/972

291. U.S. Department of Housing and Urban Development. *Biblio-- graphy on Housing, Building and Planning, for Use of Over-- seas Missions of the United States Agency for International Development.* 1969. iii + 43pp.*** (MP Series, no. 108). Designed primarily for use by the Agency for International Development in developing countries, this selection of approximately 400 current books and periodicals actually covers housing and building problems in cities and comm-- unities in the United States. Virtually every aspect of community development from credit unions to shopping centers and zoning is covered. Author index and publishers' addresses are provided, HH1.28:108

292. U.S. Department of Housing and Urban Development. *The Built Environment for the Elderly and the Handicapped: a Bibliography.* 1971. 46pp. $.50* S/N 2300–191. L.C. Card 78–616473. Contained are references to recent publications concerning housing as a total environment for the handicapped and elderly. Publications are listed by author under the following various subject headings: The Aging Process; Retirement and Income; Background of the Housing Situation; Foreign Experience; Architecture and Space Use; Fire Prevention; Senior Centers; Residential Communities; Nursing Homes; Relocation; and The Handicapped. Organizations' and Publishers' addresses are

given. Author index.
HH1.23:E12/2

293. U.S. Department of Housing and Urban Development. *Condominium and Cooperative Housing, 1960--1971, Biblio-- graphy of Economic, Financial and Legal Factors.* 1972. v + 32pp. $.45* S/N 2301--0007. L.C. Card 72--601321. Almost 250 references to books and articles touch on the economic, financial, and legal factors of condominiums and cooperative housing. Accompanying is a list of pertinent periodicals.
HH1.23:C75/960--71

294. U.S. Department of Housing and Urban Development. *Housing and Planning References, New Series.* Bimonthly. 1965 -- . No. 1--. $10.50* a year. $2.55 additional foreign mailing. Entries, most of which have a brief annotation, are arranged by subject groups that cover all aspects of architecture, building, design, planning, urbanology, home financing, etc. Author and geographical indices facilitate its use.
HH1.23/3:nos.

295. U.S. Department of Housing and Urban Development. *Operation Breakthrough, Mass Produced and Industrialized Housing, Bibliography.* 1970. iii + 72pp. $.70* L.C. Card 78--607713. The 391 references listed here are primarily aids in the construction aspects of industrialized and pre-- fabricated housing. Entries are listed by specific subject and author and geographic indices assist in locating specific information. Accompanying are lists of trade periodicals and publishers' addresses.
HH1.23:B74

295a. U.S. Forest Service. *Forest Products Laboratory, List of Publications of Interest to Architects, Builders, Engineers, and Retail Lumbermen.* 1973. 15pp.***. Publications listed deal with building materials, building structures, joints and fastenings, insulation and moisture control, and coatings and finishes for preservation and protection of the structure.
A13.27/7:Ar2/973

295b. U.S. General Services Administration. *Buildings Bibliography;*

compiled by Central Office Library. 1968. [5] + 79pp. $.50*.

This bibliography of 980 entries "provides a basic, com--prehensive reference and training tool for Government employees working in the broad areas of buildings design, construction, operation, and maintenance." As such, it is a good guide to the literature concerned with construction, architectural design, and building operation and maintenance. References are given for everything from specifications, standards, and codes to building protection. Indexed by author and subject.
GS1.17:B86

295c.   U.S. Government Printing Office. *Homes. Construction, Maintenance, Community Development.* Free*** (Price List, no. 72).

Listed are selected free and for sale publications on homes and community development. This list is revised frequently; prices are kept current; and all publications listed are supposedly available.
GP3.9:72

295d.   U.S. National Science Foundation. *Science Facilities Biblio--graphy.* 1969. v + 47pp. $.35* L.C. Card 79--602480.
See no. 295e.
NS1.13:F11/969

295e.   U.S. National Science Foundation. *Science Facilities Biblio--graphy, 1970 Supplement.* 1970. [2] + 9pp. $.10*.

Listed are articles and papers to help persons searching for data on the design of science facilities. An appendix features publishers and distribution sources for the listed references. Subject arrangement.
NS1.13:F11/970

Urban Development

296.   U.S. Department of Housing and Urban Development. *Bibliography on Housing, Building, and Planning.* 1970. 43pp.***.

Entries are arranged by subject and pertain primarily to urban community development. Author index. Address list of publishers.
HH1.23:H81/2/969

297.   U.S. Department of Housing and Urban Development. *Books*

About Cities. 1969. [1] + ii + 24pp.***.
This is a revision of *Sixty Books on Housing and Urban Planning* published in 1966. Contained are 68 references on urban problems and urban planning. Indexed by subject and author. Lists of publishers' addresses and organizations concerned with urban affairs follow.
HH1.23:C49

297a.   U.S. Department of Housing and Urban Development. *Books About Cities, 1971-73 Selective Supplement to Books About Cities, 1970.* 1973. [1] + 4pp. Free***.
HH1.23:C49/71-73supp.

298.   U.S. Department of Housing and Urban Development. *Citizen and Business Participation in Urban Affairs, a Biblio- graphy.* 1970. [3] + 84pp. $1.00* L.C. Card 67-61211.
Over 600 publications and a number of available films are referenced to assist interested persons or businesses in finding ways to help the community. A Geographic Index locates critical reviews of specific projects by place.
Arrangement is by subject with author and geographic indexes.
HH1.23:C49/2 (also H. Doc. 91-329)

299.   U.S. Department of Housing and Urban Development. *Environment and Community, an Annotated Bibliography.* 1971. iii + 66pp. $.65***.
The emphasis of the 309 annotated entries is on the en- vironment of American cities and settled communities. Entries are listed by such specific subjects as: Architecture and Urban Design; Ecology; Population Pressures; Working Conditions; and Recreation. In addition there are lists of suggested films, periodicals, concerned organizations, and publishers' addresses. Author index.
HH1.23:En8

300.   U.S. Department of Housing and Urban Development. *In- formation Sources in Housing and Community Development.* 1972. iii + 44pp. $.50* S/N 2300-0196.
Annotated are important reference sources, special subject bibliographies, and core periodicals which would assist city planners, developers, and individuals interested in community development. Special references are given to "Aid in Organizing Your Files." A list of interested organizations is provided as source reference for other materials.
HH1.23:In3

301. U.S. Department of Housing and Urban Development.
Landlord–Tenant Relationships, Selected Bibliography. 1971.
iii + 53pp. $.60* S/N 2300--0180. L.C. Card 73--613707.
Includes 314 entries, as well as lists of periodicals, publishers,
and interested organizations from which further assistance
may be obtained.
HH1.23:L23

302. U.S. Department of Housing and Urban Development.
*Neighborhood Conservation and Property Rehabilitation
Bibliography;* compiled by the Library. 1969. 78pp. $.70*
(MP Series, no. 103). L.C. Card 79--605265.
Lists 575 entries, augmented by a list of films, training aids
and courses.
HH1.28:103

303. U.S. Department of Housing and Urban Development. *New
Communities, Bibliography.* [1969. Published 1970] iv +
84pp. $.75* L.C. Card 75–606174.
Over 600 entries, grouped geographically -- Part I, American
and Canadian; Part II, Foreign Countries other than
Canada -- deal specifically with the building and problems
of new communities. Arrangement is by author. Indexed
by country, state, community and secondary author.
HH1.23:C73/969

304. U.S. Department of Housing and Urban Development. *Socio--
Physical Technology;* compiled by John Archea. 1971.
11pp.***.
The publications and periodicals listed here explore the
concept of "socio--physical technology," which encompasses
issues of mutual concern to both environmental engineers
and social scientists.
HH1.40/4:So1

305. U.S. Department of Housing and Urban Development. *Urban
Outlook, Selected Bibliography of Films, Filmstrips, Slides,
and Audiotapes.* 1969. 38pp. $.45* (MP Series, no. 95).
Purchase or loan information is provided for these audio--
visual materials, listed under specific subject categories.
Title index and a HUD audio tape index (a list representing
recordings of key Presidential and HUD Officials speeches)
complete the bibliography.
HH1.28:95

305a. U.S. National Institutes of Health. National Institute of
Mental Health. *Bibliography on Urban Crisis, Behavioral,
Psychological, and Sociological Aspects of Urban Crisis;* by
Jon K. Meyer. 1969. vii + 452pp. $3.75* L.C. Card 73-
605766.
Citations are listed under broad subject categories such as:
Racial Riots; Rioting and Social Disorders of a Non-Racial
Nature; Civil Rights; Social and Political Movements;
Socio-Economic Programs and Legislation; Intergroup
Relations. Author and Subject indices facilitate cross-
reference to specific publications.
HE20.2417:Ur1

ENVIRONMENTAL SCIENCE

General

306. U.S. Advisory Commission on Intergovernmental Relations.
*Quest for Environmental Quality, Federal and State Action,
1969-70. Annotated Bibliography;* by Rochelle L. Stanfield,
John J. Callahan, and Sandra Osbourn. 1971. v + 63pp.
$.35* L.C. Card 70-612086.
Federal and state laws concerning the environment are
cited. An annotated bibliography arranged by subject, then
author, makes this a worthwhile guide to the environmental
status of the states.
Y3.Ad9/8:2En8

307. U.S. Atomic Energy Commission. *Natural Environmental
Radioactivity, Annotated Bibliography;* by Alfred W.
Klement, jr. 1970. [1] + i + 72pp. NTIS.
Y3.At7:22/WASH-1061/supp.

308. U.S. Congress. Atomic Energy Joint Committee. *Selected
Materials on Environmental Effects of Producing Electric
Power, August 1969.* 1969. 563pp. $2.50* L.C. Card
78-604048.
Y4.At7/2:EL12/2

309. U.S. Department of the Air Force. *Selected Annotated Biblio-
graphy of Environmental Studies of Poland;* compiled by
Alvin L. Smith, jr. 1970. vii + 52pp. NTIS. (Environmental
Technical Applications Center, Technical Notes, 70-6).
L.C. Card 79-609386.
D301.40/2:70-6

309a. U.S. Department of the Air Force. Environmental Technical Applications Center. *Selected Annotated Bibliography of Environmental Studies of Iraq, Jordan, Lebanon, and Syria (1960--69);* compiled by Vincent J. Creasi, Dennis L. Boyer and Alvin L. Smith, Jr. 1970. x + 26 + [1]pp. NTIS. (Technical Notes, 70--5). L.C. Card 70--608132. D301.40/2:70--5

310. U.S. Department of the Air Force. Environmental Technical Applications Center. *Selected Annotated Bibliography of Environmental Studies of Israel (1960--69);* compiled by Vincent J. Creasi, Dennis L. Boyer, and Alvin L. Smith, Jr. 1970. NTIS (Technical Notes, 70--4). L.C. Card 71--607241. D301.40/2:70--4

311. U.S. Department of the Interior. Library. *The Concern for Conservation in the United States: a Selected Bibliography;* by J.E. Yee. 1969. NTIS (PB 185 940). (Library, Biblio-graphy Series no. 13). I22.19/2:13

312. U.S. Department of the Interior. Library. *Mercury Contamination in the Natural Environment, Cooperative Bibliography.* 1970. [3] + vi + 32pp.***. L.C. Card 75--608877.
Entries included are primarily post--1960. Arrangement is by subject with an author index.
I22.9:M53

313. U.S. Department of the Interior. Water Resources Scientific Information Center. *Oil Spillage, Bibliography.* 1973. V. 1, iv + 387pp.; V. 2, iv + 446pp. NTIS. (WRSIC 73--207). L.C. Card 73--601852.
This very comprehensive bibliography on oil spillage is a compilation of abstracts from *Selected Water Resources Abstracts.* Entries are indexed and availability is noted. This is a rather comprehensive bibliography through 1972. (Vol. 1 is through 1970; Vol. 2 is 1971--1972.)
I1.97:73--207

314. U.S. Environmental Protection Agnecy. *Bibliography of R & D Research Reports.* 1973. 101pp.*** (Socioeconomic Environmental Studies Series, no. 600/5--73--002).
This supercedes *Bibliography of R & M Research Reports,* Jan. 1973 (EPA--R5--73--012) and *Bibliography of Water*

Quality Research Reports, June 1972. Listed are the
publications in the following series: Environmental Health
Effects Research; Environmental Protection Technology;
Ecological Research; Environmental Monitoring; Socio-
economic Environmental Studies; and the Water Pollution
Control Research Series. Not indexed.
EP1.23/2:600/5--73--002

315.   U.S. Environmental Protection Agency. *EPA Reports Biblio-
graphy: a Listing of EPA Reports Available from the
National Technical Information Service as of April 1, 1973.*
1973. 959pp. $7.30* L.C. 73--602931.
Abstracted are all of the U.S. Environmental Protection
Agency and its predecessor agencies reports contained in the
National Technical Information Service (NTIS) collection
as of April 1, 1973. Entries are indexed by title, subject,
author, contract number, and accession number.
EP1.21:En8/5/973

316.   U.S. Environmental Protection Agency. *Environment: a
Bibliography of Social Science and Related Literature;* com--
piled by Denton E. Morrison, Kenneth E. Hornback, and W.
Keith Warner. 1973. 860pp. $7.45*.
"This comprehensive, unannotated bibliography contains
nearly 5,000 items covering literature related to the fields
of anthropology, communications, economics, education,
design, geography, history, human ecology, landscape
architecture, management, planning, politics and govern--
ment, population, psychology, public administration,
recreation, social psychology and sociology. The emphasis
is on literature that is substantively, methodologically or
theoretically relevant to man and his activities in relation--
ship to natural environments. The bibliography is listed
alphabetically by author, with an extensive, crosslisted
subject--by--title index under 42 categories."
EP1.23/2:600/6--74--011

317.   U.S. Environmental Protection Agency. *An Environmental
Bibliography.* 1972. 16pp. $.15* S/N5500–0058.
This particular bibliography, with some exceptions, focuses
on titles that address themselves to policy issues and inter--
disciplinary concepts of the environment. There is no
coverage of specific environmental problems or technology.
EP1.21:En8

318. U.S. Environmental Protection Agency. *Environmental Research Publications, January 1971 -- July 1973.* 1973.*** (Office of Research and Development, National Environmental Research Center, Cincinnati, Ohio).

Reports listed here are the results of studies on pollution control technology by the NERC and cooperative activities with research and industrial organizations through research grants and contracts.

EP1.21:En8/7

319. U.S. Environmental Protection Agency. *Environmental Services. Bibliography;* compiled by Bernadine E. Hoduski. Revised January 1973. iii + 26pp. Free*** (U.S. Environ-- mental Protection Agency, Region VII, 1735 Baltimore, Kansas City, Mo. 64108).

"This bibliography of environmental services is designed to be used with a slide presentation in an orientation program. It is not intended to be a comprehensive listing of environmental bibliographies. The only bibliographies, publications and information systems listed are those initiated by EPA or those which contain reference to EPA services."

EP1.21:En8/3

320. U.S. Federal Water Pollution Control Administration. *Biological Effects of Oil Pollution, Bibliography: a Collection of References Concerning Effects of Oil on Biological Systems;* by Donna R. Radcliffe and Thomas A. Murphy, 1970. iv + 46pp.** (Program no. 15080, FHU 10/69). L.C. Card 79-- 605762.

I67.13/4:DAST--19

321. .U.S. Forest Service. Pacific Northwest Forest and Range Experiment Station. *Human Behavior Aspects of Fish and Wildlife Conservation: an Annotated Bibliography;* by Dale R. Potter, Kathryn M. Sharpe, and John C. Hendee. 1973.*** (USDA Forest Service General Technical Report PNW--4).

Almost 1,000 references cover non–biological or human behavior aspects of fish and wildlife conservation. Included are sportsman characteristics, safety, law enforcement, professional and sportsman education, nonconsumptive uses, economics, and history. Key--word and author indexes.

A13.88:PNW--4

322.   U.S. Government Printing Office. *Ecology: Water and Air Pollution, Environmental Pollution, Beautification.* Free* (Price List, no. 88).
Listed are free and for sale publications on many aspects of ecology. The list is revised frequently, and all publications listed are supposed to be available.
GP3.9:88

323.   U.S. National Aeronautics and Space Administration. *Noise Pollution Resources Compendium;* by Eugene Burch. 1973. $30.00 NTIS (N73--23734).
"Contains more than 3,500 bibliographic citations -- the results of researching thousands of journals and indexes for data enabling researches to better understand noise in terms of it physical properties and its non--physical effects on human populations."
MAS1.26:131988

324.   U.S. National Technical Information Service. *Environmental Pollution, Selective Bibliography, Information for Business and Industry.* L.C. Card 72--609703.
C51.11:En8

Air Pollution

325.   U.S. Environmental Protection Agency. *Air Pollution Technical Publications of the U.S. Environmental Protection Agency.* 1973. 108pp.*** (EPA. Air Pollution Technical Information Center, Research Triangle, North Carolina. 27711).
This publication, which is to be revised semi--annually, lists all of the reports in the AP and APTD series and selected reports in the EPA–R series. Purchase information is provided. Subject index.
EP1.21:Ai7/973

326.   U.S. Environmental Protection Agency. Air Programs Office. *Air Pollution Abstracts.* Monthly. Vol. 1--. 1970--. $27.00 a year. $6.75 additional foreign mailing. Index issue $3.00.
Included in this comprehensive bibliography is all information received by the Air Pollution Technical Information Center. Subject and author indices facilitate the use of this important bibliography of air pollution abstracts.
EP4.11:Vol./No.

327–338.   The following deal with "air pollution aspects of emission
sources" of various industries. All basically have the same
format with abstracts listed under one of the following four--
teen headings: Emission Sources; Control Methods;
Measurement Methods; Air Quality Measurement;
Atmospheric Interaction; Basic Science and Technology;
Effects – Human Health; Effects -- Plants and Livestock;
Effects -- Materials; Effects – Economic; Standards and
Criteria; Legal and Administrative; Social Aspects; and
General. Indexed by subject and author.

327.   U.S. Environmental Protection Agency. Air Programs Office.
*Air Pollution Aspects of Emission Sources: Boilers -- a
Bibliography with Abstracts.* 1972. v + 125pp.***
(AP--105).
Four hundred and ninety abstracts cover air pollution from
boilers. (See note heading 327--338).
EP4.9:105

328.   U.S. Environmental Protection Agency. Air Programs Office.
*Air Pollution Aspects of Emission Sources: Cement
Manufacturing, Bibliography with Abstracts.* 1971. vii +
44pp. $.50* S/N 5503–0008. (AP–95).
One hundred and thirty abstracts. (See note heading 327--
338).
EP4.9:95

329.   U.S. Environmnetal Protection Agency. Air Programs Office.
*Air Pollution Aspects of Emission Sources: Electric Power
Production. Bibliography with Abstracts. 1971.* vii + 312pp.
$2.25* S/N 5503--0011. (AP–96). L.C. Card 77–613566.
More than 1,040 selective abstracts. (See note heading
no. 327–338).
EP4.9:96

330.   U.S. Environmental Protection Agency. Air Programs Office.
*Air Pollution Aspects of Emission Sources: Iron and Steel
Mills -- a Bibliography with Abstracts.* 1972. v + 84pp.
$1.00* (AP–107). L.C. Card 73--612229.
Three hundred and two abstracts. (See note heading no.
327–338).

331.   U.S. Environmental Protection Agency. Air Programs Office.
*Air Pollution Aspects of Emission Sources: Municipal
Incineration -- a Bibliography with Abstracts.* 1971. 95pp.

* (AP–92). L.C. Card 73–612229.
Three hundred and twenty abstracts. (See note heading no. 327–338).
EP4.9:92

332. U.S. Environmental Protection Agency. Air Programs Office.
Air Pollution Aspects of Emission Sources: Nitric Acid Manufacturing -- a Bibliography with Abstracts. 1971. 31pp. $.45* S/N 5503--0004 (AP--93). L.C. Card 73--612229.
Eighty–one abstracts. (See note heading no. 327--338).
EP4.9:93

333. U.S. Environmental Protection Agency. Air Programs Office.
Air Pollution Aspects of Emission Sources: Petroleum Refineries -- a Bibliography with Abstracts. 1972. iii + 68pp. $1.25* (AP--110). L.C. Card 73--612229.
(See note heading no. 327--338).
EP4.9:110

334. U.S. Environmental Protection Agency. Air Programs Office.
Air Pollution Aspects of Emisssion Sources: Primary Aluminum Production -- a Bibliography with Abstracts. 1973. v + 57pp. $.90* (AP--119). L.C. Card 73--612229.
Over 200 abstracts. (See note heading no. 327--338).
EP4.9:119

335. U.S. Environmental Protection Agency. Air Programs Office.
Air Pollution Aspects of Emission Sources: Primary Copper Production -- a Bibliography with Abstracts. 1973. v + 40pp. $.70* (AP–125). L.C. Card 73--612229.
(See note heading no. 327--338).
EP4.9:125

336. U.S. Environmental Protection Agency. Air Programs Office.
Air Pollution Aspects of Emission Sources: Primary Lead Production -- a Bibliography with Abstracts. 1973. v + 29pp. $.65* (AP–126). L.C. Card 73–612229.
(See note heading no. 327--338).
EP4.9:126

337. U.S. Environmental Protection Agency. Air Programs Office.
Air Pollution Aspects of Emission Sources: Pulp and Paper Industry -- Bibliography with Abstracts. 1973. iii, v + 166pp. $2.35* (AP–121). L.C. Card 73–612229.

Approximately 700 abstracts. (See note heading no. 327--338).
EP4.9:121

338. U.S. Environmental Protection Agency. Air Programs Office.
Air Pollution Aspects of Emission Sources: Sulfuric Acid Manufacturing -- Bibliography with Abstracts. 1971. vii + 58pp. $.65* S/N 5503--0007 (AP--94). L.C. Card 73--61229.
Two hundred abstracts. (See note heading no. 327--338).
EP4.9:94

339. U.S. Environmental Protection Agency. Air Programs Office.
Air Pollution Translations, Bibliography with Abstracts.
Vol. 3. 1973. vii + 250pp. $2.85* (AP--120).
See no. 340.
EP4.9:120

340. U.S. Environmental Protection Agnecy. Air Programs Office.
Air Pollution Translations, Bibliography with Abstracts, Vol. 4. 1973. vii + 144pp. $2.10* (AP--122)
These are the third and fourth in a continuing series of compilations which present abstracts and indexes of translations of technical air pollution literature. Each document listed is available in English. Entries are grouped by subject categories and are indexed by author and sub--ject. (See no. 350--351 for Vol. 1 and 2).
EP4.9:122

341. U.S. Environmental Protection Agency. Air Programs Office.
Asbestos and Air Pollution: an Annotated Bibliography.
1971. iii + 101pp.* (AP--82).
Contained are 160 abstracts which deal with the following aspects of air pollution from asbestos: Emission Sources; Measurement Methods; Control Methods; Effects -- Human Health; and Basic Science and Technology. Indexed by author, title, subject, and geographical area.
EP4.9:92

342. U.S. Environmental Protection Agency. Air Programs Office.
Beryllium and Air Pollution: an Annotated Bibliography.
1971. iii + 75pp. $.40* (AP--83). L.C. Card 74--611275.
Abstracted are 107 documents and articles on air pollution from beryllium. Covered are topics such as: Emission Sources; Atmospheric Interaction; Measurement Methods; Control Methods; Effects -- Human Health; Effects -- Plants and Livestock; and Basic Science and

Technology. Indexed by author, title, subject and
geographic area.
EP4.9:83

343. U.S. Environmental Protection Agency. Air Programs Office.
Chlorine and Air Pollution: an Annotated Bibliography.
1971. iii + 113pp. $.55* S/N 5503–0018 (AP–99).
L.C. Card 77--614058.
One hundred abstracts of articles and documents on chlorine
cover the health, economic, and technical aspects of air
pollution from the manufacture of chlorine. Indexed by
author, title, subject, and geographical location.
EP4.9:99

344. U.S. Environmental Protection Agency. Air Programs Office.
*Hydrochloric Acid and Air Pollution: An Annotated Biblio--
graphy.* 1971. ii + 105pp. $.55* S/N 5503–0019 (AP--100).
L.C. Card 76--614071.
Abstracted are 164 documents and articles on hydrochloric
acid. Abstracts are separated into the following categories:
General; Emission Sources; Atmospheric Interaction;
Measurement Methods; Control Methods; Effects – Human
Health; Effects -- Plants and Livestock; Effects -- Materials;
Effects -- Economic, Legal and Administrative; Standards
and Criteria; and Basic Science and Technology. Indexed
by author, title, subject, and geographic area.
EP4.9:100

345. U.S. Environmental Protection Agency. Air Programs Office.
*Indoor--Outdoor Air Pollution Relationships: a Literature
Review.* 1972. ix + 73pp. $1.25* (AP–112). L.C. Card
72--603656.
Tables and analysis accompany a bibliography of 77 items.
EP4.9:112

346. U.S. Environmental Protection Agency. Air Programs Office.
Mercury and Air Pollution: a Bibliography with Abstracts.
1972. v + 59pp. $1.25* (AP--114). L.C. Card 72--603649.
Same arrangement as no. 344. All entries deal with air
pollution and its effects from mercury.
EP4.9:114

347. U.S. Environmental Protection Agency. Air Programs Office.
*Municipal Incineration, Review of the Literature with Biblio--
graphies;* by James R. Stear. 1971. xiv + 187pp. $1.00*

S/N 5503–0009 (AP–79). L.C. Card 79–612339.
This review is limited to municipal refuse incineration as
practiced in the U.S. and several foreign countries. Some
400 bibliographic entries lead to articles and papers on
refuse disposal and use.
EP4.9:79

348.   U.S. Environmental Protection Agency. Air Programs Office.
Odors and Air Pollution: a Bibliography with Abstracts.
1972. v + 257pp. $3.00* (AP–113). L.C. Card 72–603601.
EP4.9:113

349.   U.S. Environmental Protection Agency. Air Programs Office.
*Photochemical Oxidants and Air Pollution: Annotated
Bibliography.* 1971. (Pt. 1. Categories A–F. iii + 813pp.
Pt. 2. Categories G–N and indexes. iii + 815 -- 1529pp.)
$6.25* set (Free to non–profit organizations***) (AP–88).
   Author, title, subject, and geographical location indices lead
   to approximately 1,900 annotated entries.
EP4.9:88/pt.1,2

350.   U.S. Public Health Service. *Air Pollution Publications, a
Selected Bibliography with Abstracts, 1966--68;* compiled
by the Science and Technology Division, Library of Congress.
1969. x + 522pp. $4.50* L.C. Card 63--60159.
   Contained are over 1,000 entries to literature generated by
   the staff and grantees of the National Air Pollution Control
   Administration. This updates earlier publications which
   cover the literature back to 1955. Arrangement is by
   broad subject categories such as: General Aspects;
   Emission Sources; Atmospheric Interaction;
   Measurement; Control Methods; Biosciences and
   Medicine; Plants; Materials Deterioration; Air Quality;
   Legal and Administrative Aspects; Social Aspects; and
   Basic Science and Technology. Subject and author
   indexes.
FS2.24:Ai7/966–68

351.   U.S. Public Health Service. *Air Pollution Translations, Biblio--
graphy with Abstracts.* Vol. 1. 1969. iii + 173pp. $1.75*.
See no. 340 for annotation.
FS2.93/3:56

352.   U.S. Public Health Service. *Air Pollution Translations, Biblio--
graphy with Abstracts.* Vol. 2. 1970. iii + 116pp. $1.00*.
(See no. 340 for annotation).

353.   U.S. Public Health Service. *Free Films on Air Pollution on Loan for Group Showing.* 1969. 23pp. $.15*.
FS2.2:Ai7/30/969

354.   U.S. Public Health Service. Division of Air Pollution. *Air Pollution and the Kraft Pulping Industry: an Annotated Bibliography;* by Paul A. Kenline and Jeremy M. Hales. 1968. 122pp.*** (AP--4).
Textual information includes a description of the kraft pulping process, a survey of mill emissions, and consideration of control measures. Following is a detailed and technical annotated bibliography of "articles concerning measurement and control of kraft mill airborne pollution currently available in the literature."
FS2.300:AP--4

355.   U.S. Public Health Service. National Air Pollution Control Administration. *Hydrocarbons and Air Pollution, Annotated Bibliography.* 1970. Pt. 1, Categories A–E, iii + 1 – 582pp.; Pt. 2. Categories F–M, and indexes, iii + 583 – 1183pp. $5.00 per set* S/N 1713--0029. (AP--75). L.C. Card 78--610871.
"This bibliography represents an effort to collect, condense and organize the literature on hydrocarbons in relation to air pollution." The approximately 2300 abstracts are arranged in thirteen subject categories ranging from pollution effects on humans, animals and materials to air quality standards and criteria. Indexed by subject, author, title, and geographic area.
HE20.1309:75/v.1, 2

356.   U.S. Public Health Service. National Air Pollution Control Administration. *Nitrogren Oxides. Annotated Bibliography.* 1970. iii + 633pp. $2.75* (AP–72). L.C. Card 75--609239.
Approximately 1,500 documents are abstracted and arranged under one of thirteen subject categories such as: Emission Sources; Measurement Methods; Effects -- Human Health; Basic Science and Technology. Indexed by author, subject, and geographic area.
HE20.1309:72

357.   U.S. Public Health Service. National Air Pollution Control

Administration. *Tall Stacks, Various Atmospheric Phenomena and Related Aspects: Annotated Bibliography and Discussion.* 1968. ii + 120pp.***. L.C. Card 74--600127.

Two hundred and fourteen abstracts and references to recent articles dealing with tall stacks and their resulting in air pollution are contained in this bibliography.
FS2.24:St1

Pesticides and Herbicides

358. U.S. Agricultural Research Service. *Bibliography of Insect--Resistant Packaging, 1913--69;* by Henry A. Highland and C.E. Metts. 1970. 16pp.*** (ARS 51–36). L.C. Card 74--608929.

This compilation of 140 entries gives one a compre--hensive view of the present status of insect resistant packaging.
A77.15:51--36

359. U.S. Department of the Interior. Water Programs Office. *DDT in Water, Bibliography.* 1971. 286pp. NTIS (WRSIC 71--211). L.C. Card 77--616489.
I1.97:71--211

360. U.S. Environmental Protection Agency. Water Programs Office. *A Catalog of Research in Aquatic Pest Control and Pesticide Residues in Aquatic Environments.* 1972. 261pp. $2.75* S/N 55--1--0355. (Pesticide Study Series, no. 1).

Abstracted are 884 projects active during the 1970–71 period. Each entry is thoroughly indexed by subject, investigator, and supporting agency.
EP2.25:1

361. U.S. National Agricultural Library. *DDT [1, 1--Dichloro--2, 2--Bis (P--Chlorophenyl) Ethylene], List of References Selected and Compiled from the Files of the Pesticides Information Center, National Agricultural Library, 1960--1969.* 1970. iii + 143pp.***. (Library List, no. 97). L.C. Card 70--606222.

"This compilation of 1,064 bibliographic citations cov--ering all aspects of the research efforts on DDT was prepared from the computerized files of the Pesticides Information Center." All items cited have appeared in the *Pesticides Documentation Bulletin.* Citations are arranged

alphabetically under the following major subjects: Entomology; Crop Protection; Livestock Protection; Commodity Protection; Environmental Contamination; Residues; Toxicology; Plant Physiology and Biochemistry; Chemistry; Engineering; and Industry. Accompanying are subject, biographical, and author indexes, with the subject index being exceptional.
A17.17:97

362. U.S. National Agricultural Library. *Toxicity of Herbicides to Mammals, Aquatic Life, Soil Microorganisms, Beneficial Insects, and Cultivated Plants, 1950--65, List of Selected References;* compiled by Patricia A. Condon. 1968. iii + 161pp.*** (Library List, no. 87). L.C. Card Agr 68–196.
The 1695 citations are arranged alphabetically within major subject groups and indexed by author and subject.
A17.17:87

Waste Management

363. U.S. Atomic Energy Commission. *Monitoring, Control, and Disposal of Tritium, Selected Bibliography.* 1973. [1] + iii + 74 + 27pp. NTIS (TID--3337).
Y3.At7:22/TID--3337

364. U.S. Atomic Energy Commission. *Radioactive Waste Management, Bibliography of Publicly Available Literature Pertaining to USAEC's Oak Ridge, Tenn., Site.* 1973. [4] + 85pp.*** (USAEC's Technical Information Center, P.O. Box 62, Oak Ridge, Tenn. 37830).
Y3.At7:22/TID--3343

365. U.S. Bureau of Solid Waste Management. *Solid Waste Management: Abstracts and Excerpts from the Literature.* 1970. (Vol. 1, xi + 308pp.; Vol. 2, vii + 147pp.). $4.00* L.C. Card 77--608288.
This was one of the first major attempts to compile a bibliography of the literature in solid waste management. Later, this is to become a serial publication. (See no. 373). Over 500 abstracts are grouped into the following major categories: Management; Collection and Transport; Disposal; Salvage; Environmental and Public Health; Pollution; and Agricultural and Food Processing Wastes. Indexed by author and subject. (For other years, see no. 369–372, 375).
HE20.1402:M31

366.   U.S. Department of the Interior. *Disposal of Brine Effluents from Inland Desalting Plants, Review and Bibliography;* by G.W. DePuy. 1969. iv + 211pp. $1.75* (Saline Water Research and Development Progress Reports, no. 454). Contained are 870 references which are indexed and cross referenced according to 18 subject areas such as: Brine Disposal; Evaporation; Seepage; Pond Linings; Mineral Recovery; and Water Pollution Regulations. I1.88:454

367.   U.S. Department of the Interior. Water Resources Scientific Information Center. *Sanitary Landfills, Bibliography;* edited by George L. Knapp. 1972. iv + 166pp. NTIS (WRSIC 72--214). L.C. Card 72--602724. I1.97:72--214

368.   U.S. Environmental Protection Agency. *Bibliography of Livestock Waste Management with List of References;* by J. Ronald Miner, Dwaine Bundy, and Gerald Christenbury. 1972. xiii + 137 + [1]pp. $2.00* L.C. Card 73--600931. Included "are references which include title, author, keywords and source data for 241 journal papers, 425 papers published as conference proceedings, 114 university or government publications, 71 magazine articles, 26 books or book chapters, 15 unpublished papers, and 53 academic theses." EP1.23/2:72--101

369--373. These volumes contain lengthy abstracts to research in solid waste management from 1941 through 1968. (See also nos. 365 and 373).

369.   U.S. Environmental Protection Agency. *Solid Waste Management, Abstracts from the LIterature, 1965;* prepared by John A. Connally and Sandra E. Stainback. 1972. vi + 216pp. $1.75* (Solid Waste Management Series, no. 66.1). L.C. 53--60514. EP1.17:66.1

370.   U.S. Environmental Protection Agency. *Solid Waste Management, Abstracts from the Literature, 1966.* 1972. vii + 197pp. $1.75* (Solid Waste Management Series, no. 66.2). EP1.17:66.2c

371.   U.S. Environmental Protection Agency. *Solid Waste*

Management, Abstracts from the Literature, 1967. 1972.
vii + 404pp. $3.00* S/N5502--0077. (Solid Waste
Management Series, no. 66.3).
EP1.17:66.3c

372. U.S. Environmental Protection Agency. *Solid Waste
Management, Abstracts from the Literature, 1968.* 1972.
vii + 286pp. $2.25* (Solid Waste Management Series, no.
66.4).
EP1.17:66.4c

373. U.S. Environmental Protection Agency. *Solid Waste Management Available Information Materials.* Quarterly.*
(Price varies fro each issue) (Solid Waste Management Series,
no. 58. nos.).
Now published quarterly, this bibliography lists reports,
and articles which are currently available from the Solid
Waste Management Office. One needs only the most
current in this series to locate available publications in the
following areas of solid waste management: Citizen
Action and General Information; Collection of Solid
Wastes; Land Disposal; Management--Planning and
Economics; Marine Disposal; Recycling and Reclamation;
and Solid Waste Processing (Composting, Incineration,
and Reduction).
EP1.17:58.nos.

374. U.S. Environmental Protection Agency. Office of Solid
Waste Management. *Accession Bulletin: Solid Waste
Information Retrieval System.* Monthly. Vol. 1--. 1970--.
***.
The purpose of this bulletin is to keep readers abreast of
the solid waste management information being published.
Included with the bibliographic accession citation is a
brief description of each document.
EP3.3/2:Vol./no.

375. U.S. Environmental Protection Agency. Office of Solid
Waste Management. *Solid Waste Management: Abstracts
from the Literature -- 1964;* prepared by John A. Connolly
and Sandra E. Stainback. 1971. vii + 280pp. $2.00*
L.C. Card 53--60514.
This publication renews the *Refuse Collection and Disposal
Annotated Bibliography* of the 1940's. The present
bibliography has been abstracted and is arranged in categories

corresponding to the various administration, engineering, and operational phases of solid waste. The literature included is both technical and general but is not all inclusive of material published in 1964. Indexed by subject, corporate author, author, and geographical location. (See nos. 369–373 for later years).
EP3.9:M31

376.   U.S. Federal Water Quality Administration. *Agricultural Utilization of Sewage Effluent and Sludge, Annotated Bibliography;* by James P. Law, jr. 1968. iv + 89pp. $.45*.
Contained are 284 well--annotated entries which are divided into the following major subject headings: Sewage Effluent as an Agricultural Water Resource; Agricultural Value of Sewage Sludge; Land Disposal of Liquid Wastes; Sanitary Aspects of Waste Water Utilization; Industrial, Recreational, and other Water Reuse Applications. Author index.
I 67.14:Ag8

377.   U.S. Geological Survey. *Subsurface Waste Disposal by Means of wells, Selected Annotated Bibliography;* by Donald R. Rima, Edith B. Chase, and Beverly M. Myers. 1971. v + 305pp. $1.50* S/N2401--1229 (Water Supply Paper, no. 2020). L.C. Card 77–179486.
Contained are 692 abstracts selected from the literature prior to 1970. About one–third of the abstracts are concerned with the disposal of oil--field brines, another third with the disposal of radioactive wastes, and the remaining with actual case histories of industries that are using injection wells. Indexed by subject and geographic area.
I19.13:2020

378.   U.S. Public Health Service. *Sanitary Landfill, Bibliography;* by R.L. Steiner and Renee Kantz. 1968. [2] + 37pp. $.35* L.C. Card 68–62415.
Publications are listed chronologically from 1925 to 1968. Not indexed.
FS2.24:L23

Water Pollution and Management
(see also nos. 481--494)

379.   U.S. Bureau of Reclamation. *Reaeration of Streams and Reservoirs, Analysis and Bibliography;* by D.I. King.

1970. 2 + ii + 131 + 4pp.** L.C. Card 75–612425.
I27.60:70–55

380–397. *Selected Water Resources Abstracts* (See no. 394) was searched to compile these computer printed bibliographies. Each entry has full bibliographic information and a lengthy annotation. They are multi--indexed by subject and author.

380. U.S. Department of the Interior. Water Resources Scientific Information Center. *Aeration of Natural Waters: a Bibliography;* Ed. by George L. Knapp. 1973. iv + 358pp. NTIS (WRSIC 73--206).
(See note heading nos. 380--397).
I1.97:73–206

381. U.S. Department of the Interior. Water Resources Scientific Information Center. *Artifical Recharge of Groundwater, Bibliography;* Ed. by George L. Knapp. 1973. iv + 309pp. NTIS (WRSIC 73--202).
(See note heading no. 380--397).
I1.97:73–202

382. U.S. Department of the Interior. Water Resources Scientific Information Center. *Cadmium in Water, Bibliography.* 1973. iv + 231pp. NTIS (WRSIC 73--209).
(See note heading no. 380--397).
I1.97:73–209

383. U.S. Department of the Interior. Water Resources Scientific Information Center. *Evaporation Suppression, a Bibliography.* 1973. iv + 478pp. NTIS (WRSIC 73--216).
(See note heading no. 380–397).
I1.97:73–216

384. U.S. Department of the Interior. Water Resources Scientific Information Center. *Irrigation Efficiency: a Bibliography.* 1973. 418pp. NTIS (WRSIC 73--214).
(See note heading no. 380–397).
I1.97:73–214

385. U.S. Department of the Interior. Water Resources Scientific Information Center. *Lake Erie, Bibliography.* 1972. iv + 240pp. NTIS (WRSIC 72–209).
(See note heading no. 380--397).
I1.97:72--209

386. U.S. Department of the Interior. Water Resources Scientific Information Center. *Lake Huron, Bibliography.* 1972. iv + 95pp. NTIS (WRSIC 72--210). (See note heading no. 380–397). I1.97:72–210

387. U.S. Department of the Interior. Water Resources Scientific Information Center. *Lake Michigan, Bibliography.* 1972. iv + 95pp. NTIS (WRSIC 72–211). (See note heading no. 380--397). I1.97:72--211

388. U.S. Department of the Interior. Water Resources Scientific Information Center. *Lake Superior, Bibliography.* 1972. iv + 127pp. NTIS (WRSIC 72--213). L.C. Card 72--602721. (See note heading no. 380–397). I1.97:72–213

389. U.S. Department of the Interior. Water Resources Scientific Information Center. *Legal Aspects of Water Pollution in New England, Bibliography.* 1971. iv + 160pp. NTIS (WRSIC 71--213). L.C. Card 75–616483. (See note heading no. 380--397). I1.97:71–213

390. U.S. Department of the Interior. Water Resources Scientific Information Center. *PCB in Water: a Bibliography.* 1973. iv + 144pp. NTIS (WRSIC 73--201). (See note heading no. 380--397). I1.97:73–201

391. U.S. Department of the Interior. Water Resources Scientific Information Center. *Phosphorous Removal, Bibliography.* 1973. (V. 1, iv + 275pp.; V. 2, iv + 465pp.). NTIS (WRSIC 73–208). L.C. Card 73–601989. (See note heading no. 380--397). I1.97:73--208

392. U.S. Department of the Interior. Water Resources Scientific Information Center. *A Selected Annotated Biblio--graphy on the Analysis of Water Resource Systems, Vol. 3.* 1972. vi + 406pp. NTIS (WRSIC 72–218). (See note heading no. 380--397 and no. 393 for further explanation). I1.97:72--218

393. U.S. Department of the Interior. Water Resources
      Scientific Information Center. *A Selected Annotated
      Bibliography on the Analysis of Water Resource Systems,
      Vol. 4.* 1973. vi + 490pp. NTIS (WRSIC 73--218).
      These two volumes contain annotations of publications
      issued in 1971 and 1972. Indexed by subject and author.
      Volume 4 has 323 annotations.
      The first two volumes of this bibliography, having the
      same title, were published by the Cornell University Water
      Resources and Marine Sciences Center, Ithaca, New York.
      They are: Publication no. 25, August 1969; and
      Publication no. 35, June 1971.
      I1.97:73--218

394. U.S. Department of the Interior. Water Resources Scientific
      Information Center. *Selected Water Resources Abstracts.*
      Semi--monthly. Vol. 1--. 1968--. $45.00 a yr. $11.50
      additional foreign mailing. NTIS.
      Included are abstracts of current and earlier pertinent
      monographs, journal articles, reports, and other publication
      formats. Indexed by subject, author, organizations, and
      accession number. Annual cumulative index.
      I1.94/2:Vol./no.

395. U.S. Department of the Interior. Water Resources Scientific
      Information Center. *Urban Water Planning, Bibliography;*
      edited by George F. Mangan and Herbert A. Swenson. 1972.
      iv + 373pp. L.C. Card 72--603335.
      (See note heading no. 380--397).
      I1.97:72--215

396. U.S. Department of the Interior. Water Resources
      Scientific Information Center. *Use of Naturally Impaired
      Water: a Bibliography.* 1973. 364pp. NTIS (WRSIC 73--217).
      (See note heading no. 380--397).
      I1.97:73--217

397. U.S. Department of the Interior. Water Resources
      Scientific Information Center. *Water Reuse: a Bibliography.*
      1973. (Vol. 1, iv + 394pp.; Vol. 2, iv + 508pp.) NTIS
      (WRSIC 73--215).
      (See note heading no. 380--397).
      I1.97:73--215

398. U.S. Environmental Protection Agency. *Annotated Bibliography of Lake Ontario Limnilogical and Related Studies. Vol. 1, Chemistry;* by Daniel Proto, Robert A. Sweeney. 1973. iii + 102 + [1] pp. $1.25* (Ecological Research Series, EPA–R3–73–028a).

One hundred and eighty–seven publications concerning the chemical aspects of Lake Ontario and influent tributaries are abstracted. Each entry is cross--indexed by author, geographic area, techniques and instrumentation, para-- meters, and subject. Also included are address lists for authors and issuing agencies.

399. U.S. Environmental Protection Agency. *Annotated Bibliography of Lake Ontario Limnilogical and Related Studies. Vol. 2, Biology;* by Elaine P. Downing, James E. Hassan, Robert A. Sweeney. 1973. iii + 236 + 1pp. $2.60* (Ecological Research Series, EPA–R3–73028b). L.C. Card 73--601692.

(See no. 398 for format). There are 596 entries concerning the biological aspects of Lake Ontario and influent tributaries.
EP1.23:73--028b

400. U.S. Environmnetal Protection Agency. *Annotated Bibliography of Lake Ontario Limnilogical and Related Studies. Vol. 3, Physical;* by John Baldwin, Robert Sweeney. 1973. 207 + [1] pp. $2.60* (Ecological Research Series, EPA–R3--73--028c).

(See no. 398 for format). There are 39 entries concerning the physical aspects of Lake Ontario and influent tributaries.
EP1.23:73--028c

401. U.S. Environmental Protection Agency. *Annotated Bibliography on Biological Effects of Metals in the Aquatic Environments;* by Donald Eisler. 1973. v + 287 + [1] pp. (Ecological Research Series, EPA--R3--73--007).

"A total of 567 references on biological effects of metals to aquatic organisms were annotated and subsequently indexed by metal and by taxa. Preference was given to articles on toxicity of heavy metals to marine, estuarine, and anadromous species."

Two indices, *Index -- Metal* and *Index -- Taxa,* efficiently direct the research to the proper publications.
EP1.23:73--007

402. U.S. Environmental Protection Agency. *Bibliography of*

Water Quality Research Reports. 1972. 6 + 45pp.
This is a cumulative list of publications in the Water
Pollution Control Research Series. Arrangement is by
broad subject area. Cost and availability are given for each
document. Not indexed. (See no.   for this
publication's replacement).
EP1.16:list 1972

403. U.S. Environmental Protection Agency. *Cost Analysis of
Water Pollution Control, Annotated Bibliography;* by
Dennis P. Tihansky. 1973. v + 393 + [1]pp. $3.95*
(Socioeconomic Environmental Studies Series, no. 73--017).
Compiled are nearly 2,000 selected publications, un--
published papers, and theses from 1960--1972 dealing with
water pollution control costs. This bibliography would
be of particular value to economists, engineers, operations
research analysts, and policy makers.
EP1.23/3:73–017

404. U.S. Environmental Protection Agency. Water Programs
Office. *Selected Urban Water Runoff Abstracts, July 1968--
June 1970.* 1970. vii + 375pp. $2.75* L.C. Card 78--
611241.
EP2.10:11024 EJC 07/70

405. U.S. Environmental Protection Agency. Water Programs
Office. *Selected Urban Water Runoff Abstracts.* Quarterly.
1971 -- .
These abstracts are classed in ten subject categories
covering all phases of storm water runoff from the
construction of drainage ditches to the treatment and
reuse of water runoff. Subject index.
EP2.10:11024 ECJ (date)

406. U.S. Environmental Protection Agency. Water Programs
Office. *Subsurface Water Pollution, Selective Annotated
Bibliography. Pt. 1, Subsurface Waste Injection.* 1972.
[1] + v + 5 + 156pp. NTIS. L.C. Card 72--603163.
EP2.27:Su1/pt.1

407. U.S. Environmental Protection Agency. Water Programs
Office. *Subsurface Water Pollution, Selective Annotated
Bibliography. Pt. 2, Saline Water Instrusion.* [1] + v + 5 +
161pp. NTIS. L.C. Card 72--603163.
EP2.27:Su1/pt.2

408. U.S. Environmental Protection Agency. Water Programs Office. *Subsurface Water Pollution, Selective Annotated Bibliography, Pt. 3, Percolation from Surface Sources.* [1] + v + 7 + 162pp. NTIS. L.C. Card 72--603163. EP2.27:Su1/pt.3

409. U.S. Federal Water Pollution Control Administration. *Current List of Water Publications, 1965--1969.* 1969. 25pp.
Listed are publications by members of the Robert A. Taft Sanitary Engineering Center. All deal with water quality and pollution.
I67.14:W29/2/965--69

409a. U.S. Federal Water Pollution Control Administration. *Selected Urban Storm Water Runoff Abstracts;* prepared by the Franklin Institute Laboratories. 1969. iv + 57 + 52pp.***.
This compilation of 573 abstracts covers the literature up to, and partially including, 1968 on storm water runoff in urban areas, storm sewers, and storm water discharge. Publications are arranged by subject and indexed by subject, author, organization, and accession number. This updates *Storm Water Runoff from Urban Areas (1966).*
(See also no. 404 and no. 405).
I67.13/2:21

409b. U.S. Federal Water Pollution Control Administration. *Water and Water Pollution Control, Selected List of Publications.* 1968. iii + 15pp.***
Listed are publications to inform the non--technical reader of the increasing problems generated by water pollution. Publications are listed primarily by issuing agency. Not indexed.
I67.14:W29

410. U.S. National Technical Information Service. *Chemical Wastewater Treatment, Selected Abstracts.* 1973. NTIS (NTIS--PK--153).
C51.11:W28

GEOSCIENCE

General

411. U.S. Bureau of Mines. *New Publications, Monthly List.* ***

I28.5/2:nos.

412.   U.S. Bureau of Mines. *List of Bureau of Mines Publications and Articles, January 1, 1965, to December 31, 1969, with Subject and Author Index;* compiled by Rita D. Sylvester. 1970. 437pp. $3.75* (Its: Special List). L.C. 61--64978. This supplements two former cumulative lists of Bureau of Mines publications – *List of Bureau of Mines Publications and Articles, July 1, 1910, to January 1, 1960,* and *List of Bureau of Mines Publications and Articles, January 1, 1960, to December 31, 1964.* Compiled here are the annual lists (see below) from 1965--1969. Bureau of Mines series publications are listed numerically by series. Also listed are Bureau articles which are published in professional and non--government journals, open--file reports, patents, co–operative reports, and available reprints. Most entries have lengthy annotations. Indexed by subject, author, and place.
I28.5:965--69

413.   U.S. Bureau of Mines. *List of Bureau of Mines Publications and Articles, 1970.* 1971. $1.50*.
(Same format as no. 412).
I28.5:970

414.   U.S. Bureau of Mines. *List of Bureau of Mines Publications and Articles, 1971.* 1972. $1.25*.
(Same format as no. 412).
I28.5:971

415.   U.S. Bureau of Mines. *List of Bureau of Mines Publications and Articles, 1972.* 1973. $1.25*.
(Same format as no. 412).
I18.5:972

416.   U.S. Department of the Army. Corps of Engineers. *An Annotated Bibliography of Aerial Remote Sensing in Coastal Engineering;* by Donald B. Stafford, Richard O. Bruno, and Harris M. Goldstein. 1973. v + 122pp.*** (U.S. Coastal Engineering Research Center. Miscellaneous Paper 2--73).
About 200 references published since 1934 are representative of the literature covering the applications of aerial remote sensing techniques to coastal engineering. Accompanying

each entry is a concise and informative summary of the references describing the characteristics of each remote sensor in coastal engineering investigations. Computer indexes of authors, titles, and keywords.
D103.42/2:73–2

417.   U.S. Department of the Army. Corps of Engineers. *Bibliography on Snow, Ice, and Frozen Ground, with Abstracts.* (Title varies). Annual. 1947--. Vol. 1--. NTIS and *** L.C. 53--60024.
This bibliography is a "current and comprehensive coverage of basic and applied scientific research on snow, ice, and frozen ground, as well as living and working in polar regions and other cold areas." Entries are annotated and indexed in the older issues; but in the newer volumes entries are entered by author, indexed by subject, and have no annotation.
D102.22:12/vol.

418.   U.S. Department of the Army. Quartermaster General. *Annotated Bibliography and Evaluation of Remote Sensing Publications Relating to Military Geography of Arid Lands;* by W.G. McGinnies. 1970. iv + 103pp. NTIS (ES--61).
"A comprehensive review has been made of remote sensing publications relating to military geography of arid lands. These have been abstracted or annotated and arranged in tables relating devices and processes to geographic features, flora, fauna, weather, climate, coastal zones, and general geography. . . . Each reference is rated as especially useful, useful, or of little value."
D106.21:71--27–ES

419.   U.S. Department of the Interior. Water Resources Scientific Information Center. *Aerial Remote Sensing, Bibliography;* edited by Donald B. Stafford. 1973. iv + 482pp. NTIS (WRSIC 73–211).
Selected Water Resources Abstracts (see no. 394) was searched to compile this computer printed bibliography. Each entry has full bibliographic information and is multi--indexed by subject and author.
I1.97:73–211

420.   U.S. Department of the Interior. Water Resources Scientific Information Center. *Avalanches, Including Debris Avalanches, Bibliography.* 1972. iv + 87pp. NTIS (WRSIC 72--216).

L.C. Card 73–600703.
(Same notation as for no. 419).
I1.97:72–216

421–426. Listed in these annual bibliographies are publications "that appeared during (the year) concerning the geology of the North American continent, Greenland, the West Indies and adjacent islands, Hawaii, Guam, and other island possessions but not the trust territories of the United States." Arranged by author and indexed by subject and geographic location.

421.   U.S. Department of the Interior. *Bibliography of North American Geology, 1963.* 1968. v + 1105pp. $3.00* (U.S.G.S. Bulletin, no. 1233).
I19.3:1233

422.   U.S. Department of the Interior. *Bibliography of North American Geology, 1966.* 1970. xi + 1069pp. $4.75 (U.S.G.S. Bulletin, no. 1266)
I19.3:1266

423.   U.S. Department of the Interior. *Bibliography of North American Geology, 1967.* 1970. xxxx + 1029pp. $4.75* (U.S.G.S. Bulletin, no. 1267).
I19.3:1267

424.   U.S. Department of the Interior. *Bibliography of North American Geology, 1968.* 1971. xli + 1301pp. $5.25* (U.S.G.S. Bulletin, no. 1268).
I19.3:1268

425.   U.S. Department of the Interior. *Bibliography of North American Geology, 1969.* 1972. xl + 1434pp. $6.00* (U.S.G.S. Bulletin, no. 1269).
I19.3:1269

426.   U.S. Department of the Interior. *Bibliography of North American Geology, 1970.* 1973. v + 1276pp. $8.70* S/N2401–2420.
I19.3:1370

427.   U.S. Geological Survey. *New Publications of the Geological Survey, Monthly List.* Free***.
Made cumulative by no. 430.
I19.14/4:date

428.   U.S. Geological Survey. *Popular Publications of the United States Geological Survey.* 1972. 19pp. Free***.

Listed and described are popular non--technical publications
by the Geological Survey to inform the general public
about geology, hydrology, topographic mapping and related
resources subjects. Most publications listed can be obtained
free and the rest can be purchased inexpensively from the
Government Printing Office.
I19.14/2:P96/972

429.   U.S. Geological Survey. *Publications of the Geological Survey,*
       1962--1970. iv + 586pp. Free***.
       As a permanent supplement to *Publications of the Geological*
       Survey, 1879--1961, this bibliography lists all U.S.G.S.
       from 1962--1970, plus all U.S.G.S. publications which
       have gone out--of--print since the 1879--1960 Catalog.
       Publications are listed by series and indexed by subject,
       author, and geographic area.
       I19.14:962–970

430.   U.S. Geological Survey. *Publications of the Geological*
       Survey, (year). Annual. Free***.
       This is an annual cumulation of the monthly listing of
       U.S.G.S. publications. Publications are listed by series
       and indexed by subject and geographic area. This is
       made cumulative by editions such as no. 429.
       I19.14:yr.

431--434. This series, which covers the period from 1951 forward,
       is international in scope and includes significant material
       on the Antarctic. Each volume contains approximately
       2,000 abstracts that are arranged by 13 subject categories:
       Biological Sciences; Cartography; Expeditions; Geological
       Sciences; Ice and Snow; Logistics; Equipment and
       Supplies; Medical Sciences; Meteorology; Oceanography;
       Atmospheric Physics; Terrestrial Physics; and Political
       Geography. Indexed by author, title, and geographic area.

431.   U.S. Library of Congress. Science and Technology Division.
       Antarctic Bibliography, 1951–1961; compiled by H.
       Thomas Bowker and others. 1970. vii + [1] + 349pp. $4.75*
       L.C. Card 65--61825.
       LC33.9:951–961

432.   U.S. Library of Congress. Science and Technology Division.
       Antarctic Bibliography, v. 3, 1968; edited by Geza T.
       Thuranyi. 1968. vii + 491pp. $6.00*.
       LC33.9:3

433. U.S. Library of Congress. Science and Technology Division. *Antarctic Bibliography, v. 4;* edited by Geza T. Thuranyi. 1971. vii + 491pp. $5.75*. LC33.9:4

434. U.S. Library of Congress. Science and Technology Division. *Antarctic Bibliography, v. 5;* edited by Geza T. Thuranyi. 1972. vii + 499pp. $5.75* S/N 3018--0013. LC33.9:5

435. U.S. National Ocean Survey. *List of Seismological Publications.* 1971. 12pp. Free***. C55.413:Se4

436. U.S. Smithsonian Institution. *Bibliography of Salvage Archeology in the United States;* compiled by Jerome E. Petsche, with foreword by John O. Brew. [1] + iv + 162pp.*** (Smithsonian Institution Publications in Salvage Archeology, no. 10). L.C. Card 68–67086.
"This bibliography is primarily a guide to appraisals and reports of archeological and paleontological remains lost or threatened as a result of the numerous projects for irrigation, flood control, hydroelectric power, and nagivation improvement in the river basins of the United States." Publications are listed by state.
SI1.22:10

Cartography

437. U.S. Department of the Navy. National Oceanographic Office. *Catalog of Nautical Chart; Special Purpose Navigational Charts and Publications.* 1971. 33pp.***.
This listing has been superceded by a similarly titled 1974 publication of the U.S. Defense Agency Army Mapping Service.
D203.22:1--N–A

438. U.S. Library of Congress. *Guide to the History of Cartography: an Annotated List on the History of Maps and Mapmaking;* compiled by Walter W. Ristow. 1973. 96pp. $.75* S/N 3001--00055. L.C. Card 73--9776.
A revised edition of a 1954 and 1960 *Guide,* this work has six times as many entries as the 1960 publication. Listed and described are 398 outstanding general works and ref- erence books relating to individual countries and to specialized aspects of cartography. Entries are arranged

alphabetically by author or title and are indexed by subject, author, and place.
LC5.2:H62/2/973

439. U.S. National Archives and Records Service. *Cartographic Records of the Bureau of Agricultural Economics;* compiled by William J. Heynen. 1971. 110pp.*** (Special Lists, no. 28). L.C. Card 70--182578.
GS4.7:28

440. U.S. National Archives and Records Service. *Guide to Cartographic Records in the National Archives;* prepared by Charlotte Ashby and others. 1971. xi + 444pp. $3.25*
L.C. Card 76--611061
"This bibliographic guide was planned as a central source of information about the cartographic holdings of the National Archives; the maps and aerial photographs described are those that were in the Cartographic Branch on July 1, 1966." A subject index leads one to the proper source.
GS4.6/2:C24

441. U.S. National Archives and Records Service. *List of Selected Maps of States and Territories;* compiled by Janet L. Hargett. 1971. vii + 112pp.*** (Special List, no. 29). L.C. Card 78--183183.
GS4.7:29

442. U.S. National Archives and Records Service. *Pre--Federal Maps in the National Archives: an Annotated List;* comp. by Patrick D. McLaughlin. 1971. 42pp.*** (Special Lists, no. 26). L.C. Card 73--175628.
GS4.7:26

Climatology and Meteorology

443. U.S. Department of the Air Force. Environmental Technical Applications Center. *Annotated Climatological Bibliography of Benelux Countries, (1960--69);* compiled by Dennis L. Boyer and Alvin L. Smith, jr. 1970. ix + 67pp.**
(Technical notes, 70--2). L.C. Card 78--607240.
D301.40/2:70--2

444. U.S. Department of the Air Force. Environmental Technical Applications Center. *Annotated Climatological Bibliography of India;* by Dennis L. Boyer and Alvin L. Smith, jr. 1969.

vi + 55pp.** (Technical notes, 69--6).
D301.40/2:69--6

445. U.S. Department of the Air Force. Environmental Technical
Applications Center. *Selected Annotated Bibliography on
Lightning;* by Alvin L. Smith, jr. and Dennis L. Boyer. 1969.
iii + 13pp. NTIS. (Technical Notes, 69--8). L.C. Card 77--
605026.
D301.40/2:69--8

446. U.S. Department of the Air Force. Environmental Technical
Applications Center. *Selected Bibliography on the Climate
of Central American Countries;* by Vincent J. Creasi. 1969.
vii + 27pp.** (Technical Note, 69--7).
D301.40/2:69--7

447. U.S. Department of the Air Force. Environmental Technical
Applications Center. *Selected Climatological Bibliography
for Thailand;* by Alvin L. Smith, jr. 1969. vii + 39pp. NTIS
(Technical Notes, 69--1).
D301.40/2:69--1

448. U.S. Department of the Army. Earth Sciences Laboratory.
*Bibliography on Atmospheric (Cyclic) Sea--Salts; by William
B. Brierly.* 1970. NTIS (ES--57).
Contained are "more than 600 references covering all
phases of the sea--salt cycle; the origin of the particles in
salt lakes, playas, and oceans; the processes by which the
salt particles are jetted into the air from sea and lake surfaces
by bursting bubbles, their transport inland over the
continental landmasses, their impingement, incrustment,
and fallout either as dry salt particles or in various forms
of precipitation, and their eventual return in rivers to
the sea. Selected references are also included on the
historic development of the subject, methods of chemical
analysis, and techniques of instrumentation and experimental
research leading to the formulation of current theories and
postulations." Indexed by subject.
D106.21:70--63--ES

449. U.S. Department of the Interior. Water Resources Scientific
Information Center. *Weather Modification: Precipitation
Inducement, a Bibliography.* 1973. 246pp. NTIS (WRSIC
73--212).

"This is another in a series of planned bibliographies in water resources to be produced solely from material available for listing in *Selected Water Resources Abstracts (SWRA)."* Material is abstracted and indexed. Availability is provided.
I1.97:73--212

450.   U.S. Environmental Science Services Administration. *Bibliography of Weather and Architecture;* by John F. Griffiths and M. Joan Griffiths. 1969. v + 72pp. NTIS. (PB--184--969). C52.15/2:EDSTM--9

451.   U.S. Environmental Science Services Administration. *Selective Guide to Climatic Data Sources.* 1969. 90pp. $1.00* L.C. Card 71--602769.
More than a bibliography, this is an excellent guide to published and unpublished climatological data. Each recurring pbulication is discussed in detail with samples given of every table or chart occurring in them. An index of published data lists separate categories -- rainfall, tem--perature, wind speed, etc., -- by time periods. Availability, price and/or subscription rates are given for each publication.
C30.66/2:4.11/2

452.   U.S. Environmental Science Services Administration. *Guide to Soviet Literature Accessions in the Atmospheric Sciences Library and the Geophysical Sciences Library, January -- February 1970;* trans. by Irene A. Donehoo. 68pp. NTIS (WB/TA Series, no. 24). L.C. Card 72--607236.
A bi--monthly publication. For Additional listings check *Government Reports Announcements.*
C51.21/2:24

453.   U.S. Environmental Science Services Administration. *Publications from ESSA Office of Public Information.* 1969. 10pp. Free***.
Popular informational publications on weather, meteorology, and other aspects of the Earth's environment are annotated. Purchase information is provided. (See no. 456 for similar title).
C52.21/2:P96

454.   U.S. Government Printing Office. *Weather, Astronomy, and Meteorology.* Free* (Price List no. 48).
Listed are free and for sale publications on many aspects of weather, astronomy, and meteorology. This list is revised frequently; prices are supposedly current; and all publications listed are available from the GPO.

455.   U.S. National Oceanic and Atmospheric Administration.
       Drought Bibliography; by Wayne C. Palmer and Lyle M.
       Denny. 1971. xi + 236pp. NTIS (NOAA Technical
       Memorandum, EDS--20). L.C. Card 73--614160.
       C55.13/2:EDS--20

456.   U.S. National Oceanic and Atmospheric Administration.
       Publications from NOAA Office of Public Affairs. 1972.
       12pp. Free***.
          Most of the publications listed here are inexpensive,
          popular items dealing with weather phenomena such as
          floods, hurricanes, tornadoes, and earthquakes. Price (if
          any) and availability are given.
       C55.26:P96

457.   U.S. Public Health Service. National Air Pollution Control
       Administration. *Climate of the Cities, Survey of Recent
       Literature (with List of References);* by James T. Peterson.
       1970. v + 48pp. $.55* (AP--59). L.C. Card 70–604448.
          "This report is a survey of the literature on city climatology,
          with emphasis on that written since the series of articles
          published by Dr. H. Landsberg, from 1956 to 1962. Those
          meteorological aspects that have been most frequently
          investigated are discussed herein; they are temperature,
          humidity, visibility, radiation, wind, and percipitation."
          The literature is followed by a complete bibliography of
          the references mentioned.
       HE20.1309:59

Energy and Energy Resources

458.   U.S. Atomic Energy Commission. *NSF–RANN Energy
       Abstracts: a Monthly Abstract Journal of Engery Research.*
       Monthly. Vol. 1--. 1973--. Free*** (Atomic Energy
       Commission, Oak Ridge National Laboratory, Publications
       Division, Oak Ridge, Tennessee. 37830). (ORNL--EIS--yr.--54/
       Vol.–no.). Back issues available from NTIS.
          This bibliography which is sponsored by the Research
          Applied to National Needs Program (RANN) of the
          National Science Foundation (NSF), is for disseminating
          rapidly the results of research performed under the
          Energy Research and Analysis category of RANN. Covered
          are the results of research on energy sources, electric power,

and energy production, consumption, supply and demand, and policy. Arranged by subject. Computer--generated indexes are issued twice a year.
Y3.At7:22/ORNL--EIS--yr.--54/v.--no.

459.   U.S. Bureau of Mines. *List of Bureau of Mines Publications on Oil Shale and Shale Oil, 1917--68;* compiled by Marianne P. Rogers. [1969]. [3] + 61pp. $.65* (IC–8249). L.C. Card 74--605044.
I28.27:8429

460.   U.S. Bureau of Mines. *Selected List of Bureau of Mines Publications on Petroleum and Natural Gas, 1961--1970;* by V. Vern Hutchison. 1972. [3] + 263pp. $1.75* S/N 2404--1050 (IC--8534). L.C. Card 72--601663.
This bibliography supplements Bureau of Mines Circular 8240, issued in 1964, and contains 829 separate entries on petroleum and natural gas publications of the Bureau of Mines Mines from 1961–1970. Entries are thoroughly indexed by subject and author.
I28.27:8534

461.   U.S. Congress. Senate. Committee on Interior and Insular Affairs. *A Bibliography of Congressional Publications on Energy from the 89th Congress to July 1, 1971.* 1971. xvii + 45pp.*** (Serial 92–6).
Entries were drawn from the *Monthly Catalog of U.S. Government Publications* and the Congressional Research Service Data Base. Publications are arranged by subject and are not indexed.
(See also no. 462 and no. 463).
Y4.In8/13:92–6

462.   U.S. Congress. Senate. Committee on Interior and Insular Affairs. *A Bibliography of Non--Technical Literature on Energy.* 1971. [3] + 99pp.*** (Serial 92–7).
Compiled through the use of the computer--stored data base of the Congressional Research Service, this bibliography covers July 1, 1969, through July 1, 1971. Publications are listed by subject with all phases of energy sources from fusion to wind being covered. In addition to energy sources, the following areas of energy technology are covered: Production of Fuels; Transportation of Fuels; Utilization of Fuels; and Environmental Effects on the Natural Resources.

Y4.In8/13:92--7

463. U.S. Congress. Senate. Committee on Interior and Insular
Affairs. *Supplemental Bibliography of Publications on
Energy;* compiled by Dana C. Ellingen. 1972. ix + [1] +
26pp.*** (Serial 92--29). L.C. Card 72–602697.
Supplements no. 461 and no. 462.
Y4.In8/13:92–29

464. U.S. Geological Survey. *Bibliography and Index of U.S.
Geological Survey Publications Relating to Coal, 1882–
1970;* by Paul Averitt and Lorreda Lopez. 1972. v + 173pp.
$.75* S/N 2401–2175. (Bulletin 1377). L.C. Card 72--
600257.
This is a compendium of about 1,300 geological reports,
maps, and statistical summaries relating to coal.
Arrangement is by author. Geographical location index.
I19.2:1377

465. U.S. Government Printing Office. *Mines, Explosives, Fuel,
Gasoline, Gas, Petroleum, Minerals.* Free* (Price List, no.
58).
Listed are selected for sale and free publications on mines,
explosives, etc. This list is revised frequently, and all items
are supposedly available and at the price indicated.
GP3.9:58

Geology and Natural Resources

466. U.S. Bureau of Reclamation. *Tunnel Geology Bibliography;*
compiled by G.W. DePuy. 1969. 1971. 3 + 50pp.
$2.25*** L.C. Card 71--611660.
I27.10/5:245

467. U.S. Department of the Army. Quartermaster General.
Desert Research, II: Selected References 1966--70; compiled
by Patricia Paylore. 1970. iv + 169pp. NTIS (ES--60).
The 594 references, many of them annotated at length,
place emphasis on arid lands aspects of such topics as
geomorphology, weather and climate, vegetation, fauna,
surface materials, hydrology, and geography. Indexed by
subject.
D106.21:71–20–ES

468. U.S. Department of the Interior. Library. *Natural Resources*

in Foreign Countries, Contribution Toward Bibliography of Bibliographies; compiled by Mary Anglemyer. 1968. vii + 113pp 113pp.*** (Bibliography Series, no. 9).
Annotated are 526 bibliographies on the natural resources of foreign countries. Publications are listed alphabetically by author under the country to which the bibliography pertains.
I22.9/2:9

469. U.S. Department of the Navy. Naval Oceanographic Office. *Selected Bibliography of Geology and Geophysics for the Gulf of Mexico;* by Henry R. EEnsminger and William T. Morton. 1968. [3] + 18 + 2pp.** (Informal Report, 68--69). D203.26/2:68--69

470. U.S. Geological Survey. *Bibliography of Geology and Mineral-ogy of Rare Earths and Scandium to 1971;* by John W. Adams and Eleanor R. Iberall. 1973. xxx + 195pp. $2.10*
S/N 2401--2154 (Bulletin, no. 1366). L.C. Card 73--600026.
Cited are 2092 publications intended to aid researchers interested in geologic occurrence, geochemistry, and mineralogy of the rare earths and scandium. Also included are some references in areas of analytical chemistry, ore benefication, uses, physical properties, and certain artificial rare--earth compounds that resemble minerals. Entries are arranged by author and indexed by subject and geographic areas.
I19.3:1366

471. U.S. Geological Survey. *Bibliography of Geology of the Green River Formation, Colorado, Utah, and Wyoming, to March 1, 1973;* by Marjorie C. Mullens. 1973. iii + 20pp.***
(Circular, no. 675).
"This bibliography, which contains 597 references, was compiled to aid studies on the geology and resources of the Green River Formation. References included are mainly on the areal geology, stratigraphy, paleontology, geo--chemistry, and mineralogy of the Green River Formation, but some concern exploitation of the oil--shale deposits."
I19.4/2:675

472. U.S. Geological Survey. *Bibliography of Reports Resulting from Geological Survey Participation in the United States Technical Assistance Program, 1940--67;* by Jo Ann Heath and Nancy B. Tabacchi. 1968. v + 68pp. $.35* (Bulletin

no. 1263). L.C. Card GS--236.

Listed are publications which resulted from the U.S.G.S. and foreign country counterparts investigations of developing countries. This bibliography, which covers 1940--1967, updates U.S.G.S. Bulletin 1193. Entries are arranged alphabetically by author under each individual country and are indexed by subject and author.

I19.3:1263

473.   U.S. Geological Survey. *Bibliography on Geology and Resources Resources of Vanadium to 1968;* by R.P. Fischer and Jane P. Ohl. 1970. xxxii + 168pp. $1.00* (Bulletin, no. 1316). L.C. Card 73--606274.

Contained are nearly 1400 bibliographic references to the geology and resources of vanadium which cover the literature through 1967. "Most references included are to original sources of informationof the distribution and occurrence of vanadium--bearing deposits, on the geo--chemical relations of vanadium in rocks and deposits, and on vanadium mineralogy." Arrangement is by author with a geographical--subject index.

I19.3:1316

474.   U.S. Geological Survey. *Glaciological Notes, Acquisitions of World Data Center A.* Quarterly. 1960--. No. 1--. *** (Geological Survey, 1305 Tacoma Ave. South, Tacoma, Washington. 98402).

I19.60:no.

475.   U.S. Geological Survey. *Remote Sensing for Earth Resources, 1969;* by J.P. Glasby and D.G. Lowe. 1971. xiv + 182pp.***.

I19.14/2:R28/969

476.   U.S. Geological Survey. *Selected Annotated Bibliography on Asphalt--Bearing Rocks of the United States and Canada, to 1970;* by Marjorie C. Mullens and Albert E. Roberts. 1972. iv + 218pp. $1.25* S/N 2401--2110 (Bulletin, no. 1352). L.C. Card 72--600019.

Contained are about 600 selected annotated references pertaining to the geology and occurrence of asphalt--bearing rocks.

I19.3:1352

477.   U.S. Geological Survey. *Selected Annotated Bibliography of Minor--Element Content of Marine Black Shales and*

Related Sedimentary Rocks, 1930–65; by Elizabeth B. Tourtelot. 1970. xv + 118pp. $.60* (Bulletin, no. 1293). L.C. Card 75--604512.

Included are about 375 abstracts which present minor--element data from analyses of black shales and related organic--rich sedimentary rocks. In addition, there are selected discussions on the source of the minor elements. Indexed by subject and geographic area.
I19.3:1293

478.   U.S. Geological Survey. *Selected Annotated Bibliography on the Geochemistry of Gold;* by Margaret Cooper. 1971. [3] + 63pp. $.35* (Bulletin, no. 1337). L.C. Card 77--611048.

Approximately 200 references deal with genesis and geo--chemistry of gold and with geochemical prospecting for gold deposits. A number of the references are also bibliographies. Indexed by subject and author.
I19.3:1337

479.   U.S. Geological Survey. *Terrestrial Impact Structures, Bibliography 1965–68;* by Jacquelyn H. Freeberg, 1969. iv + 39pp. $.30* (Bulletin, no. 1320). L.C. Card 74--650225.

This bibliography supplements Bulletin 1220 which covered the literature relating to impact structures up to 1964. At that time there were 110 known such structures. This supplements adds 17 new sites and extends the lit--erature coverage through 1968. The 269 entries are grouped alphabetically by author according to site. Author index.
I19.3:1320

480.   U.S. Government Printing Office. *Geology.* Free* (Price List, no. 15).

Listed are for sale and free publications on all aspects of geology. This list is revised frequently; prices are kept current; and all publications are supposedly available.
GP3.9:15

481.   U.S. National Aeronautics and Space Administration. *Remote Sensing of Earth Resources, Literature Survey with Indexes.* 1970. 1227pp. NTIS (NASA SP--7036). L.C. Card 79--609221.

Abstracted are 3684 publications "related to the

identification and evaluation by means of sensors in spacecraft and aircraft of vegetation, minerals, and other natural resources, and the techniques and potentialities of surveying and keeping up--to-date inventories of such riches." Entries are listed according to such subjects as: Agriculture and Forestry; Environmental Changes and Cultural Resources; Geogesy and Cartography; Geology and Mineral Resources; Oceanography and Marine Resources; Hydrology and Water Management; Data Processing and Distribution Systems; and Instrumentation and Sensors.

Five indexes -- subject, personal author, corporate source, contract number and report/accession number -- aid in locating information. NAS1.21:7036

Hydrology
(see also no. 379--409)

482. U.S. Department of the Interior. *Salinity Problems in Arid Lands Irrigation, Literature Review and Selected Bibliography;* by Hugh E. Casey. 1972. 316pp.*** L.C. Card 73--601000. I1.12:Sa3/7

483. U.S. Department of the Interior. Office of Saline Water. *Abstracts of Literature on the Distillation of Seawater and on the Use of Nuclear Energy for Desalting;* by K.O. Jonhsson. 1970. vii + 280pp. $2.00* (Research and Development Progress Report, no. 589).
      Over 1100 lengthy abstracts are divided into the following subject areas: (1) Energy Sources; (2) Energy Utilization (Coupling); (3) Seawater Distillation Processes; (4) Other Desalting Processes; (5) Overall Plant Studies; (6) Siting Considerations; (7) Industrial Applications; and (8) Water Utilization. Keyword and author indices. I1.88:589

484. U.S. Department of the Interior. Office of Saline Water. *Bibliography of Desalting Literature, 1969;* by Columbia Software, Inc. 1970. iv + 465pp. $3.25* (Research and Development Progress Report, no. 552).
      Almost 5,000 entries are arranged under the following subject categories: (1) Desalting Processes; (2) Chemical Recovery Processes; (3) Dynamic Phenomena; (4) Development Status; (5) Membranes; (6) Chemical Properties; (7) Water; and (8) Energy Sources. Author

and Descriptor indices.
I1.88:552

485.   U.S. Department of the Interior. Water Resources Scientific
        Information Center. *Water Resources Research Catalog.*
        Pt 1, 2. Vol. 1--. 1965--. (Annual). (The 1972 two volume
        set was $16.25* S/N 2400–0734).
        This annual catalog, initiated in 1965, presents summary
        descriptions of current research on water resources
        problems. "The Catalog also makes readily available to all
        who are engaged in water--related research, or otherwise
        concerned with water resources problems, information
        on what is being done, by whom, and where." Indexes
        by subject, investigator, contractor, and supporting agency.

486.   U.S. Forest Service. *Southeastern Forest*
        Experiment Station. Annotated Bibliography of Publications
        on Watershed Management by the Southeastern Forest
        Experiment Station, 1928--70; by James E. Douglass. 1972.
        47pp. Free*** (Research Paper, SE--93).
        Contained are 209 annotated citations of publications on
        watershed management and the influence of various types
        of forest cover on streamflow and water yield.
        Citations are arranged alphabetically and chronologically
        by author. A subject index guides to specific areas of
        interest.
        A13.78:SE--93

487.   U.S. Geological Survey. *Annotated Bibliography on*
        Artificial Recharge of Ground Water, 1955–67; by D.C.
        Signor, D.J. Growitz, and William Kam. 1970. iii + 141pp.
        $.65* (Water--Supply Paper, no. 1990). L.C. Card 70--
        603551.
        This is a sequel to Water--Supply Paper no. 1447 and contains
        well–annotated references to the technical literature on
        artificial ground--water recharge from 1955–67.
        Arrangement is alphabetical by author with a subject--
        geographic index to facilitate its use.
        I19.13:1990

488.   U.S. Geological Survey. *Bibliography of Hydrology of the*
        United States and Canada, 1964; compiled by J.R. Randolph,
        N.M. Baker, and R.G. Deike. 1969. xxi + 232pp. $1.00*
        (Water--Supply Paper, no. 1864). L.C. Card GS68–391.
        Listed are references to publications in the field of hydrology

published in the U.S. and Canada during 1964. Entries are listed alphabetically by author, and complete bibliographic information is given. A subject--geographic index facilitates its use.

Since this bibliography has been sponsored by various agencies and organizations over the years, there is a bibliographic listing of all former similar bibliographic titles in the "Introduction."

(See no. 493–494 for later editions).

I19.13:1864

489. U.S. Geological Survey. *Bibliography of Tritium Studies Related to Hydrology Through 1966;* by Edward C. Rhodehamel, Veronica B. Kron, and Verda M. Dougherty. 1971. 3 + 174pp. $.75* (Water--Supply Paper, no. 1900). L.C. Card 76--608171.

"The bibliography consists of a main list of references classified as to the principal subject matter of each item, and an auxiliary bibliography containing background knowledge about radioactivity, analytical techniques, and various environments in which tritium exists."

I19.13:1900

490. U.S. Geological Survey. *Reports for California by the Geological Survey, Water Resources Division;* compiled by J.S. Bader and Fred Kunkel. Menlo Park, Calif. 1969. v + 95pp.*** L.C. Card 78–606629.

I19.2:C12/3

491. U.S. Geological Survey. *Reports for California by the Geological Survey, Water Resources Division.* 1971. vii + 104pp.*** L.C. Card 74--616480.

I19.2:C12/3/971

492. U.S. Geological Survey. *Reports for California by the Geological Survey, Water Resources Division.* 1973. viii + 111pp.***. L.C. Card 73–602287.

I19.14/2:C12/2

493. U.S. Government Printing Office. *Water Power, Hydrology, Saline Water Conversion.* Free* (Price List, no. 42).

Listed are for sale and free publications on all aspects of water power, hydrology, and saline water conversion. This list is revised frequently; prices are kept current; and all publications listed are supposedly available.

494. U.S. Water Resources Council. *Annotated Bibliography on Hydrology and Sedimentation, 1963--65, United States and Canada.* 1969. xi + 527pp. $4.50*.
See no. 495 for notation.
Y3.W29:9/9

495. U.S. Water Resources Council. *Annotated Bibliography on Hydrology and Sedimintation, 1966--68, United States and Canada.* 1970. xi + 613pp. $5.25*.
"The Hydrology and Sedimentation Committee, Water Resources Council, have sponsored this Bibliography as a guide to literature on hydrology and sedimentation for the use of Government agencies and the public." Every effort has been made to cover all such literature published in the U.S. and Canada during the period indicated. Entries are indexed by subject and geographic area.
(See also no. 487).
Y3.W29:9/10

HISTORY

496. U.S. Civil War Centennial Commission. *The Civil War Centennial: a Report to the Congress.* 1968. [5] + 69pp. $2.25*.
In addition to the report, there is a bibliography of 240 items dealing with the Civil War. These are arranged alphabetically by author with bibliographic notations.
Y3.C49/2:1/968

497. U.S. Department of the Air Force. Pacific Air Forces. *United States Air Force History: an Annotated Bibliography;* compiled by Mary Ann Cresswell and Carl Berger. 1971. v + 106pp. $.50* S/N 0870--0307. L.C. Card 77–616261.
D301.62/2:H62

498. U.S. Department of the Army. *Bibliography of Military History, Selected Annotated Listing of Reference Sources in the United States Military Academy Library;* compiled by J. Thomas Russel. 1969. [1] + xvii + 57pp.**
(United States Military Academy Library Bulletin, no. 7).
D109.10:7

499. U.S. Department of the Army. *Fort Leavenworth, 1823--80.* 1970. [1] + 6pp.** (U.S. Army Command and

General Staff College, Library Division, Fort Leavenworth, Kansas, Special Bibliography, no. 18).
D101.76:18

500. U.S. Department of the Army. *Fort Leavenworth.* 1973. i + 38pp.** (U.S. Army Command and General Staff College, Library Division, Fort Leavenworth, Kansas, Special Bibliography, no. 34).
Several hundred references, some of them annotated, are concerned with Fort Leavenworth since its conception. Entries are listed alphabetically under eleven subject headings such as: Cavalry and Dragoon; Churches and Schools; Expeditions and Exploration; Indian Affairs; and Military Frontier and Westward Expansion.
D101.76:34

501. U.S. Department of the Army. Office of Military History. *Publications of the Office of the Chief of Military History.* Annual. Free*** L.C. Card 76--605851.
A descriptive list of available publications.
D114.10:yr

502. U.S. Department of the Navy. Marine Corps. *Annotated Bibliography of Marine Corps' Artillery;* by Ralph W. Donnelly. 1970. ix + 68pp. Free*** (Marine Corps Historical Bibliography). L.C. Card 73--607594.
Approximately 400 references to books, periodicals, manuscripts, and pictures (most of which are annotated) show the use of artillery from the conception of the Marines to the present day.
D214.15:Ar7

503. U.S. Department of the Navy. Marine Corps. *Annotated Bibliography of the United States Marines in the Civil War;* by Michael O'Quinlivan and Rowland P. Gill. 1968. [3] + 15pp. Free*** (Marine Corps Historical References Bibliography). L.C. Card 68--62467.
Most of the 78 annotated references deal specifically with the Marines of both sides in the Civil War. Additionally, a few general works have been included to give one an overview of the Civil War.
D214.15:C49

504. U.S. Department of the Navy. Marine Corps. *Annotated Reading List of Marine Corps History;* compiled by Jack

B. Hilliard and Harold A. Bibins. 1971. [1] + v + 55pp.
Free*** L.C. Card 77--614145.
Nearly 600 briefly annotated entries comprise this
bibliography. Listings are by subject categories such as:
Bibliographies; Biographies; Pictorial Histories; Aviation;
and Marine Corps History by Period (treated individually
from the Revolutionary War through the present day).
Author index.
D214.14/2:H62/7

505.   U.S. Department of the Navy. Office of Naval Operations.
United States Naval History, Bibliography. 6th ed. 1972.
vi + 34pp. $.70* S/N 0846--0067. L.C. Card 73--601146.
Revised frequently, this keeps up with the literature being
published in the field of naval history. Arrangement is by
broad categories such as: General Histories; Biographies;
Naval History by Period; Marine Corps History; Coast
Guard History; and Special Subject. Author index.
D207.11:H62/972

506.   U.S. Government Printing Office. *American History.*
Free* (Price List, no. 50).
Listed are free and for sale publications on American
history. This list is revised frequently; prices are current;
and publications are supposedly available from the GPO.
GP3.9:50

507.   U.S. Library of Congress. *American Revolution, Selected
Reading List;* prepared by Stefan M. Harrow et al. 1968.
iv + [1] + 38pp. $.50* L.C. Card 68--67236.
Prepared more as a reading guide than a reference source
book, this bibliography cites all types of materials dealing
with the Revolution from eye witness accounts to scholarly
evaluations. Virtually every aspect of the Revolution is
touched upon from the initial controversy with Great
Britain to the Confederation Period of the 1780's.
Arranged according to subject and indexed by author.
LC1.12/2:R32

508.   U.S. Library of Congress. General Reference and Bibliography
Division. *Creating Independence, 1763--89, Background
Reading for Young People: Selected Annotated Bibliography;*
compiled by Margaret N. Coughlan. 1972. [8] + 62pp.
$.75* S/N 3001--0046. L.C. Card 72--3573.
The attractive format and illustrations of this bibliography

make it worth owning solely for its esthetic qualities. Publications are listed according to subject divisions which describe the colonial period, political tension of the times, advocates and dissenters of the revolution, the war years, and the birth of the Constitution. Annotations are interesting and informative.
LC2.2:in2/5/763--89

509. U.S. Library of Congress. General Reference and Bibliography Division. *Periodical Literature on the American Revolution, Historical Research and Changing Interpretations, 1895--1970, Selective Bibliography;* compiled by Ronald M. Gephart. 1971. [iv] + 2 + 93pp. $1.00* L.C. Card 74--609228.
Over 1,000 entries are divided into the following areas: The Confederation, 1777--1778; Society and Culture in Revolutionary America; The Making of the Constitution; Political Thought and Legal Development; Economic Development; Social and Cultural Development. Indexed by author and subject.
LC2.2:Am3/3/895--970

510. U.S. Library of Congress. General Reference and Biblio-- graphy Division. *Presidential Inaugurations, Selected List of References;* compiled by Ruth S. Freitag. 3d edition, revised and enlarged. 1969. vii + 230pp. $2.00* L.C. Card 76--602825.
Nearly 1500 citations to books, parts of books, and periodical articles cover the Presidential inaugurations from Presidents Washington through Nixon. Entries are grouped according to President and special subject matter, such as inaugural balls, bibles, music, and weather. Indexed by name and subject.
LC2.2:P92/3/969

511. U.S. Library of Congress. Geography and Map Division. *Detroit and Vicinity Before 1900, Annotated List of Maps;* compiled by Alberta G. Auringer Koerner. iv + [2] + 84pp. $.45* L.C. Card 68--67060.
"This bibliography describes 239 maps and atlases which depict the city of Detroit, Michigan, its vicinity, the Detroit River, Wayne County, other towns in Wayne County during the 18th and 19th centuries, and the adjacent shore in Canada regardless of the date of publication." Entries are arranged chronologically by the date on the map and then alphabetically by cartographer or title. Indexed by

subject, place, and cartographer.
LC5.2:D48

512. U.S. National Archives and Records Service. *Administration of Modern Archives, Select Bibliographic Guide;* compiled by Frank B. Evans. 1970. (Pub. 1971). xiii + 213pp. $3.25* S/N 2202--0032. L.C. Card 76--611061.
An effort has been made in this guide "to include all writings that have contributed to or illustrate the develop- ment in the United States of archival principles and techniques." Only the most pertinent English language materials published through 1969 have been included. Entries are arranged primarily by archival function. Indexed by subject.
GS4.17/3:Ad6

513. U.S. National Archives and Records Service. *Franklin D. Roosevelt, Selected Bibliography of Periodical and Disser-- tation Literature, 1945--66;* compiled and annotated by William J. Stewart. 1967. [1] + iii + 175pp. $2.50***
(Franklin D. Roosevelt Library, Hyde Park, N.Y. 12538).
Excluded are publications concerned primarily with military operations, newspaper articles, and unsigned articles. Annotated entries are divided into the following sections; Franklin D. Roosevelt; New Deal; World War II; and Archives, Bibliography and Historiography. Indexed by author and subject.
GS4.17/3:R67/945–66

514. U.S. National Archives and Records Service. *Select List of Publications of the National Archives and Records Service.* 1973. ii + 51pp.*** (General Information Leaflet, no. 3).
Included are currently available publications of the National Archives and Records Service. Publications are gouped by series or type of material covered, and purchase information is provided. Not indexed.
G4.22:3/973

515. U.S. National Historical Publications Commission. *Writings on American History; 1959; Volume II of the Annual Report of the American Historical Association for the Year 1961;* compiled by the National Historical Publications Commission, James R. Masterson, editor, Joyce E. Eberly, Assistant Editor. 1969. xv + 737pp. $4.75* (Also issued as H. Doc.

386, pt. 2, 87th Cong., 2nd Sess.). L.C. Card 4--18261. See no. 516 for notation.
SI4.1:961/v.2

516. U.S. National Historical Publications Commission. *Writings on American History, 1959; Volume II of the Annual Report of the American Historical Association for the Year 1962.* 1972. xvi + 962pp. $5.25* (Also issued as H.Doc. 110, pt. 2, 88th Cong. 2nd Sess.).
These are continuations of a series begun in 1902. "In 1951 the National Historical Publications Commission assumed responsibility for the preparation of the *Writings* and seeing it through the press."
This series purposes to cite every book and article published in the U.S. or its territories which pertains to U.S. history during a given calendar year. Publications are grouped according to subject and state, region, or locale, and are indexed by author and place. Also included is a list of serials cited.
SI4.1:962/v.2

LITERATURE AND THE ARTS

Arts and Crafts

517. U.S. Department of the Air Force. Pacific Air Forces. *Manual Arts and Crafts;* prepared by Helen M. Thompson. 1969. Free***.
Annotated references are divided into such subject groups as: Automotive Hobbies; Boatbuilding; Ceramics; Drawing and Painting (different types are treated individually); Graphic Arts; Hi--Fi and Stereo; Jewelry Making; Leather--craft; Sculpture; and Woodworking. Publications are treated critically, and this serves as a good buying guide for building a collection of arts and crafts literature. Purchase information is generally provided, and supplements keep the bibliography current.
D301.62:M31/969

518. U.S. Department of the Air Force. Pacific Air Forces. *Manual Arts and Crafts, Supp. 1.* 1970. [1] + v + 40pp. Free***.
D301.62:M31/969/supp.1

519. U.S. Department of the Air Force. Pacific Air Forces. *Manual Arts and Crafts, Supp. 2.* 1971. [1] + v + 35pp.

Free***.
D301.62:M31/969/supp.2

520. U.S. Department of the Air Force. Pacific Air Forces. *Photo--graphy, Supp. 1;* prepared by Mary T. McCullough. 1969.
iv + 46pp. Free***.
D301.62:P56/2/967/supp.1

521. U.S. Department of the Air Force. Pacific Air Forces. *Photo-graphy, Supp. 2;* prepared by Mary T. McCullough. 1970.
[1] + 22pp. Free***.
Supplements keep current the information on particular
aspects and techniques of photography. Also covered
are the photographic professions. Annotations are
lengthy, and publications are treated critically. Indexed
by author and title.
D301.62:P56/2/967/supp.2

522. U.S. Department of the Interior. Indian Arts and Crafts
Board. *Art of the Eskimo and the Northwest Coast Indian.*
1967. 2pp. Free***. (Bibliography Series, no. 2).
I1.84/5:2

523. U.S. Department of the Interior. Indian Arts and Crafts
Board. *Native American Arts and Crafts of the United
States.* 1971. 6pp. Free*** (Bibliography Series,
no. 1).
"The selected readings listed in this bibliography are
suggested as an introduction to the richly varied arts and
crafts created from prehistoric to modern times by
Native American peoples of the United States." Not
indexed.
I1.84/5:1

524. U.S. Small Business Administration. *Handicrafts;* by
Robert W. Gray. Rev. 1973. 8pp.*** (Small Business
Bibliography, no. 1).
Listed are government and non--government publications
to assist prospective and current owners of handicrafts to
plan, organize, direct, coordinate, and control their
business. Government publications are lumped together,
and non--government publications are listed according to
type of craft -- ceramics, enameling, woodcarving, etc.
SBA1.3:1/6

525. U.S. Small Business Administration. *Hobby Shops;* by Milton K. Grey. 1971. 8pp. Free*** (Small Business Bibliographies, no. 53).
Listed are selected books and other publications which provide information on the hobby and craft merchandise offered by hobby retailers. Names and addresses of hobby clubs are given.
SBA1.3:53/3

Literature Lists and Guides

526. U.S. Department of the Army. *Recommended Books for a Military Library.* 1972. 57pp.** (U.S. Army Command and General Staff College, Library Division, Fort Leavenworth, Kansas, Special Bibliography,no. 8).
D101.76:8

527. U.S. Department of the Army. Military Academy. *Bibliography of Military History; a Selected, Annotated Listing of Reference Sources in the United States Military Academy Library;* compiled by J. Thomas Russel. 1969. 57pp.*** (U.S. Military Academy, West Point).
Patterened after Winchell's *Guide to Reference Books* (8th edition), books are grouped by broad subjects. Annotations have been adapted from Winchell, and works were chosen for their "practical, informational value as sources for the beginning researcher in the field of military history." As such, this also makes a good selection guide for a military history collection.
D109.10:7

528. U.S. Department of the Interior. Indian Arts and Crafts Board. *Indian and Eskimo Folktales.* 1967. 4pp. Free*** (Bibliography Series, no. 3).
I1.84/5:3

529. U.S. Department of the Air Force. Pacific Air Force. *Basic Religious Books and Chaplains' Services;* prepared by Mae L. Johnson. 1970. [1] + iv + 86pp. Free*** (PACAF Basic Bibliographies). L.C. Card 70–609306.
D301.62:R27/970

530. U.S. Department of the Air Force. Pacific Air Force. *Black*

Literature; prepared by Norman E. Dakan. 1970. 69pp.
Free*** (PACAF Basic Bibliographies). L.C. 76--611246.
"This bibliography is an attempt to bring together
critically annotated titles by and about black writers in
America. It is, insofar as possible, a fairly comprehensive
listing for the years after 1940." Indexed by author and
title.
D301.62:B56

531. U.S. Department of the Air Force. Pacific Air Forces. *Fiction
Men Read;* prepared by Julie M. O'Brien. 1970. [1] + iii +
34pp. Free*** (PACAF Basic Bibliographies).
Since the titles listed here are representative of what men
read, this is a good selection aid for general reading
materials.
D301.62:F44/970

532. U.S. Department of the Air Force. Pacific Air Forces.
Non--fiction Men Read; prepared by Frances Lum. 1971.
[1] + iv + 17pp. Free*** (PACAF Basic Bibliographies).
This a librarian's aid to the non--fiction titles which would
interest men.
D301.62:N73

533. U.S. Department of the Air Force. Pacific Air Forces.
Reference Books; prepared by Eleanor F. Ballou. 1968.
Free*** (PACAF Basic Bibliographies).
All areas from the applied sciences to recreation are
covered by this annotated, critical buying and selection
guide to reference books which is kept current by
supplements. This is an excellent free tool for any library
with a general type collection.
D301.62:R25/968/supp.2

534. U.S. Department of the Air Force. Pacific Air Forces.
Reference Books, Supp. 1. 1970. [1] + iv + 37pp. Free***
(PACAF Basic Bibliographies).
D301.62:R25/968/supp.1

535. U.S. Department of the Air Force. Pacific Air Forces.
Reference Books, Supp. 2. 1971. [1] + iv + 21pp. Free***
(PACAF Basic Bibliographies).
D301.62:R25/968/supp.2

536. U.S. Department of the Air Force. Pacific Air Forces. *When*

to Buy What, Buying Calendar for Annual Publications; prepared by Eleanor F. Ballou and Gloria D. Dean. 1972.
[1] + ii + 146pp. Free*** (PACAF Basic Bibliographies).
L.C. Card 79--611402.
This lists and tells the frequency of publications and when
to order numerous annual and serial publications. Purchase
information, current as of 1972, is included.
D301.62:B98/972

537. U.S. Department of the Navy. Naval Personnel Bureau.
*Guide for Professional Reading for Officers of the United
States Navy and Marine Corps.* 21st edition. 1970. [2] + v + 3
31pp. Free*** L.C. Card 61--61559.
D208.15:P94/968

538. U.S. Government Printing Office. *Government Periodicals
and Subscriptions Services.* Free* (Price List, no. 36).
Listed are periodicals and subscription publications
distributed by the Government Printing Office. A
brief annotation and price of subscription accompany
each publication.
GP3.9:36

539. U.S. Government Printing Office. *Monthly Catalog of
United States Government Publications.* $19.35* a yr., including
including annual index; $4.85 additional foreign mailing.
L.C. Card 4--18088.
This is the primary bibliographic guide to U.S. government
publications. It provides complete bibliographic infor--
mation, as well as price, availability, and Superintendent of
Documents classification number, for each item.
Publications are listed alphabetically by issuing agency
and are indexed by subject, author, and title indexes.
(Prior to 1974, indexing was primarily by subject.)
Special features include: (1) an appendix in the February issue entitled "Directory of United States Government Periodicals and Subscription Publications"; (2) an
appendix in the September issue listing all depository
libraries by state and city with depository number and
year of depository designation; (3) a "Preview" section
each month for forthcoming publications; (4) a monthly
section headed "New Classification Numbers" which also
contains discontinued series and classification corrections;
and (5) an annual cumulative index in the December issue.
GP3.8:date

540. U.S. Government Printing Office. *Selected United States Government Publications* [List]. Biweekly, with supplements issued irregularly. Free*.

Listed with a brief annotation are publications which the Government Printing Office thinks might be of interest to the public. The subject matter varies immensely, and the type of material ranges from highly technical to coloring books. All items have the current price and are available from the GPO.

GP3.17:Vol./no.

541. U.S. Library of Congress. *Children and Poetry, Selective, Annotated Bibliography;* compiled by Virginia Haviland and William J. Smith (Children's Book Section). 1969. x + 67pp. $.75* L.C. Card 70--603744.

Included are noteworthy and enjoyable anthologies and books of poetry of the past, the present, and the world. One entire section is devoted to rhymes. Each selection is thoroughly annotated, and frequently a poem or section of a poem is included in the annotation. Delight-- ful illustrations enhance the work. Indexed by title and author.

LC1.12/2:P75

542. Library of Congress. *Library of Congress Catalogs in Book Form and Related Publications.* 1971. [2] + 17 + [2] pp. Free***.

The primary book catalogs issued by the Library of Congress are described in some detail. Information about each catalog includes: contents and arrangement; frequency of publication; and number of issues to date. Following are a few of the publications described: *The National Union Catalog* (various parts); *Library of Congress Catalog -- Books: Subjects;* and *The National Register of Microform Masters.*

LC1.12/2:C28/971

543. U.S. Library of Congress. *Library of Congress Publications in Print, March 1973.* vii + 41pp. Free*** (Revised Annually). L.C. Card 6--35005.

Complete purchase and availability information is given for each title listed.

LC1.12/2:P96/973

544. U.S. Library of Congress. Catalog Publication Division.

Newspapers in Microform: Foreign Countries, 1948--1972.
1973. xix + 269pp. $10.00*** L.C. Card 73--12976.
Originally published as a part of a single volume, *News--papers on Microfilm (1967)*, "this publication is the seventh in a continuing cumulative series designed to bring under bibliographic control foreign newspapers that have been reduced to microform and are housed permanently in United States, Canadian, and other foreign libraries as well as in the vaults of domestic and foreign commercial producers of microforms. . . . This volume lists 8,620 titles, with 833 cross references, in 1,935 localities." Indexed alphabetically by title. Arranged alphabetically by country and by place within the country.
LC18.2:N47/4/972

545. U.S. Library of Congress. Catalog Publication Division. *News--papers in Microform: United States, 1948--1972.* 1973. xxiii + 1056pp. $30.00*** L.C. Card 73--6936.
Originally published as a part of a single volume, *News--papers on Microfilm (1967)*, "this publication is the seventh in a continuing series designed to bring under bibliographic control United States newspapers that have been reduced to microform and are housed permanently in United States, Canadian, and other foreign libraries as well as in the vaults of domestic and foreign commercial producers of micro--forms. . . . This volume lists 34,289 titles, with 2,308 cross references, in 7,457 localities of the United States and its territories and possessions." Indexed alphabetically by title. Arranged alphabetically by state and by city within the state.
LC18.2:N47/3/972

546. U.S. Library of Congress. Division for the Blind and Physically Handicapped. *Books on Magnetic Tape.* 1968. 48pp. Free***. Free***.
LC19.2:T16/2/no.1

547. U.S. Library of Congress. Division for the Blind and Physically Handicapped. *Books on Open--Reel Tape* [Catalog]. 1973. 63pp. Free***.
Included in this catalog are books on open--reel tape which are available on loan from the Library of Congress and regional libraries which cooperate in distributing recorded reading materials free on loan to persons who cannot read because of visual or physical disability.

548. U.S. Library of Congress. Division for the Blind and Physically Handicapped. *Cassette Books.* 1971. vii + 75pp. Free***.
Listed and described are about 700 titles which are on cassette tapes and available from regional libraries which cooperate with the Library of Congress Division for the Blind and Physically Handicapped in loaning, free of charge, cassette books to those who cannot read because of visual or physical disability. Like a library, the books on cassettes run the full range of subjects from the best of fiction to books on medicine and economics. Even children's books are included.
Indexed by author and title.
LC19.2:C27

549. U.S. Library of Congress. Division for the Blind and Physically Handicapped. *Talking Books to Profit By.* 1971. 3 + 11pp. Free***.
The titles listed are a part of the Library of Congress's program for those who cannot read because of visual or physical disability. Each book or magazine listed is on a record or tape and is concerned with some form of self improvement. Topics covered include cooking, earning a living, handling money, family relationships, and getting along with others.
LC19.2:T14/13

550. U.S. Library of Congress. General Reference and Bibliography Division. *Children's Books, (Annual), a List of Books for Preschool Through Junior High School Age;* compiled by Virginia Haviland and Lois Watt. (Annual). $.25* (S/N 3001–00054). L.C. Card 65--60014.
This is an annotated listing of picture books, stories for older children, folklore, biography, poetry, plays, Bible stories, histories, and science books for children which were published during the year. Not indexed.
LC2.11:yr.

551. U.S. Library of Congress. General Reference and Biblio--graphy Division. *Children's Literature, Guide to Reference Sources, 1st Supplement;* compiled by Virginia Haviland with assistance of Margaret N. Coughlan. 1972. viii + 316pp. $3.00* S/N 3001--0044. L.C. Card 6–35005.
As a supplement to the original title published in 1966, this

contains publications primarily issued from 1966 through 1969. Annotations are alphabetical under definitive subject headings of the following major subject headings: History and Criticism; Authorship, Illustration; Bibliography; Books and Children; The Library and Children's Books; International Studies; and National Studies. There is a general index by subject, author, and title.
LC2.8:C43/supp.

552.   U.S. Library of Congress. General Reference and Bibliography Division. *Folklore of North American Indians, Annotated Bibliography;* compiled by Judith C. Ullom. 1969. x + 126pp. $2.25* L.C. Card 70--601462.
This selective bibliography of North American Indian folklore is arranged by eleven cultural groups. Each title has a lengthy annotation which fully describes the work. Many black and white illustrations enhance the book. Indexed by author, title, and subject.
LC2.2:In25/2

553.   U.S. Library of Congress. General Reference and Bibliography Division. *French--Speaking Central Africa: a Guide to Official Publications in American Libraries;* compiled by Julian W. Witherall. 1973. xiv + 314pp. $3.70* S/N 3001--0051. L.C. Card 72--5766.
A number of American libraries hold government records and publications of French--speaking Central African countries. Notations are made beside each publication to indicate which libraries hold particular documents. Some 3270 entries are grouped by country and then arranged by author and title. Indexed by subject and author.
LC2.8:Af8/3

554.   U.S. Library of Congress. General Refernce and Bibliography Division. *Louisa May Alcott, Centennial for Little Women, Annotated, Selected Bibliography;* compiled by Judith C. Ullom. 1969. vii + [3] + 91pp. $.55* L.C. Card 76--600591.
This bibliography was prepared primarily to serve as an attractive, annotated catalog of the Library of Congress's Louisa May Alcott holdings. In celebrating her centennial of *Little Women,* the Library exhibited many items, which are so noted in the bibliography.
LC2.2:Al1/2

555.   U.S. Library of Congress. General Reference and Bibliography
Division. *Sub–Saharan Africa: a Guide to Serials.* 1970.
xx + 409 + [2]pp. $5.25* L.C. Card 70–607392.
Included in this Guide are 4670 titles "relating to Africa
south of the Sahara that are issued in Western languages
or in African languages that use the Roman alphabet."
Most titles are either held by the Library of Congress or
other American libraries. Location symbols indicate which
libraries have the individual titles. Indexed by subject and
organization.
LC2.8:Af8/2

556.   U.S. Library of Congress. Hispanic Foundation. *Latin
America, Spain, and Portugal: an Annotated Bibliography of
Paperback books.* 1971. (Published 1972) [4] + 180pp. $.75*
(Bibliographical Series, no. 13). L.C. Card 71–37945.
"The bibliography lists 1512 paperback books currently
in print on the social sciences and humanities. The entries
are arranged alphabetically by author within each section
and include full bibliographic information, price of the
publication, and a brief descriptive comment. To enhance
the bibliography's utility, a list of publishers and a subject
index are appended."
LC24.7:13

557–564. *These Assessions Lists* are records of the publications
acquired by the Library of Congress from the various countries
participating in this exchange aspect of Public Law 480
(The Agricultural Trade Development and Assistance Act
of 1954, as amended).

557.   U.S. Library of Congress. Processing Department. *Accessions
List: Ceylon.* V.1–. 1967–. Quarterly. Free to libraries***
(P.L. 480 Project, Library of Congress, American Libraries B
Book Procurement Center, New Delhi, India). L.C. Card
SA 67–7489.
LC1.30/7:Vol./no.

558.   U.S. Library of Congress. Processing Department. *Accessions
List: Eastern Africa.* Vol. 1–. 1968. Quarterly. Free
to libraries*** (National Program for Acquistions and
Cataloging, Library of Congress, Nairobi, Kenya).
LC1.30/8:Vol./no.

559.   U.S. Library of Congress. Processing Department. *Accessions*

List: India. Vol. 1--. 1962--. Monthly. Free to libraries***
(P.L. 480 Project, Library of Congress, American Libraries
Book Procurement Center, New Delhi, India). L.C. Card 63--
24164.
LC1.30:Vol./no.

560.   U.S. Library of Congress. Processing Department. *Accessions
List: Indonesia, Malaysia, Singapore, and Brunei.* Vol. 1--.
1966--. Monthly. Free to libraries*** (National Program
for Acquisitions and Cataloging, Library of Congress,
Djakarta, Indonesia). L.C. Card SA--66--444.
LC1.30/5:Vol./no.

561.   U.S. Library of Congress. Processing Dpartment. *Accessions
List: Israel.* Vol. 1--10. 1964--1973. Monthly. L.C. Card
HE 66--1615.
LC1.30/4:Vol./no.

562.   U.S. Library of Congress. Processing Department. *Accessions
List: Middle East.* Vol. 1--. 1963. Monthly. Free to
libraries*** (P.L. 480 Project, Library of Congress, American
Libraries Book Procurement Center, Cairo, Egypt).
L.C. Card 63--24163.
LC1.30/3:Vol./no.

563.   U.S. Library of Congress. Processing Department. *Accessions
List: Nepal.* Vol. 1--. 1966. Three times a year. Free to
libraries*** (P.L. 480 Project, Library of Congress, American
Libraries Book Procurement Center, New Delhi, India). L.C.
Card AS 66--4579.
LC1.30/6:Vol./no.

564.   U.S. Library of Congress. Processing Department. *Accessions
List: Pakistan.* Vol. 1--. 1962--. Monthly. Free to
libraries*** (P.L. 480 Project, Library of Congress, American
Libraries Book Procurement Center, Karachi--Dacca). L.C.
Card 63--24162.
LC1.30/2:Vol./no.

565.   U.S. Library of Congress. Processing Department. *Monthly
Checklist of State Publications.* Vol. 1--. 1910--. Monthly.
$12.80 a yr.*, $3.20 additional foreign mailing. L.C. Card
10--8924.
    This continuing bibliography is of state publications
received by the Library of Congress. It is arranged

alphabetically first by state, then by issuing agencies within the state. Full bibliographic information is provided. Annual cumulative index.
LC30.9:Vol./no.

566. U.S. Library of Congress. Processing Department. *Monthly Index of Russian Accessions.* 1948--1970. Monthly. L.C. Card 48--46262.
This accessions list, which is no longer published, listed Russian language books and periodicals published both in and out of the Soviet that were received by the Library of Congress. Subject index with annual author index.
LC30.10:Vol./no.

567. U.S. Library of Congress. Processing Department. *Non--GPO Imprints.* Annual.
Listed are federal publications which are not published by the Government Printing Office but are available for public distribution.
LC30.2:Im7/date

568. U.S. Library of Congress. Reference Department. *Half Century of Soviet Serials, 1917--68: a Bibliography and Union List of Serials Published in the USSR;* compiled by Rudolf Smits. 1968. 2v. $16.00* L.C. Card 68--62169.
Contained are all known serial publications, 29761 entries which have appeared in the Soviet Union since 1917 with the exception of oriental language publications, serials published outside the Soviet Union, and newspapers. Complete bibliographic history and data pertaining to library holdings in the U.S. and Canada are given for each title. Cross referenced.
LC29.2:So8/3/Vol.1&2

569. U.S. Library of Congress. Serials Division. *Newspapers Currently Received and Permanently Retained in the Library of Congress.* 3rd ed. 1972. 23pp. $.35* S/N 3005--0005. L.C. Card 68--61877.
Revised every two years, this edition lists 286 U.S. and 951 foreign newspapers received and retained by the Library of Congress on a permanent basis, plus an additional 350 U.S. and 65 foreign newspapers retained on a current basis only.
LC6.7:1972

570. U.S. Library of Congress. Slavic and Central Europe Division. *USSR and Eastern Europe, Periodicals in Western Languages;* compiled by Paul L. Horecky and Robert G. Carlton. 3rd ed., rev. and enl. 1968. 89pp. $.55* L.C. Card 68–60045.

Listed are periodicals currently published in or dealing with Albania, the Baltic countries, Bulgaria, Czechoslovakia, Hungary, Poland, Rumania, the Soviet Union, and Yugoslavia. Periodicals are listed alphabetically under the country. Full bibliographic information, purchase price, and a brief description are given for each item. Indexed by title, issuing organization, and subject.
LC35.2:P41/967

571. U.S. Smithsonian Institution. *Reading is Fundamental: RIF's Guide to Book Selection.* 1972. vi + 80pp.*** (Smithsonian Institution, A&I Bldg., Room 2407, Washington, D.C. 20560).

This is a selection guide to inexpensive books and paperbacks for the elementary grades and various ethnic groups. Title, author, publisher, grade level, and a brief annotation accompany each entry. Source guides and publishers are listed.
SI1.17/2:R22

572. U.S. Smithsonian Institution. *Reading is Fundamental: RIF's Guide to Book Selection. Supp. 1.* 1972. iv + 20pp.***
SI1.17/2:R22/supp.1

573. U.S. Smithsonian Institution. *Reading is Fundamental: RIF's Guide to Book Selection. Supp. 2.* 1972. iv + 64pp.***.
SI1.17/2:R22/supp.2

MARINE SCIENCES

General

574. U.S. National Bureau of Standards. *Oceanography, Bibliography of Selected Activation Analysis Literature;* G.J. Lutz, editor. 1970. 43pp. $.50* (NBS Technical Note, no. 534). L.C. Card 78–608118.

Fish, shellfish, seaweed, marine sediments and seawater are included in this special application of activation analysis.
CI3.46:534

575. U.S. National Oceanic and Atmospheric Administration. Environmental Data Service. *Interim Lists of the Periodicals in the Collections of the Atmospheric Sciences Library and Marine and Earth Sciences Library.* 1971. iv + 60 + ii + 58pp.***.

Divided into two sections, the periodical holdings of the two libraries are listed separately in alphabetical order by title. Projected is a consolidated list which is periodically updated.

D55.224:971

576. U.S. National Oceanic and Atmospheric Administration. Environmental Data Service. *Marine Science Newsletters, 1973, Annotated Bibliography;* compiled by Charlotte Ashby. 1973. ii + 26pp. NTIS. (NOAA Technical Memorandum EDS NODC--3).

Compiled are 94 newsletters containing news about the marine sciences or of interest to marine scientists. Part I lists the newsletter alphabetically. Availability, frequency, and cost (if any) are given for each listing. Part II is an alphabetical listing of publishers, indexed to the appropriate newsletter and an index to the newsletters by type of publisher (i.e. Academic, Sea--Grant, or Business).

C55.13/2:EDS NODS–3

577. U.S. National Oceanic and Atmospheric Administration. Environmental Data Service. *Sea Grant Publications Index, 1968--1972.* 2 vols. 1973. (V. 1, 289pp.; V. 2, 341pp)*** (NOAA Technical Memorandum EDS ESIC/8 and 9).

Listed are all materials received by the National Sea Grant Depository (NSGD) through January 1973, except for newsletters which appear in the *Sea Grant Newsletter Index.* Vol. 1 contains the Document listing; and Vol. 2 contains the Key--Word--In--Context, Author, Corporate Author, Gran Grant Number, NTIS Number, and Additional Report Number Indexes. Complete bibliographic information and availability are given for all reports.

C55.13/2:EDS/ESIC/8&9

578. U.S. Naval Oceanographic Office. *Catalog of Publications, 1971.* 1971. 73pp. $.75* S/N 0842--0054.

Publications are listed by subject and briefly annotated.

D203.22:1--P/971

579. U.S. Naval Oceanographic Office. *Selected Readings in the Marine Sciences, Fall 1969;* compiled by Norman T. Edwards

and Suzanne E. DeCarre. 1969. 32pp. $.45* (Special
Publications, no. 129). L.C. Card 79--604627.
This publication was prepared for the general public with
an interest in the marine sciences. Complete bibliographic
information, including interest levels – juvenile, adult,
technical, is given for each citation. Publications are listed
according to the following areas: Oceanography; Marine
Biology; Marine Geology; Diving; and Government
Publication.
D203.22/3:129

580.   U.S. Naval Research Office. *Ocean Science and Technology
Division Report Availability Notice.* 1972. ii + 218pp***
(ONR Report ACR--181).
This is a collection of abstracts of reports which were
produced totally or in part by the ONR Ocean Science
support and which are currently available from the author
or NTIS. Topics cover: Physical Oceanography; Air--
Sea Interaction; Oceanic Biology; Marine Geology and
Geophysics; and Ocean Technology. Not indexed.
D210.14:ACR--181

Marine Biology

581.   U.S. Department of the Army. Corps of Engineers. *Annotated
Bibliography on Effects of Salinity and Salinity and Salinity
Changes on Life in Coastal Waters;* by S.H. Hopkins. 1973.
ix + 411 + [2]pp.*** (U.S. Army Engineer Waterways
Experiment Station, Vicksbur, Mississippi) (Contact Report
H–73--2). L.C. Card 73--603119.
"References with annotations are given for about 1,400
published and unpublished reports, dated 1972 and earlier,
on physiological and ecological effects of salinity, salinity
differences, and changes in salinity on organisms living in
estuaries and other coastal waters. A subject index with
cross–indexing is provided."
D103.24/9:H–73–2

582.   U.S. Department of the Interior. Bureau of Sport Fisheries
and Wildlife. *Sport Fishery Abstracts.* Vol. 1--. 1955--.
Quarterly.***.
Contained are abstracts of recently published articles on
limnology, ecology, natural history, and other specialized
areas which pertain to the conservation and management
of sport fishery resources. Each issue is indexed by author

and subject. The final issue in each volume has cumulative author and subject indexes.
I49.40/2:Vol./no.

583. U.S. Department of the Interior. Fish and Wildlife Service. *Annotated Bibliography of Zooplankton Sampling Devices;* by Jack W. Jossi. 1970. iii + 90pp.** (Special Scientific Report – Fisheries, no. 609).
Presented are references to the literature published since 1873 on zooplankton sampling devices. Arrangement is by author with a Key--Work--In--Context index to facilitate rapid retrieval.
I49.15/2:609

584. U.S. Department of the Interior. Fish and Wildlife Service. *Annotated References on the Pacific Saury, Cololabis Aira;* by Steven E. Hughes. 1970. iii + 12pp.** (Special Scientific Report – Fisheries, no. 606).
Seventy--two annotated references describe the research and summarize the results in developing a fishery for saury. Three–fourths of the references are of Japanese or Soviet reports on their saury stocks and fishing industries. Extensive annotations accompany those references which have not been translated. Indexed by subject.
I49.15/2:606

585. U.S. Department of the Interior. Fish and Wildlife Service. *Available Leaflets on Fisheries.* 1969. Free*** (Fishery Leaflet, no. 626).
I49.28:626

586. U.S. Department of the Interior. Fish and Wildlife Service. *Bibliography of Lobsters, Genus Homarus;* by R.D. Lewis. 1970. i + 47pp*** (Special Scientific Report -- Fisheries, no. 591).
Over 1300 references, eighty per cent of which are located in the Woods Hole Marine Biological Laboratory, are listed alphabetically according to author.
I49.15/2:591

587. U.S. Department of the Interior. Fish and Wildlife Service. *Bibliography of Oyster Parasites and Diseases;* by Carl J. Sindermann. 1968. [2] + 13pp.** (Special Scientific Report -- Fisheries, no. 563).
"The bibliography is oriented toward the diseases that

affect oysters and is not concerned with human disease that may be transmitted by raw shellfish." Of particular concern are disease states resulting from an infectious agent or parasite invasion. Author arrangement. Not indexed. I49.15/2:563

588. U.S. Department of the Interior. Fish and Wildlife Service. *Books and Articles on Marine Mammals;* by Ethel I. Todd. 1968. iii + 14pp.*** (Commercial Fisheries Bureau, Circular, no. 299). L.C. Card 70--60116.
Listed are contemporary titles of books and articles on the identification, biology, and commercial use of seals, sea lions, walrus, whales, and dolphins. Publications are both popular and technical. Not indexed. I49.4:299

589. U.S. Department of the Interior. Fish and Wildlife Service. *Efficacy of Methylpentynol as Anesthetic on 4 Salmonid; Toxicity of Methylpentynol to Selected Fishes: Annotated Bibliography on Methylpentynol (with list of references);* by Robert M. Howland and others. 1969. iii + 11 + 7 + 7pp. $.35* (Investigations in Fish Control, no. 29--31). I49.70:29--31

590. U.S. Department of the Interior. Fish and Wildlife Service. *Fishery Publications Index, 1955--64: Publications of the Fish and Wildlife Services by Series, Authors, and Subjects;* compiled by George Washington University. 1969. 240pp. $1.75* (Commercial Fisheries Bureau Circular, no. 296).
Indexed by author and subject. (See also no. 605--611). I49.4:296

591. U.S. Department of the Interior. Fish and Wildlife Service. *Selected Bibliography on the Sea Otter;* by Ethel I. Todd and Karl W. Kenyon. 1972. [1] + 40pp. $.50* S/N 2410-0311 (Special Scientific Report – Wildlife, no. 149). L.C. Card 72--601902.
The 172 references listed here supplement and update the bibliography accompanying the 1969 publication "The Sea Otter in the Eastern Pacific Ocean," (North American Fauna Series, no. 68). I49.15/3:149

592. U.S. Department of the Interior. Fish and Wildlife Service. *Selected Fish Disease Publications in English;* prepared by

S.F. Snieszko and others. 1970. 7pp. Free*** (Fish Disease Leaflet, no. 26).
I49.28/3.26

593. U.S. Department of the Interior. Fish and Wildlife Service. *Some Publications on Fish Culture and Related Subjects.* 1968. 16pp.*** (Fishery Leaflet, no. 448).
I49.28:448/4

594. U.S. Department of the Interior. Fish and Wildlife Service. *Supplementary Bibliography on Eelgrass, Zostera Marina;* by C. Peter McRoy and Ronald C. Phillips. 1968. [2] + 14pp. $.15* (Special Scientific Report -- Wildlife, no. 114).
The 204 references included here update to 1966 an earlier list (Special Scientific Report – Wildlife, no. 114). Arrangement is alphabetical by author, Not indexed.
I49.15/3:114

595. U.S. Department of the Interior. Library. *Automation of Fish Processing and Handling: a Bibliography;* by Garland L. Standrod. 1969. NTIS. (PB 183 980) (Library, Bibliography Series, no. 11).
I22.19/2:11

596. U.S. Department of the Interior. Water Resources Scientific Information Center. *Estuarine Pollution, Bibliography.* 1973. iv + 27 + 477pp. NTIS (WRSIC 73–205).
"This is another in a series of planned bibliographies in water resources to be produced solely from material available for listing in *Selected Water Resources Abstracts.*" Material is abstracted and indexed. Availability is given.
I1.97:73--205

597. U.S. Forest Service. Pacific Northwest Forest and Range Experiment Station. *An Annotated Bibliography of the Effects of Logging on Fish of the Western United States and Canada;* by Dave R. Gibbons and Ernest O. Salo. 1973.***
(USDA Forest Service General Technical Report, PNW--10).
Annotated is "the scientific and non--scientific literature published on the effects of logging on fish and aquatic habitat of the western United States and Canada. It includes 278 annotations and a total of 317 references. Subject areas include erosion and sedimentation, water quality, related influences upon salmonids, multiple logging

effects, alteration of streamflow, stream protection, multiple–use management, streamside vegetation, stream improvement, and description of studies on effects of logging." Author and subject indexes.
A13.88:PNW--10

598.   U.S. Geological Survey. *Neogene Marine Mollusks of the Pacific Coast of North America, Annotated Bibliography, 1797--1969;* by Warren O. Addicott. 1973. iii + 201pp. $1.50* (U.S.G.S. Bulletin, no. 1362). L.C. Card 72--600313.
Annotated citations are given for reports dealing with marine mollusks of the Neogene (Miocene and Pliocene) age from the Pacific and Arctic coasts of North America. Reports are listed alphabetically by author and are indexed by subject and geographic area.
I19.3:1362

599.   U.S. Geological Survey. *Tertiary Marine Mollusks of Alaska, Annotated Bibliography;* by W.O. Addicott. 1971. iii + 30pp. il. $.25* S/N 2401--1195 (U.S.G.S. Bulletin, no. 1343). L.C. Card 74--177921.
"Included are 135 papers accompanied by brief annotations pertaining to Tertiary marine mollusks of Alaska published up to and including 1970." Indexed by subject.
I19.3:1343

600.   U.S. Government Printing Office. *Fish and Wildlife.* Free* (Price List, no. 21).
Listed are selected for sale and free publications on fish and wildlife. This list is revised frequently; prices are kept current; and all publications are supposedly available.
GP3.9:21

601.   U.S. National Oceanic and Atmospheric Administration. National Marine Fisheries Service. *An Annotated Biblio-- graphy of Attempts to Rear the Larvae of Marine Fishes in the Laboratory;* compiled by Robert C. May. 1971. iii + 24pp. $.35* (NOAA Technical Report NMFS SSRF--632).
This highly specialized bibliography covers from 1878 to 1969. "Annotations summarize each paper, and appendixes list the species of fishes studied and the types of food used in the attempts to rear them." Arrangement is alphabetical by author.
C55.13:NMFS--SSRF--632

602. U.S. National Oceanic and Atmospheric Administration . National Marine Fisheries Service. *Annotated Bibliography of Cunner, Tautogolabrus Adspersus (Walbaum);* by Frederick M. Serchuk and David W. Frame. 1973. ii + 43pp. $.75* (NOAA Technical Report NMFS SSRF–668).

"This annotated, indexed bibliography of the cunner contains contains 347 entries including references on taxonomy, distribution, life history, physiology, behavior, commercial and sport fisheries, and related fields." It is current through June 1972. A subject–geographic index facilitates its use.
C55.13:NMFS SSRF--668

603. U.S. National Oceanic and Atmospheric Administration. National Marine Fisheries Service. *Annotated Bibliography of Inter-specific Hybridization of Fishes of the Subfamily Salmoninae;* by James R. Dangel, Paul T. Macy, and Fred C. Withler. 1973. iv + 48pp.* (NOAA Technical Memorandum NMFS NWFC–1).

"This bibliography of 611 annotated references lists published and unpublished material on hybridization between species of the subfamily Salmoninae and crosses of salmonids with non–salmonids. It does not include crosses within a species. The bibliography is indexed by species for the genera Brachnmystax, Hucho, Ocyrhynchus, Salmo, Salmothymus, and Salvelinus and certain non--salmonid species."
C55.13/2:NMFS NWFC--1

604. U.S. National Oceanic and Atmospheric Administration. National Marine Fisheries Service. *Annotated Bibliography on Fishing Industry and Biology of the Blue Crab, Callinectes Sapidus;* by Marlin E. Tagatz and Ann Bowman Hall. 1971. 2 + 94pp. $1.00* S/N 9318–0009. (NOAA Technical Report NMFS--SSRF–640). L.C. Card 70--614841.

"References are given on 742 publications, published before 1970, on classification, distribution abundance, life history, morphology, physiology, ecology, fishery, and industry. Annotations and subject index are also provided."
C55.312:640

605--611. Each *Fisheries Publications* provides for the calendar year numerical lists (with abstracts) and indexes by author, subject, and geographical area, the following series of publications of the National Marine Fisheries Service: Circular; Data Report; Fishery Leaflet; and Special

Scientific Report – Fisheries. (See also no. 587).

605. U.S. National Oceanic and Atmospheric Administration. National Marine Fisheries Service. *Fishery Publications, Calendar Year 1965, Lists and Indexes.* 1973. [iv] + 12pp. $.30* (NOAA Technical Report NMFS CIRC--383).
C55.13:NMFS CIRC--383

606. U.S. National Oceanic and Atmospheric Administration. National Marine Fisheries Service. *Fishery Publications, Calendar Year 1966, Lists and Indexes.* 1973. [iv] + 19pp. $.35* (NOAA Technical Report NMFS CIRC–382).
C55.13:NMFS CIRC–382

607. U.S. National Oceanic and Atmospheric Administration. National Marine Fisheries Service. *Fishery Publications, Calendar Year 1967, Lists and Indexes.* 1973. [iv] + 22pp. $.35* (NOAA Technical Report NMFS CIRC--381).
C55.13:NMFS CIRC--381

608. U.S. National Oceanic and Atmospheric Administration. National Marine Fisheries Service. *Fishery Publications, Calendar Year 1968, Lists and Indexes.* 1973. [iv] + 24pp. $.35* (NOAA Technical Report NMFS CIRC--380).
C55.13:NMFS CIRC–380

609. U.S. National Oceanic and Atmospheric Administration. National Marine Fisheries Service. *Fishery Publications, Calendar Year 1969, Lists and Indexes.* 1973. [iv] + 31pp. $.45* (NOAA Technical Report NMFS CIRC–379).
C55.13:NMFS CIRC--379

610. U.S. National Oceanic and Atmospheric Administration. National Marine Fisheries Service. *Fishery Publications, Calendar Year 1970, Lists and Indexes.* 1972. [iv] + 24pp. $.45* (NOAA Technical Report NMFS CIRC–377).
C55.13.NMFS CIRC--377

611. U.S. National Oceanic and Atmospheric Administration. National Marine Fisheries Service. *Fishery Publications, Calendar Year 1971, Lists and Indexes.* 1972. [iv] + 24pp. $.30* (NOAA Technical Report NMFS CIRC–372).
C55.13:NMFS CIRC–372

612. U.S. National Oceanic and Atmospheric Administration. National

Marine Fisheries Service. *Indexed Bibliography of the Eggs and Young of Tunas and Other Scombrids (Pisces, Scombridae), 1880–1970;* by William J. Richards and Witold L. Klaw. 1973. iv + 107pp. $1.00* (NOAA Technical Report NMFS SSRF–652).

"This bibliography enumerates reports on the early life history of tunas and other scombrid fishes published before 1971. All entries are indexed, usually by species, but on occasion by a larger taxonomic unit, and within each taxonomic unit the entries are indexed by one or more subjects." Each item appears in English, Spanish, French, and German.

C55.13:NMFS SSRF–652

613. U.S. National Oceanic and Atmospheric Administration. National Marine Fisheries Service. *Marine Fishery Abstracts.* (Formerly *Commercial Fishery Abstr.*). V. 1--. 1948–. Monthly. $6.50 a year*; $1.75 additional foreign mailing.

Contained are abstracts of current research in the biological and technical apsects of fisheries which have been reported in the trade, engineering, and scientific journals dealing with fishery science. This publication purposes to meet the needs of fishery scientists, engineers, and managers in industry, academic institutions, and research by keeping them abreast of current progress in fishery research and technology.

(see also *Sport Fishery Abstracts,* no. 582).

C55.310/2:Vol./no.

614. U.S. National Oceanic and Atmospheric Administration. National Marine Fisheries Service. *Revised Annotated List of Parasites from Sea Mammals Caught Off West Coast of North America with a List of Literature Cited;* by L. Margolis and M.D. Dailey. 1972. iii + 23pp. $.35* (NOAA Technical Report NMFS SSRF–647).

In addition to a substantial bibliography, parasite--host and host–parasite lists of the ecto– and endoparasites recorded from marine mammals of the North American west coast are provided.

C55.13:NMFS SSRF--647

615. U.S. National Oceanic and Atmospheric Administration. National Oceanographic Data Center. *Cooperative Investigation of the Caribbean and Adjacent Regions (CICAR). Volume II, Bibliography on Marine Biology;* prepared by the Franklin

Research Institute Laboratory. 1972. vi + 238pp. $7.45*.
Numerous research centers and libraries throughout the
world have been searched to gather the information
compiled in this annotated bibliography on marine biology.
Nearly 3500 references arranged chronologically from
1794--1971 cover marine biology in the Caribbean Sea,
Gulf of Mexico, Greater and Lesser Antilles Regions, and
the Adjacent coastal areas of North, South, and Central
America. Indexed by subject, author, and geographical
area.
(See no. 617 and no. 621 for other volumes of *CICAR*
bibliography).
C55.292:C19/v.2

616.   U.S. Smithsonian Institution. *Bibliography and Zoological
Taxa of Paul Bartsch* [with list of literature cited] ; by
Florence A. Ruhoff; with biographical sketch by Harald
Rehder. 1973. v + 166pp. $2.85* (Smithsonian Contri--
butions to Zoology, no. 143).
"A compilation, alphabetically arranged, of all zoological
taxa proposed by Dr. Paul Bartsch from 1901 to 1955,
most of them phylum Mollusca, but also including one
subspecies of bird and two genera in the Tunicata. The
catalog of taxa is preceded by a biographical sketch of
Dr. Bartsch and a complete list of his publications. The
last section is a list of species and subspecies described
by Bartsch arranged alphabetically by genera and subgenera."
SI1.27:143

Physical Oceanography

617.   U.S. National Oceanic and Atmospheric Administration. National
Oceanographic Data Center. *Cooperative Investigation of
the Caribbean and Adjacent Regions (CICAR), Volume III,
Bibliography on Marine Geology and Geophysics.* 1972.
vi + 238pp. $7.45*.
Numerous research centers and libraries throughout the
world were searched to gather the information compiled
in this annotated bibliography on marine geology and
geophysics. Almost 3300 references arranged chrono--
logically from 1796 to 1971 cover the geology and geo--
physics in the Caribbean Sea, Gulf of Mexico, Greater and
Lesser Antilles Regions, and the adjacent coastal areas of
North, South, and Central America. Indexed by subject,
author, and geographical area.

(See no. 615 and no. 621 for other volumes of *CICAR* bibliography).
C55.292:C19/v.3

618. U.S. National Oceanic and Atmospheric Administration. World Data Center A. *Oceanography: Catalogue of Accessioned Publications.* Annual supplements.***.
International in scope, the publications listed are grouped by country of origin and indexed by keyword and author. The supplements update the original publication entitled *Catalogue of Accessioned Publications, 1957–1967* (Washington, D.C. 1967).
C55.220/4:P96/supp.

619. U.S. National Oceanic and Atmospheric Administration. World Data Center A. Oceanography: *Catalogue of Assessioned Soviet Publications, 1957--1968.* 1971. ix + 380pp.***.
This list, which is indexed by keywords and author, is of the Russian holdings in the World Data Center A coordination offices and subcenters. Each entry pertains to oceanography.
C55.220/2:957–68

620. U.S. Naval Oceanographic Office. *Bibliography of Reports, Articles, and Data References Resulting from Scientific Operations Aboard Navy Pool (T–AGOR) Ships, 1963--69;* compiled by D.E. Tidrick and R.E. Morris. 1970. v + 39 + [4] pp.** (IR 70--25).
D203.26/2:70--25

621. U.S. Naval Oceanographic Office. *Cooperative Investigation of the Caribbean and Adjacent Regions (CICAR), Vol. I, Bibliography on Meteorology, Climatology, and Physical Chemical Oceanography;* prepared by the American Meterological Society. 1970. Vol. 1, 380pp.; Vol. 1/Index 381--614pp. $13.00 (set)*** L.C. Card 72--609667.
"This abstracted bibliography has been compiled from the files of the American Meteorological Society (AMS) and from files of Government libraries in the Washington, D.C., area." It is to provide a reasonably comprehensive and timely review of the published literature in physical/chemical oceanography and in meteorology/climatology concerned with the Caribbean Sea, Gulf of Mexico, Greater and Lesser Antilles Regions, and the adjacent coastal areas of North, Central, and South America. The 3079 entries are divided into two sections, "Meteorology"

and "Oceanography" and therein arranged chronologically.
Indexed by subject, author, and geographical area.
(See also no. 615 and no. 617 for other volumes of
CICAR bibliography).
D203.24/3:M56/V. 1 and Index

622.   U.S. Naval Oceanographic Office. *Films on Oceanography;*
by R.P. Cuzon du Rest. 1969. 99pp. $1.00* (Catalog
Series, C–4).
Films are listed under the following categories: General
Oceanography; Biology; Chemistry; Engineering;
Geology; and Physics. Each film is described physically
and includes a brief summary, a note as to audience type
for which intended,and the price and source. Indexed by
title.
D203.24:C--4/3

623.   U.S. Naval Oceanographic Office. *Guide to the Technical
Literature of Oceanography, Annotated Bibliography;* by
Suzane E. DeCarre. 1970. 3 + 69 + 2pp.** (IR, no. 70–34).
D203.26/2:70--34

624.   U.S. Naval Research Office. *Ocean Science and Technology
Division Report Availability Notice.* 1972. ii + 218pp.***
(ONR Report ACR--181).
This is a collection of abstracts of reports which were
produced totally or in part by the ONR Ocean Science
upport program and which are currently available from
the author or NTIS. Topics cover: Physical Oceanography;
Air--Sea Interaction; Oceanic Biology; Marine Geology
and Geophysics; and Ocean Technology. Not indexed.
D210.14:ACR--181

625.   U.S. Smithsonian Institution. *Central Western Indian Ocean
Bibliography;* by A.J. Peters and J.F.G. Lionnet. 1973.
6 + 322pp.*** (Atoll Research Bulletin, 165).
This lengthy bibliography provides a key to four and a half
centuries of Indian Ocean exploration and research. It
"is an annotated and indexed list of published scientific
work bearing on the smaller British--held islands and
included seas in the western Indian Ocean." Indexed by
subject, region, and taxa.
SI1.25:165

MEDICINE AND HEALTH

General

626. U.S. National Archives and Records Service. *List of U.S. Government Medical and Dental 8mm Films for Sale by the National Audiovisual Center.* 1970. 57pp.*** L.C. Card 73–610066.
This list was compiled for use by people in medical and health related fields. Films are divided into two major divisions -- medical and dental – and there subdivided by subject. Title, order number, running time, price, and a summary of contents accompany each film title.
GS4.2:M46

627. U.S. National Bureau of Standards. *Man, His Job, and the Environment: a Review and Annotated Bibliography of Selected Recent Research on Human Performance;* by William G. Mather, III, Boris V. Kit, Gail A. Bloch, and Martha F. Herman. 1970. vi + 101pp. $1.00*) (Special Publication, no. 319). L.C. Card 77--604124.
"Recent scientific literature was searched to review pro--cedures currently being used to study human reactions to work and environmental stress." Considered were task variables, environmental factors, individual characteristics, physiological variables, psychophysical measures, and socio--logical factors. The research reviewed included analyses of on--the--job performance, simulations of real--life situations, laboratory experiments with human and non--human subjects, and clinical studies.
Accompanying the extensive bibliography are detailed abstracts of 190 research reports.
C13.10:319

628. U.S. Public Health Service. *Annotated Bibliography on Vital and Health Statistics.* 1970. ix + 143pp. $1.25* (PHS Bibliography Series, no. 82). L.C. Card 76–608017.
The bibliography is divided into five major subjects and eleven minor categories covering the various aspects of morbidity, mortality, maternal and infant studies, and methodology. Indexed by author.
HE20.11:82

629. U.S. Public Health Service. Center for Disease Control. National Clearinghouse for Smoking and Health. *What's*

New on Smoking in Print and on Film. 1973. 13pp. $.25*.
Listed are educational materials on smoking and health that
are available from member agencies of the National Inter--
agency Council on Smoking and Health. Materials listed
cover a wide range of interests and are directed to many
audiences, including young people and adults, smokers and
non--smokers. All are free or inexpensive.
HE20.7002:Sm7

630. U.S. Public Health Service. Health Services and Mental
Health Administration. National Institute for Occupational
Safety and Health. *NIOSH Publications.* 1973. [8]pp.
Free***.
HE20.2812:N21/973

631. U.S. Public Health Service. National Institutes of Health.
*Film Guide on Reproduction and Development: a Guide to
Selected Films on Reproduction and Developmental Biology
for Graduate and Undergraduate Programs in the Biomedical
Sciences.* 1969. 66pp. $1.25* L.C. Card 76--603672.
Twenty–six carefully selected films are discussed at
length, and suggestions are given to instructors who may
use the films in teaching. Complete descriptions are
provided for each film along with rental or purchase infor--
mation.
FS2.22/15:R29

632. U.S. Public Health Service. National Institutes of Health.
Bureau of Health Manpower Education. *Division of Dental
Health Catalog, 1972.* 1972. iii + 31pp. Free***.
Listed are publications, posters, and films produced by
the Division of Dental Health. Purchase information is
given.
HE20.3113:D43/972

632a. U.S. Public Health Service. National Institutes of Health.
Bureau of Health Manpower Education. *Division of Nursing
Selected Publications.* 1971. 8pp. Free***.
Only available publications are included.
HE20.3113:N93/971

632b. U.S. Public Health Service. National Institutes of Health.
Bureau of Health Manpower Education. *Educational
Technology and the Teaching--Learning Process, Selected
Bibliography;* prepared by Jeanne Saylor Berthold, Mary

Alice Curran, Diana Y. Barhyte. Rev. 1969. 1970.
5 + 56pp.*** L.C. Card 73--608611.
"This bibliography is intended to serve as an introduction
to the literature on the teaching--learning process and on
the various new approaches in the field of teaching
technology. Much of the bibliography is devoted to such
aspects of educational technology as multimedia approaches,
films and television, programmed instruction, and computer
assisted instruction. Not indexed.
HE20.3113:T22/969

632c.   U.S. Public Health Service. National Institutes of Health.
Bureau of Health Manpower Education. *Literature Relating
to Neurological and Neurosurgical Nursing;* prepared by
Margaret Hulburt. 1970. [6] + 95pp. $.60* L.C. Card 70--
609772.
Entries are listed alphabetically by author under nine
specific subject headings. "The first section contains text--
books on neuroanatomy and neurophysiology. The second
through fifth cover four nursing situations: the medical
examination, neurological nursing, and the intensive care
unit. The sixth section lists documents on the nursing care
of patients with specific neurological disorders and diseases;
and the seventh covers conditions that present special
nursing care problems, such as aphasia and paraplegia.
The last two sections contain resources for the instructor
and non--English documents."
HE20.3113:N39

632d.   U.S. Public Health Service. National Institutes of Health.
Bureau of Health Manpower Education. *Research in
Nursing 1955--1968.* [Rev. 1969]. 1970. v + 91pp.***.
Publications and projects described are classified in three
broad areas: Organization, Distribution, and Delivery of
Nursing Service; Recruitment, Selection, Education, and
Characteristics of the Nurse Supply; and Nursing Research
Development. Indexed by author and subject.
HE20.31--2:N93/7/955--68

633.   U.S. Public Health Service. National Institutes of Health.
John E. Fogarty International Center for Advanced Study
in Health Sciences. *A Bibliography of Chinese Sources on
Medicine and Public Health in the People's Republic of China,
1960--1970.* 1973. [2] + xxiv + 486pp. $5.55* S/N 1753--
00013. L.C. Card 73--602181.

Covered are books, monographs, and articles from medical journals, newspapers and magazines. Entries are arranged by subject category -- accupuncture, cardiovascular, etc. Part I covers articles, and Part II covers monographs. Not indexed.
HE20.3711:C44/960--70

634. U.S. Public Health Service. National Institutes of Health. John E. Fogarty International Center for Advanced Study in Health Sciences. *Soviety Medicine, Bibliography of Bibliographies.* 1973. vii + 46pp. $.80*. L.C. Card 73--602784.
This bibliography was compiled to provide U.S. biomedical scientists interested in Soviet medicine with a selected list of Soviet medical bibliographies and reference aids. "It contains approximately 425 items and includes information on 30 medical categories." Arranged by subject. Not indexed.
HE20.3711:So8

635. U.S. Public Health Service. National Institutes of Health. National Health Professions Education and Training Bureau. *Foreign Medical Graduate, Bibliography.* 1972. (Pub. 1973). v + 107pp. $1.75* S/N 1741--0050.
Citations deal with several aspects of the foreign medical graduate in the United States, including the education of foreign medical graduates abroad, the flow of foreign medical graduates to the U.S., and their training and utilization in American medicine. Each entry is arranged by author, key-word--in--context, and source of reference.
HE20.3113:F76

636. U.S. Public Health Service. National Institutes of Health. National Institute of Child Health and Human Development. *Selected Bibliography on Death and Dying;* by Joel C. Vernick. 1970. v + 61pp. $.65* L.C. Card 75--607348.
Nearly 1500 entries represent articles and books on the subjects of death and dying. Indexed by subject and author.
HE20.3361:D34

637. U.S. Public Health Service. National Institutes of Health. National Institute of Neurological Disease and Stroke. *Brain Death: a Bibliography with Key--word and Author Indexes.* 1972. 30pp.*** (NINDS Bibliography Series,no. 1). L.C. Card 72--602933.

This bibliography grew as a result of a literaure search which was conducted in order to try to redefine the death of an individual in terms of brain death. The 340 entries are indexed by key--word and author.
HE20.3513/3:1

638. U.S. Public Health Service. National Institutes of Health. National Library of Medicine. *Abridged Index Medicus.* V. 1--. 1970--. Monthly. $21.90 a yr.*, $5.50 additional foreign mailing.
One hundred English language titles are indexed by this publication, which is a mini--version of *Index Medicus.* Entries are arranged by specific subject headings and indexed by author. This publication is cumulated annually, but not at the subscription cost. (See no. 642--644).
HE20.3612/2:Vol./no.

639. U.S. Public Health Service. National Institutes of Health. National Library of Medicine. *Bibliography of the History of Medicine, 1964--1969.* vi + 1475pp. $12.00*.
"This cumulative volume, which covers material published from 1964--1969, is the fifth of a series of bibliographies of medicine. The bibliography focuses on the history of medicine and its related sciences. Entries are given for (1) Biographies, (2) Subjects, and (3) Authors.
HE20.3615:5

640. U.S. Public Health Service. National Institutes of Health. National Library of Medicine. *Bibliography of the History of Medicine, no. 6, 1970.* 1973. vi + 295pp. $3.70* S/N 1752--o138.
A continuing series, the bibliography focuses on publications which deal with the history of medicine and its related sciences, professions, and institutions.
HE20.3615:6

641. U.S. Public Health Service. National Institutes of Health. National Library of Medicine. *Bibliography of the History of Medicine, no. 7, 1971.* 1973. $3.00* S/N 1752--00147.
HE20.3615:7

641a. U.S. Public Health Service. National Institutes of Health. National Library of Medicine. *A Catalogue of Incunabula and Sixteenth Century Printed Books in the National Library of Medicine. 1st Supp.* 1971. v + 51pp. $2.75*.

"This present catalogue, listing 27 incunabula and 272 sixteenth century books, supplements *A Catalogue of Incunabula and Manuscripts in the Army Medical Library (1950)*, prepared by Dorothy M. Schullian, and *A Catalogue of Sixteenth Century Printed Books in the National Library of Medicine (1967)*, compiled by Richard J. Darling."
HE20.3614:Si9/supp.1

642. U.S. Public Health Service. National Institutes of Health. National Library of Medicine. *Cumulated Abridged Index Medicus, Vol. 1, 1970.* 1971. 1159pp. $10.00* L.C. Card 77--610781.
HE20.3612/2+3:1

643. U.S. Public Health Service. National Institutes of Health. National Library of Medicine. *Cumulated Abridged Index Medicus, Vol. 2, 1971.* 1972. 1128pp. $10.00*.
HE20.3612/2--2:2

644. U.S. Public Health Service. National Institutes of Health. National Libraryof Medicine. *Cumulated Abridged Index Medicus, Vol. 3, 1972.* 1973. 1075pp. $12.20*.
HE20.3612/2--2:3

645. U.S. Public Health Service. National Institutes of Health. National Library of Medicine. *Film Reference Guide for Medicine and Allied Sciences, 1970.* 1970. vi + 214 + 34 + 63pp. $2.75* L.C. Card 56--60040.
This catalog, which is sponsored and published by the Federal Advisory Council on Medical Training Aids, describes selective audiovisuals used in biomedical education by the following member agencies: Air Force, Army, Navy, Veterans Administration, Armed Forces Institute of Pathology, and the National Library of Medicine. Besides a brief summary of the contents, each film is completely described physically, and the producer, sponsor, country of origin, year of release, and distributor are noted. Indexed by subject.
HE20.3608/2:970

646. U.S. Public Health Service. National Institutes of Health. National Library of Medicine. *Index Medicus, Including Bibliography of Medical Reviews.* V. 1--. 1960--. Monthly.

$155.00 a year*, $38.75 additional foreign mailing. (Annual cumulative volumes are sold separately). L.C. Card 61--60337.

As one of the foremost medical indexes in the world, this bibliography lists references to the current literature from approximately 2500 medical journals from all over the world. Entries are listed by specific subject and facilitated by both a subject and a name listing. Each issue also contains a section entitled "Bibliography of Medical Review," which is also published separately. (See no. 766).
HE20.3612:Vol./no.

647.   U.S. Public Health Service. National Institutes of Health. National Library of Medicine. *International Bibliography of Medicolegal Serials, 1736–1967;* by Jaroslav Nemec. 1969. vii + 110pp. $1.25*.

Listed according to the most current title are 333 medi--colegal serial titles in the National Library of Medicine. Place of first publication and basic bibliographic infor--mation (frequency, opening and closing dates, series, etc.) are provided. Current titles, of which there are 75, are starred. Six indexes and a history of medicolegal literature makes this a worthwhile bibliographic tool.
FS2.209:M46/736--967

648.   U.S. Public Health Service. National Institutes of Health. National Library of Medicine. *List of Journals Indexed in Index Medicus, 1971.* 1971. 92pp. $1.25*.
S/N 1752--0718

This is an excellent listing of current medical periodicals. Lists are by title, subject, and geographic area.
HE20.3612/4:971

649.   U.S. Public Health Service. National Institutes of Health. National Library of Medicine. *National Library of Medicine Current Catalog, 1965–1970.* 1971. 8 vols. $71.75* S/N 1752–0131.

Monographic publications cataloged by the National Library of Medicine are listed here by author, joint author, title, and subject.
HE20.3609/3:965--70

650.   U.S. Public Health Service. National Institutes of Health. National Library of Medicine. *National Medical Audiovisual Center 1973 Motion Picture and Videotape Catalog: Selected*

Audiovisual for the Health Scientist. 1973. viii + 180pp.
$1.95*.
Listed and described are 16mm motion pictures and video-
tapes available on free loan from the National Medical
Audiovisual Center (NMAC) for health sciences professional
educational use. Motion pictures and tapes are listed
separately by subject and are then fully described in separate
alphabetical listings by title.
HE20.3608/4:973

The Aged and Aging

651. U.S. Congress. Senate. Special Committee on Aging.
Publications List, 87th--93rd Congresses, 1961--1973. 1973.
(Printed 1974). 11pp. Free***.
This is an alphabetical listing of the Committee publications
with availability information provided for each item.
Y4.Ag4:P96/973

652. U.S. Public Health Service. *Comprehensive Review of
Geronto--Psychiatric Literature in the Postwar Period, Review
of the Literature to January 1, 1965 With List of References;*
by L. Ciompi. 1969. vi + 97pp. $1.00* L.C. Card 70–601679.
Contained are 2747 citations, both foreign and English,
which are arranged alphabetically by author under broad
subject headings. This is considered to be a comprehensive
"review of current thinking about aging."
FS2.22:G31/3/965

653. U.S. Social and Rehabilitation Service Administration.
Administration on Aging. *AOA Publications.* 1973. 11pp.
Free***.
Order and purchase information are given for all available
AOA publications.
HE17.311:P96/973

654. U.S. Social and Rehabilitation Service Administration.
Administration on Aging. *Nutrition and Aging, Selected
Annotated Bibliography, 1964--1972;* compiled by
Margaret D. Simko and Karen Colitz. [1973]. v + 42pp.
$.75*.
Publications are arranged by author within the following
subject categories: Nature of Aging; Nutrition Status;
Metabolic and Nutritional Research; Illness and Aging;

Nutrition Problems; Feeding the Elderly; Nutrition and Consumer Education; Meal–Delivery Systems; and Agencies and Food Programs for the Elderly. HE17.311:N95/964–72

656. U.S. Social and Rehabilitation Service Administration. Administration on Aging. *More Words on Aging, Bibliography of Selected 1968–70 References, Supplement, May 1971.* 1971. vi + 108pp. $.55* S/N 1762–0040.
Supplements the 1970 edition of *Words on Aging* (see below).
HE17.311:Ag4/supp.

657. U.S. Social and Rehabilitation Service Administration. Administration on Aging. *Words on Aging: a Bibliography;* compiled by Dorothy M. Jones. 1970. vi + 190pp. $.75* L.C. Card 76–610099.
This seventh edition of selected references on aging is divided into broad subject categories such as: Process of Aging; Economic Aspects of Aging; Health and Medical Care; and Social Relationship and Social Adjustment. Indexed by author and subject.
HE17.311:Ag4

Drugs and Drug Abuse

658. U.S. Bureau of Narcotics and Dangerous Drugs. *Illicit Use of Dangerous Drugs in the United States: a Compilations of Studies, Surveys, and Polls;* by Dorothy F. Berg. 1970. 37pp. ***.
In addition to giving bibliographic information, this work provides actual statistics derived by the work. Particularly covered is the illicit us of hallucinogens, stimulants, de-- pressants, opiates, and glue.
J24.2:D84/2

659. U.S. Department of the Air Force. Air University Library. *Drugs and Drug Abuse, Selected References;* com- piled by Gaye Byars. 1972. 26pp.*** (Special Biblio- graphy, no. 199).
Current books, articles, and documents are cited which refer to the following aspects of drugs and drug abuse: Drugs in the Military; Drug Education; Rehabilitation Treatment; and Marihuana. Not indexed.
D301.26/11:199

660. U.S. National Clearinghouse for Drug Abuse Prevention. *Bibliography of Drug Abuse Literature, 1971;* prepared by Susan B. Lachter, Eileen Marchak, and Angela L. Theophile. 1972. v + 39pp. $.50* L.C. Card 73–600628.
Included in this bibliography are all citations which appeared in the biweekly lists of *DACAS* (Drug Abuse Current Awareness System) from Dec. 1970-- Dec. 1971. "This bibliography is more specialized and technically-- oriented than most general bibliographies. The citations from the current scientific literature can provide good background material for developing research papers on the college and postgraduate level, and can also be useful as an overview of the published research of investigators in the field."
PrEx13.10:D84/2/971

661. U.S. National Clearinghouse for Drug Abuse Prevention. *Drug Dependence and Abuse, Selected Bibliography.* 1971. vi + 51pp. $.60* L.C. Card 73--611414.
Material included in this bibliography is current and is intended for a broad audience. Both scientific and popular materials which could be used in speeches, debates, and papers are listed by specific subject.
PrEx13.10:D84/971

662. U.S. National Clearinghouse for Drug Abuse Prevention. *The Effect of the Drugs of Abuse on the Reproductive Processes.* 1972. 31pp.** (Selected Reference Series, no. 4/1).
References to significant research concerned with the effect that drugs of abuse have on reproduction comprise this bibliography. No conclusions can be drawn from the material included, but the "citations can be helpful in outlining past research and the general direction of current studies in this area."
PrEx13.10/2:4/1

663. U.S. National Clearinghouse for Drug Abuse Prevention. *Methaqualone.* 1973. 13pp.** (Selected Reference Series, 7, no. 1).
Material listed is current, readily available, and significant in the study of methaqualone.
PrEx13.10/2:7/1

664. U.S. National Clearinghouse for Drug Abuse Prevention.

Selected Bibliography on the Use of Drugs by Young People. 1971. 4pp.** (Selected Reference Series, no. 1/1). Publications are informative and non-technical. PrEx13.10/2:1/1

665. U.S. Public Health Service. U.S. Health Services and Mental Health Administration. National Institute of Mental Health. *Alcoholism Treatment and Rehabilitation.* 1972. ix + 201pp. $.75* S/N 1724–0239. L.C. Card 73–601040.
This collection of selected abstracts "covers a wide range of modalitites, treatment and rehabilitation programs, and innovative treatment techniques and methods published in the world literature since 1960. Such an up-to-date compendium should serve as an invaluable aid to persons directly engaged in treatment, rehabilitation, research, program planning, and administration in the alcoholism field."
HE20.2417:Al 1

666. U.S. Public Health Service. Health Services and Mental Health Administration. National Institute of Mental Health. *Anti–depresseant Drug Studies 1955–1966: Bibliography and Selected Abstracts;* by Aaron Smith and others. 1969. 659pp. $5.50* L.C. 70–601845.
Of more than 2,000 articles screened and evaluated, only 918 were selected for inclusion in this bibliography, and of those 918 approximately half were abstracted. Those abstracted contain the following details: purpose of the study; subjects; procedure; instruments; results; and dosage. This is considered to be a comprehensive listing of all reports published in English from 1955 to 1966 concerning drugs used in the treatment of psychiatric depression. Not indexed.
FS2.22/13:An8/955--66

667. U.S. Public Health Service. Health Services and Metnal Health Administration. National Institute of Mental Health. *Bibliography on Drug Dependence and Abuse, 1928–66.* 1969. 5 + 1 -- 85d, 86 -- 258pp.*** L.C. Card 70–600726.
The more than 3,000 citations are divided into eight categories: (1) General Discussions, Reviews, and History, (2) Incidence and Prevalence; (3) Sociological Factors; (4) Treatment and Rehabilitation; (5) Attitudes and Education; (6) Pharmacology and Chemistry; (7) Psycho–

logical Factors, and (8) Production, Control, and Legal
Factors. Not indexed.
FS2.22/13:D84/928--66

668. U.S. Public Health Service. Health Services and Mental Health
Administration. National Institute of Mental Health.
Government Publications on Drug Abuse. 1970. [1] + 16pp.
Free*** L.C. Card 73--606747.
Publications are listed by government issuing agency. A
good abstract is given for each publication, but there is
no bibliographic information other than the title. Not
indexed.
HE20.2417:D84

669. U.S. Public Health Service. Health Services and Mental Health
Administration. National Institute of Mental Health.
Selected Bibliography on Drugs of Abuse. 1970. 25pp.
Free*** L.C. Card 71–606583.
Listings are alphabetical by author under the following
subject headings: General Drug Abuse Information;
Hallucinogens (Includes Marihuana); and Amphetamines
and Barbiturates. The approximately 400 entries represent
the best of the periodical, book, and government report
literature current as of 1969.
HE20.2417:D84/2

Health Services and Medical Care

670. U.S. Congress. House. *Resolved: That the Federal
Government Should Enact a Program of Comprehensive
Medical Care for All United States Citizens: a Collection of
Excerpts and Bibliography Relating to the Intercollegiate
Debate Topic, 1972–73;* prepared by the Congressional
Research Service, Library of Congress. 1972. v + 418pp.
$2.25* S/N 5271--00327. (H. Doc. No. 92–325).
Only 18 pages of bibliography accompany a select group
of readings relating to medical care concepts.
H. Doc. 92--325

671. U.S. Department of the Air Force. Pacific Air Forces. *Health
and Hygiene;* prepared by Ardys M. Asper. 1971. [1] + iv +
59pp.*** (PACAF Basic Bibliographies).
This selective bibliography contains annotated listings of
new titles in the fields of health and hygiene. Areas
covered ranged from pediatrics to geriatrics and from
alcoholism to surgery. An author–title index facilitates its

use.
D301.62:H34/971

672. U.S. Government Printing Office. *Health and Medical Service. Hospitals and Nursing, First Aid, Industrial and Occupational Health, and Sanitation.* Free* (Price List, no. 51).
Listed are free and for sale publications on all aspects of health and medical service. This list is frequently revised; prices are kept current; and all publications are supposedly available.
GP3.9:51

673. U.S. Office of Economic Opportunity. *Bibliography on the Comprehensive Health Service Program.* 1970. iii + [1] + 31pp.*** L.C. Card 70--60646.
Annotated references are made to 67 reports on the Comprehensive Health Services projects. Accompanying is a listing of OEO--assisted projects, as of Jan. 1, 1970.
PrEx10.15:C73

674. U.S. Public Health Service. *Comprehensive Health Planning, Selected Annotated Bibliography.* 1968. iv + 31pp.***
(PHS Publication 1753). L.C. Card 68--61469.
Contained are 157 annotations of books, articles, and pamphlets relating to total health planning which includes manpower, facilities, services, theory and techniques. Address lists for obtaining information are provided.
FS2.24:H34/4

675. U.S. Public Health Service. *Public Health Engineering Abstracts.* 1939--1968. (Monthly). L.C. Card 70--600422.
At the time this publication was replaced by specialized abstracts, it represented a monthly review of more than 800 domestic and foreign journals of science and engineering reports of State and Federal Governments, and reports and proceedings of scientific research groups. Topics covered (1) Atmospheric Pollution, (2) Insects and Insect--Borne Diseases, (3) Milk and Other Feeds, (4) Occupational Health, (5) Public Health Practices, (6) Radiological Health and Safety, (7) Sewerage, Industrial Wastes, and Water Pollution, and (8) Water Supplies, Plumbing. Annual subject--author index.
FS2.13:47

676. U.S. Public Health Service. Health Services Administration. Community Health Services Bureau. *Selected Annotated Bibliography on Health Maintenance Organizations (HMO s) and Organized Health Care Systems.* 1973. [2] + 29pp. $.65* S/N 1741–0062.

This bibliography supplements a similar 1971 bibliography and attempts to include the better publications in the field. Entries are arranged by subjects and include such topics as HMO s in general, group medical practice, and sources of information on HMO s. Availability information is generally provided.
HE20.5110:H34

677. U.S. Public Health Service. Health Services and Mental Health Administration. Community Health Service. *Community Health Service Publications Catalog, 1971--1972.* 1971. 56pp. $.35* S/N 1726–0020.

Briefly described by subject category are the publications by the Community Health Service during the year. Indexed by title.
HE20.2560:971–972

678. U.S. Public Health Service. Health Services and Mental Health Administration. Emergency Health Services. *Emergency Health Services Selected Bibliography.* 1970. [3] + 175pp. $1.25* L.C. Card 78--606811.

A good subject index assists one in using this bibliography which deals with day--to–day medical emergencies and disasters. Also listed are audio–visual and catalog materials.
HE20.2013:A–1

679. U.S. Public Health Service. Health Services and Mental Health Administration. Emergency Health Services. *Emergency Health Services, Selected References.* [Rev. 1972]. [2] + 22pp.***.

Publications listed here should be especially helpful in the development of hospital emergency department and ambulance services and the training of emergency medical technicians. Sources of material are provided, and pertinent periodicals are listed.
HE20.2012/2:Em3

680. U.S. Public Health Service. Health Services and Mental Health Administration. Emergency Health Services. *Spanish--Language Health Communications Teaching Aids, List of*

Printed Materials and Their Sources; compiled by Robert
N. Isquith and Charles T. Webb. Reprinted Jan. 1973.
vii + 55pp.***.
Publications are arranged by publisher and indexed by
subject.
HE20.2012/2:Sp2

681. U.S. Public Health Service. Health Services and Mental Health
Administration. Federal Health Programs Service. *Auto--
mated Multiphasic Health Testing, Bibliography, Vol. 1, No. 1.*
1970. [3] + 175pp. $1.50*. L.C. Card 77–608927.
Four hundred and sixty--three annotated entries dealing
with the various aspects of automation and computerization
in the health and medical fields are listed here. Author
and subject indices enhance the use of this computerized
bibliography.
HE20.2710:1/1

682. U.S. Public Health Service. Health Services and Mental Health
Administration. Federal Health Programs Service. *Index
to Clinical Research in the Federal Health Programs Service,
Bibliography of Published Papers, Presentations, Current
Studies.* 1970. v + 79pp. $.45* L.C. 76--610458.
HE20.2710/2:C61

683. U.S. Public Health Service. Health Services and Mental Health
Administration. Health Care Facilities Service. *Publications
of the Health Care Facilities Service, Hill–Burton Program.*
6th Edition. [1972]. v + 45pp. $.45*.
Listed are available publications of guidelines on design,
construction, and operations of hospital and medical
facilities. Included are both the physical and personnel
aspects of hospital operation.
HE20.2512:P96

684. U.S Public Health Service. Health Services and Mental Health
Administration. Health Care Facilities Service. *Publications
of the Health Facilities Planning and Construction Service,
Hill–Burton Program.* 1970. v + 41pp. $.30* L.C. Card
67--61255.
HE20.2511:G–3

685. U.S. Public Health Service. Health Services and Mental Health
Administration. Health Care Facilities Service. *Selected
References on Hospital Equipment.* 1973. v + 48pp. $.80*

S/N 1725–00023.
The publications listed here purpose to assist planners in determining hospital equipment needs as a systems approach to overall hospital planning.
HE20.251:H79/2

686. U.S. Public Health Service. Health Services and Mental Health Administration. Health Care Facilities Service. *Selected References on Hospital Outpatient and Emergency Activities.* 1973. v + 28pp. $.55*.
This bibliography is a companion document to *Hospital Outpatient and Emergency Activities: Functional Programming* and *Selected References on Hospital Equipment.* References are grouped under the following headings: Functional Programming; Equipment Planning; and Architectural and Engineering Design Considerations. Not indexed.
HE20.2512:H79

687. U.S. Public Health Service. Health Services and Mental Health Administration. Health Care Facilities Planning and Construction Service. *Selected Studies in Building Research Applicable to the Design and Construction of Health Facilities.* v + 2 + 63pp. $.65*.
Over 600 references dealing with the design and construction of health facilities are indexed by keyword.
HE20.2511:D–26

688. U.S. Public Health Service. Health Services and Mental Health Administration. Maternal and Child Health Service. *Annotated Bibliography on Maternal Nutrition.* 1970. [4] + 199pp. $1.50* L.C. Card 70–608164.
This bibliography is a supplement to *Maternal Nutrition and the Course of Pregnancy* (NAS–NRC Publication 1761). Citations are to the literature from 1958 to 1968 and are arranged by such topics as: Birth Weight; Adolescence; Diet and Its Effect on the Course and Outcome of Pregnancy; Iron Status and Iron–Deficiency Anemia; Pre–gravid Weight and Gain in Weight During Pregnancy; and Social, Economic, and Other Variables That Affect Pregnancy. Not indexed.
HE20.2759:M41

689. U.S. Public Health Service. Health Services and Mental Health Administration. Maternal and Child Health Service. *Publications of the Maternal and Child Health Service.*

1971. 21pp. $.20* S/N 1730--0012.
A briefly annotated bibliography with purchase and
availability information. Indexed by subject and title.
HE20.2759:P96/971

690. U.S. Public Health Service. Health Services and Mental
Health Administration. National Center for Health Services
Research. *Catalog of Health Services Research: Abstracts of
Public and Private Projects, 1967--1970.* 1971. vii + 193 +
144 + 5 + 10 + 2pp. NTIS.
This thoroughly indexed work is a comprehensive catalog
of research and demonstration projects directly or
indirectly addressed to the improvement of health care
services. Arrangement is by specific subject area under
major subject headings.
HE20.2110:71--20

691. U.S. Public Health Service. Health Services and Mental
Health Administration. National Center for Health Services
Research. *Catalog of Health Services Research and
Development, Reports, Abstracts, and Data, 1967--71.*
1972. vi + [56] pp. NTIS.
This is a multiple index catalog of recently announced
Health Services research and development reports.
HE20.2102:C29/967--71

692. U.S. Public Health Service. Health Services and Mental
Health Administration. National Center for Health Services
Research. *Ethical Issues in Health Services, Report and
Annotated Bibliography;* by James Carmody. 1970.
(Published in 1971). 3 + 43pp.*** (RD 70--32).
Covered by this bibliography are the following aspects of
medical service: (1) The Fight to Health Care; (2) Death
and Euthanaisa; (3) Human Experimentation; (4) Genetic
Engineering; and (5) Abortion. Not indexed.
HE20.2110:70--32

693. U.S. Public Health Service. Health Services and Mental
Health Administration. National Center for Health Services
Research. *Health Services Research, Bibliography 1972--73;*
by John W. Williamson and James B. Tenney. 1972. [2] +
v + 58pp. $3.00***.
"This bibliography is prepared to provide a revised and
updated list of articles, monographs, and books of value
to beginners and relatively new investigators in the area of

of health services research." Contained are 478 entries
on all aspects of health services and medical care.
HE20.2113/2:H34/972--73

694. U.S. Public Health Service. Health Services and Mental Health
      Administration. National Center for Health Services Research.
      *Interorganizational Research in Health, Bibliography (1960--
      70);* by Paul E. White and George J. Vlasak. 1972. [1] +
      vii + 80pp.***.
      "The bibliography reflects the field as reported in the
      periodical literature in the decade 1960--1970. The biblio--
      graphy encompasses all known and pertinent items" dealing
      with interorganizational relationships in health which
      fulfill the following criteria: "(a) they were research under--
      takings, (b) they focused on inter--organizational relation--
      ships, and (c) they dealt with health services."
      HE20.2113/2:H34/2/960--970

695. U.S. Public Health Service. Health Services and Mental Health
      Administration. National Center for Health Services Research.
      Multiphasic Health Testing Systems: Reviews and Annotations;
      by Anna C. Gelman. 1971. 155pp.*** (HSRD, 71--1).
      L.C. Card 77--614007.
      Those items chosen for inclusion were carefully selected
      and thoroughly annotated. Subject arrangement. Not
      indexed.
      HE20.2110:71--1

696. U.S. Public Health Service. Health Services and Mental Health
      Administration. National Center for Health Services Research.
      *Planning for Hospital Discharge, Bibliography with Abstracts
      and Research Reviews;* by August Le Rocco. 1970. ix +
      85pp. NTIS (PB 193 520) (Report HSRD 70--17). L.C.
      Card 73--609292.
      The well--annotated publications included here have been
      listed by one of three groups: Hospital Discharge Planning;
      General, Progressive Patient Care; and Home Care. Author
      and detailed subject indices help locate specific areas of
      interest. Also included is a list of journals researched.
      HE20.2110:70--17

696a. U.S. Public Health Service. Health Services and Mental Health
      Administration. National Center for Health Services Research.
      Publications Report. No. 1. 1970--. Annual.
      This is an annual listing, accompanied by purchase

information, of research reports by the National Center
for Health Services Research and Development. Entries are
annotated. New to the 1973 edition (no. 4) is an author
index and a listing of conference reports.
HE20.2113:no.

697. U.S. Public Health Service. Health Services and Mental Health
Administration. National Center for Health Services Research.
*Utilization of Health Services: Indices and Corrolates, Research
Bibliography;* by LuAnn Aday, Robert Eichhorn. 1972.
(Published in 1973).
Two hundred and seven lengthy abstracts are approached
via the following sections: (1) Classification of and key to
the Indices and Correlate of Utilization; (2) Indices of
Utilization; and (3) Correlates of Utilization. Such a
bibliography will assist the researcher in finding dependable
information on which to base national health care policy
decisions.
HE20.2113/2:H34/3/972

697a. U.S. Public Health Service. Health Services and Mental Health
Administration. National Center for Health Statistics.
*Catalogue of Publications of the National Center for Health
Statistics, 1962--1971.* iii + 86pp. $.70*.
Presented is a complete listing and brief description of NCHS
publications from 1962--1971. Publications are grouped in
15 subject categories and purchase information is provided.
Indexed by title.
HE20.2213:N21/967--71

698. U.S. Public Health Service. Health Services and Mental Health
Administration. National Center for Health Statistics.
*Catalogue of Publications of the National Center for Health
Statistics, 1972 Supplement.* 1973. [3] + 33pp.
HE20.2213:N21/972/supp.

698a. U.S. Public Health Service. Health Services and Mental Health
Administration. National Center for Health Statistics.
Current Listing of Vital and Health Statistics Series. 1972.
7pp. Free***.
Listed by each of the 22 series are the titles in each series.
All publications listed may be obtained free.
HE20.2213:V83

699. U.S. Public Health Service. Health Services and Mental Health

Administration. Regional Medical Programs Service.
Selected Bibliography of Regional Medical Programs.
2d Rev. 1970. [3] + 103pp.***
HE20.2611:970

700. U.S. Public Health Service. Health Services and Mental Health
Administration. Regional Medical Programs Service. *Selected
Bibliography of Regional Medical Programs, Rev. 1972.* 1972.
[1] + iii + 35pp. L.C. Card 72--602242.
Publications are divided into two groups according to
whether they pertain to (1) regional medical programs
in general and (2) specific regional medical programs. A
brief subject index does assist the user in locating some
specifics.
HE20.2611:972

701. U.S. Social Security Administration. *Impact of Medicare,
Annotated Bibliography of Selected Sources;* prepared by
Mary McGee. 1970. v + 70 + [1]pp. $.40* L.C. Card
70--604540.
This is a collection of publications on *Medicare* written
between 1965 and 1968. Entries are arranged alphabetically
within the following subject areas: Administration and
Planning; Hospital Reimbursement; Home Health,
Extended Care, and Psychiatric Services; Physicians'
Services; Private Health Insurance; Public Policy and
Issues; Standards; Use and Financing of Medical Care
Services; Utilization Review; and ORS publications.
Author index.
HE3.38:M46/2

702. U.S. Social Security Administration. *Medicare, Bibliography
of Selected References, 1966–67.* 1968. [5] + 88pp.
$.35* L.C. Card HEW68–56.
Listed are significant books, pamphlets, and articles on
Medicare that were added to the Social Security Admini--
stration Library during Medicare's first year. Publications
are listed by specific subject. Author index.
FS3.38:M46

Medical Research

703. U.S. Atomic Energy Commission. *Bibliography of Medical
Uses of Technetium–99m, 1965–71;* compiled by Ruth M.
Stemple. 1973. 2 + [3] + 251pp. $7.60 NTIS (ORAU–121).
Y3.At7:22/ORAU--121

704. U.S. Atomic Energy Commission. *Effects of Human Exposure to Ionizing Radiation, Bibliography;* by Ann D. Nevill, A.P. Jacobson, K.A. McDermott. 1968. [1] + 70pp. NTIS (NP–17232).
Y3.At7:22/NP--17232

705. U.S. Atomic Energy Commission. *Nuclear Medicine, Supplement Supplement 1, Bibliography from Nuclear Science Abstracts, Vol. 22, June 29.* [3] + 172 + [1]pp. NTIS (TID--3319 Supp. 1).
Y3.At7:22/TID–3319/Supp.1

706. U.S. Atomic Energy Commission. *Nuclear Medicine, Supp--lement 2, Nuclear Science Abstracts, Vol 23, June 1970.* iv + 227 + 99pp. NTIS (TID–3319 Supp. 2).
Y3.At7:22/TID--3319/Supp.2

707. U.S. Atomic Energy Commission. *Nuclear Medicine, Supp--lement 3, Nuclear Science Abstracts, Vol. 24, June 1971.* iv + 189 + 88pp. NTIS. (TID--3319 Supp. 3)
Y3.At7:22/TID--3319/Supp.3

708. U.S. Atomic Energy Commission. *Research and Devlopment in Progress: Biomedical and Environmental Research Program.* 2d ed. 1972. v + 245pp. NTIS.
Y3.At7:22/TID--4060

709. U.S. Department of the Army. Army Medical Service. *Bibliography, Medical Research and Development Articles, FY 1968.* [1969]. [93]pp.***.
D103.10/2:M46/968

710. U.S. Federal Aviation Administration. *Circadian Rhythms, Selected References;* compiled by Louise Annus Heller. 1968. [3] + 82pp.*** (Bibliography List, no. 15).
Listed are over 400 bibliographic entries of books, periodi-cals, and reports on "circadian rhythm," a term used to describe a condition of living organisms in which certain phenomena recur regularly at about the same time each day. Some entries are annotated. Arrangement is by subject. Indexed by author.
TD4.17/3:15

711. U.S. Federal Avaiation Administration. Aviation Medicine Office. *Aviation Medicine Translations, Annotated Biblio--*

graphy of Recently Translated Material, 5; by Mary Ellen Allen and Ruth Ann Mertens. 1968. [3] + 7 + [1]pp. NTIS (FAA AM no. 68–7). TD4.210:68–7

712. U.S. Federal Aviation Administration. Aviation Medicine Office. *Aviation Medicine Translations, Annotated Bibliography of Recently Translated Material, 6;* by Ruth Ann Mertens and others. 1971. [5] + 5pp. NTIS (FAA AM no. 71–5). TD4.210:71–5

713. U.S. Federal Aviation Administration. Aviation Medicine Office. *Aviation Medicine Translations, Annotated Bibliography of Recently Translated Material, 7;* by Karen N. Jones, D.R. Goulden, and E. Jean Grimm. 1972. [6] + 7 + [1]pp. NTIS (FAA AM 72–16). TD4.210:72–16

714. U.S. Federal Aviation Administration. Aviation Medicine Office. *Aviation Medicine Translations, Annotated Bibliography of Recently Translated Material, 8;* by Gregory N. Constant, D.R. Goulden, and E. Jean Grimm. 1973. NTIS (FAA AM no. 73–19). TD4.210:73–19

715. U.S. Government Printing Office. *Diseases and Physical Conditions: Alcoholism, Dentistry, Drugs and Narcotics Addiction, Smoking, and Vital and Health Statistics.* Free* (Price List, no. 512A).
Listed are for sale and free publications on the items mentioned in the title. This list is revised frequently; prices are kept current; and all publications listed are supposedly available from the GPO.
GP3.9:51A

716. U.S. Joint Publications Research Service. *Bibliography on Aerospace Medicine and Bioastronautics for 1967, USSR;* by L.I. Boreava, et al. 1968. 56pp. NTIS (JPRS–46947). Y3.J66:13/46947

717. U.S. National Aeronautics and Space Administration. *Aerospace Medicine and Biology, Continuing Bibliography with Indexes, Selection of Annotated References to Unclassified Reports and Journal Articles That Were*

157

Introduced into the NASA Information System During (date). Monthly. NTIS (NASA SP--7011 (Nos.). NAS1.21:7011(no.)

718.	U.S. Public Health Service. *Bibliography on Smoking and Health with English Language Abstracts of Foreign Items, 1968 Cumulation.* 1968. v + 296pp. $2.00* (Bibliography Series, no. 45). L.C. Card 68--60300.
Included in this annual publication are all items which were added to the collection of the National Clearinghouse for Smoking and Health during the year. Publications are arranged alphabetically within eleven subject categories. Indexed by author and subject.
FS2.21:45/3

719.	U.S. Public Health Service. *Bibliography on Smoking and Health with English Language Abstracts of Foregin Items, 1969 Cumulation.* 1969. v + 321pp. $2.00*.
FS2.21:45/4

720.	U.S. Public Health Service. *Bibliography on Smoking and Health with English Language Abstracts of Foreign Items, 1969 Cumulation, Pt. 2.* 1970. 362pp. $3.25* (Bibliography Series, 45).
HE20.11:45/pt.2

721.	U.S. Public Health Service. *Bibliography on Smoking and Health, 1970.* 1971. 351pp. $3.25* S/N 1727–0024.
HE20.11:45/2

722.	U.S. Public Health Service. *Bibliography on Smoking and Health, 1971.* 1972. [3] + 342pp. $2.50*.
HE20.11:45/3

723.	U.S. Public Health Service. *Bibliography on Smoking and Health, 1972.* 1973. [3] + 314pp. $3.20*.
HE20.11:45/4

724.	U.S. Public Health Service. *Endocarditis, Bibliography Com--piled from English Language, 1965–1966;* compiled by Lucille T. Shoop. 1969. iv + 13pp.*** L.C. Card 63--65422.
The 237 entries listed here comprise the second supp--lement (first supplement, 1966) to this title which was first issued in 1963. Not indexed. Biennial supplements

are planned.
FS2.24:En2/Supp.2

725.   U.S. Public Health Service. *Readings on Cancer, Annotated Bibliography.* 1969. iv + 23pp. $.25* (Bibliography Series, no. 14). L.C. Card 70--600690.
"This annotated and graded bibliography is designed to serve the needs of all persons interested in the problem of cancer, particularly cancer patients and their families, students, and teachers." The selections provide information on cancer as a disease and as an area of biomedical research. Publications are rated (E) easy, (M) Moderately difficult, and (D) difficult.
FS2.21:14/4

726.   U.S. Public Health Service. *Selected References on Rheumatic Fever, Gloumerulonephritis, and Streptococcal Infections, Bibliography Compiled from English Language, 1965;* by Lucille T. Shoop. 1968. v + 37pp.** (Bibliography Series, no. 76).
FS2.21:76

727.   U.S. Public Health Service. *Selected References on Rheumatic Fever, Gloumerulonephritis, and Streptococcal Infections, Bibliography Compiled from English Language, 1966.* 1968. [2] + 32pp.** (Bibliography Series, no. 77).
FS2.21:77

728.   U.S. Public Health Service. *Selected References on Rheumatic Fever, Gloumerulonephritis, and Streptococcal Infections, Bibliography Compiled from English Language, 1967.* 1968. v + 32pp.** (Bibliography Series, no. 78).
Included are all articles included in *Index Medicus* written in English on rheumatic fever and related subjects during the given year. Arranged by subject. Indexed by author.
FS2.21:78

729.   U.S. Public Health Service. Food and Drug Administration. Bureau of Radiological Health. *Low and Very Low Dose Influences of Ionizing Radiations on Cells and Organisms, Including Man: a Bibliography;* by Benjamin P. Sonnenblick. 1972. vii + 325 + 1pp. NTIS.
"A bibliography of more than 3400 citations on low and very low level (respectively, below 50 or 10 roentgen, rads, or rems) ionizing radiation effects on biological systems.

Divided into eleven categories, the citations cover a period
from the early 1950's to mid--1969."
HE20.4114:72--1

730.   U.S. Public Health Service. Food and Drug Administration.
Bureau of Radiological Health. *Publications Index.* 1971.
265pp.*** (BRH/OBD 72--1). L.C. Card 77--614504.
HE20.4111:72--1

731.   U.S. Public Health Service. Food and Drug Administration.
Bureau of Radiological Health. *Publications Index (July 1972).*
1972. 336pp.*** (BRH/OBD 73--4).
HE20.4111:73--4

732.   U.S. Public Health Service. Health Services and Mental Health
Administration. Center for Disease Control. *Current
Literature on Venereal Disease, Abstracts and Bibliography.*
(Issued 3 or 4 times a year).** L.C. 53--61360.
With the use of *Medlars*, this bibliography is able to keep
up with the current literature in the field. Indexed annually.
HE20.2311:yr./no.

733.   U.S. Public Health Service. Health Services and Mental Health
Administration. Center for Disease Control. *Selected* ✦
*References on Behavioral Aspects of Venereal Disease Control,
Annotated Bibliography for Behavioral Scientists, Epi--
mediologists, and Venereal Disease Casefinding Personnel;*
prepared by William W. Darrow. 1972. [3] + 59pp.**
L.C. Card 70--614395.
Entries are thoroughly annotated. Subject index.
HE20.2315:V55

734.   U.S. Public Health Service. Health Service and Mental Health
Administration. Federal Health Programs Service. *Index to
Clinical Research in the Federal Health Programs Service,
Bibliography of Published Papers, Presentations, Current
Studies.* 1970. v + 79pp. $.45* L.C. Card 76--10458.
See no. 736 for notation.
HE20.2710/2:C61

735.   U.S. Public Health Service. Health Service and Mental Health
Administration. Federal Health Programs Service. *Index to
Clinical Research in the Federal Health Programs Service,
Bibliography of Published Papers, Presentations, Current
Studies, 1971.* 1972. v + 101pp. $.45* S/N1730--0016.

See no. 736 for notation.
HE20.2710/2:C61/971

736.　U.S. Public Halth Service. Health Service and Mental Health
Administration. Federal Health Programs Service. *Index to
Clinical Research in the Federal Health Programs Service,
Bibliography of Published Papers, Presentations, Current
Studies, 1972.* 1973. v + 58pp.*.
This bibliography is in three separate sections, each of
which has its own author, investigator, and subject index.
The parts are: (1) Published Clinical Research Papers;
(2) Presentations on Clinical Research; and (3) Current
Clinical Research Projects.
HE20.2710/2:C61/972

737.　U.S. Public Health Service. Health Services and Mental Health
Administration. Maternal and Child Health Service.
Galactosemia, Annotated Bibliography; compiled by
Donough O'Brien, M.D. 1971. [6] + 37pp. $.30*
S/N 1791--0158.
Medlars search service was used to update the 1963 edition
of this bibliography. Included are English references
through March 1971. Entries are arranged under the
following categories: Clinical Studies and Review; Pathology;
Biochemistry; Laboratory Detection and Screening
Studies; Genetics; and Treatment. Author index.
HE20.2759:G13

738.　U.S. Public Health Service. Health Services and Mental Health
Administration. Maternal and Child Health Service.
*Publications of the Centre International de l'Enfance
Coordinated Growth Studies, 1951--68* [with list of
references; compiled by Frank Falkner.] 1969. [1] + 22pp.
*** L.C. Card 74--606581.
This is a list of publications which emanated from nine
centers throughout the world engaged in research on
human development.
HE20.2759:En2/951–68

739.　U.S. Public Health Service. Health Services and Mental Health
Administration. National Center for Health Statistics.
*Annotated Bibliography on Robustness Studies of Statistical
Procedures;* by Z. Govindarajulu and R.T. Leslie. 1972.
viii + 51pp. $.60* (Data Evaluation and Methods Research,
Series, no. 2, no. 51). L.C. 70--190003.

Contained are 360 entries on robustness. Each item is classified under a broad classification scheme which distinguishes estimation from testing hypotheses, parametric from nonparametric, among various departures from postulated assumptions and theory from the Monte Carlo Study.
HE20.2210:2/51

740.   U.S. Public Health Service. National Institutes of Health. *Bibliography of Gonadotropins for 1966* [reports on reproduction and population research;] prepared by Martin L. Peller and Frederick G. Dhyse. 1968. xii + 175pp. $1.50.
An effort was made to make this a comprehensive listing of gonadotropin literature for 1966 and thus assist the scientist and clinician engaged in reproduction and population research in keeping up with the literature. The 849 entries are listed under broad subject headings and indexed by author and subject.
FS2.22/13--7:1

741.   U.S. Public Health Service. National Institutes of Health. *Down's Syndrome (Mongolism), a Reference Bibliography;* by Rudolf F. Vollman. 1969. iv + 88pp. $.45* L.C. Card 70–605926.
The 692 entries, mostly post--1950, on Down's syndrome have been selected from a review of the world literature. Citations are arranged alphabetically by author and indexed by subject.
HE20.3012:D75

742.   U.S. Public Health Service. National Institutes of Health. *Scientific Directory, 1973, an Annual Bibliography, 1972.* 1973. v + 321pp. $2.35* S/N1740--00359. Annual. L.C. Card 57–62015.
This is a directory of scientific personnel affiliated with the NIH. However, the primary purpose is to provide a bibliography, with subject and author indices, of all publications of the NIH. Those publications listed deal primarily with medicine and biomedicine.
HE20.3017:973

743.   U.S. Public Health Service. National Institutes of Health. John E. Fogarty International Center for Advanced Study in the Health Sciences. *Social and Psychological Aspects of Applied Human Genetics Bibliography;* by James R. Sorenson.

1973. [1] + iv + 98pp. +1.25*.
This selective compilation of books and articles focuses on
the psychological and social issues of applied human
genetics. Entries are listed under forty--two specific
subjects, of which a few are: Genetic Counseling; Twin
Studies; Down's Syndrome; Medical Genetics; Eugenics;
Genetics and Law; and Genetic Engineering.
HE20.3711:G28

744.   U.S. Public Health Service. National Institutes of Health.
National Cancer Institute. *Partial Bibliography on Human
Cancer Involving Viruses, Jan. 1966--Dec. 1969.* 1970.
L.C. Card 71--608072.
Two hundred and seventy--seven entries with key word
descriptors are arranged by author and indexed by subject,
and author, including secondary authors.
HE20.3165:H88/966--69

745.   U.S. Public Health Service. National Institutes of Health.
National Cancer Institute. *Partial Bibliography on Type--B
and Type--C Viruses in Relation to Animal Neoplasia.*
1971. [5] + 103pp.***.
The 1427 entries cover the period of Jan. 1967–Dec. 1970.
They are indexed by author, animal, neoplas, and virus.
HE20.3165:V81/967--70

746.   U.S. Public Health Service. National Institutes of Health.
National Heart and Lung Institute. *Fibrinolysis, Thrombolysis,
and Blood Clotting, Bibliography.* V. 1--. 1966--. Monthly
with annual cumulation.*** L.C. Card 67–62840.
With the use of *Medlars,* the entries for both the monthly
and annual cumulative bibliography are selected and
arranged under specific subject headings. Complete entries
are given in a subject section and in an author section.
Cross--references are made through a separate subject index.
HE20.3209:Vol.

747.   U.S. Public Health Service. National Institutes of Health.
National Institute of Arthritis and Metabolic Disease.
Artificial Kidney Bibliography. V. 1--. 1967–. Quarterly.
$2.70 a yr.*, $.70 additional foreign mailing.
Medlars is searched periodically to compile this specific
bibliography on kidney failure and the dialysis methods –
hemodialysis and peritoneal dialysis, used to treat the
kidney patient. Publications are listed by such subjects as:

Kidney Failure, Acute; Anuria; Uremia; Hemodialysis; Peritoneal Dialysis; Kidney Transplantation; Kidney, Artificial; and Membranes, Artificial. Author index. HE20.3311:Vol./no.

748. U.S. Public Health Service. National Institutes of Health. National Institute of Arthritis and Metabolic Disease. *Diabetes Literature Index.* V. 1–. 1966–. Monthly. $2.50 a yr.*, $5.50 additional foreign mailing.
This bibliography is produced from the *Medlars* system, and it includes literature citations on diabetes which appear in *Index Medicus.* Since this publication deals only with diabetes, the subject headings under which items and the hierarchiacal subject index are much more extensive and complete than for Index Medicus. In addition to the Hierarchical Index, there are Keyword and Author indices. HE20.3310:Vol./no.

749. U.S. Public Health Service. National Institutes of Health. National Institute of Arthritis and Metabolic Disease. *Endocrinology Index.* V. 1–. 1968–. Bimonthly. $38.00* a year, $9.50 additional foreign mailing.
Produced from *Medlars,* this bimonthly bibliography is a current awareness tool for scientists and physicians working in endocrinology. Publications are listed in the following broad categories: Pituitary; Thyroid; Adrenal; Gonads; Neuroendocrinology; Placenta; Parathyroid; and Cyclic Nueleotides. Author and Subject indices make information easily accessible. HE20.3309:Vol./no.

750. U.S. Public Health Service. National Institutes of Health. National Institute of Arthritis and Metabolic Disease. *Gastroenterology Abstracts and Citations.* V. 1–. 1966–. Monthly. $29.00 a yr.*, $7.25 additional foreign mailing. L.C. Card 67–1468.
Prepared with the use of *Medlars* these abstracts cover the printed research and findings concerning the digestive system. Author and subject indices facilitate the use of this publication. Cumulative annual indices. HE20.3313:Vol./no.

751. U.S. Public Health Service. National Institutes of Health. National Institute of Arthritis and Metabolic Disease. *Index of Dermatology, Monthly Guide to the Literature in*

*Clinical Dermatology, Investigative Dermatology, and
Dermatopathology.* V. 1--. 1973--. $14.50* a year., $3.55
additional foreign mailing.

Citations are computer--selected from the current month's
input of *Medlars* and corresponds to the same month of
Index Medicus. All citations for this publication are selected
"solely on the basis of their relevance to dermatology."
There are five main sections: Subject Headings; Review;
General; Bio--science; and Author. Citations are listed
completely in all except the subject section which is just a
listing of all subjects covered in a particular month's Index.
HE20.3315:Vol./no.

752. U.S. Public Health Service. National Institutes of Health.
National Institute of Child Health and Human Development.
Populations Sciences: Index of Biomedical Research.
V. 1, no. 1 --. Oct. 1973--. Monthly. $15.00* a year.
Produced in conjuction with the National Library of
Medicine, this bibliography is based on citations selected
for the corresponding monthly issue of *Index Medicus.*
Citations are divided into subjects, some of which are:
Anatomy and Physiology; Drug and Radiation Effects;
Microbiology – Sterility; Immunology; Reproductive
Behavior; Contraceptive Drugs and Devices; and Steroids
and Non--Steroids. Indexed by author.
HE20.3362/5:Vol./no.

753. U.S. Public Health Service. National Institutes of Health.
National Institute of Child Health and Human Development.
*Sudden Infant Death Syndrome: a Selected Annotated
Bibliography, 1960--1971.* 1972. 1 + 58pp. $.65* L.C.
Card 73--601230.

The 239 annotated entries cover the "literature concerned
with SIDS and, in some cases, the general phenomenom
of sudden, unexpected infant death as it might relate to
SIDS." Indexed by subject and author.
HE20.3361:In3/960--71

754. U.S. Public Health Service. National Institutes of Health.
National Institute of Neurological Disease and Stroke.
*Biblio--Profile on Human Communication and Its Disorders,
Capsule State--of--the--Art Report with Bibliography: No. 1
Neuroanatomy of Speech, 159 References, 1950--70, Period
of Search, 1965--70.* 1971. [3] + vii + 17pp. $.35*.
HE20.3513/2:1

755.   U.S. Public Health Service. National Institutes of Health.
National Institute of Neurological Disease and Stroke.
*Biblio--Profile on Human Communication and Its Disorders,
Capsule State--of--the--Art Report with Bibliography: No.
2 Otitis Media: Diagnosis, Therapy, and Prevention and
Control;* by Francis L. Catlin. 1971. [7] + 47pp. $.55*.
Contained are 400 references from 1964--1970. Subject
arrangement with author index.
HE20.3513/2:2

756.   U.S. Public Health Service. National Institutes of Health.
National Institute of Neurological Disease and Stroke.
*Biblio--Profile on Human Communication and Its Disorders,
Capsule State--of--the--Art Report with Bibliography: No.
3 Surgical Treatment of Deafness;* by Patrick Brookhouser,
John E. Boardley and E. Louise Worthington. 1971. 4 +
ix + 71pp.***.
Contained are 579 references from 1968 through July
1971. Subject arrangement with author index.
HE20.3513/2:3

757.   U.S. Public Health Service. National Institutes of Health.
National Institute of Neurological Disease and Stroke.
Bibliography of Scrapie; compiled by Clarence J. Gibbs, Jr.,
D. Carleton Gajdusek, and Juliette Harvey. 1969. [1] +
67pp.***.
Author arrangement. Not indexed.
FS2.22/13:Scr16

758.   U.S. Public Health Service. National Institutes of Health.
National Institute of Neurological Disease and Stroke.
*Blood Level Determinations of Antiepileptic Drugs, Clinical
Value and Methods: a Bibliography with Key--Word and
Author Indexes.* 1972. iii + [2] + 50pp. $.80*.
Five hundred and eleven citations are listed under 12 major
categories. Key--word in context and author indices aid
in finding a desired publication quickly.
HE20.3513/3:2

759.   U.S. Public Health Service. National Institutes of Health.
National Institute of Neurological Disease and Stroke.
*Cerebrovascular Bibliography, Including Neurological,
Vascular, Hematological Aspects.* Vol. 13, no. 2. April--June
1973.***.
This pbulication is scheduled to begin regular publication

with V. 14, no. 1, January -- March 1974 at $8.50 a year*,
$2.20 additional foreign mailing.

Another *Index Medicus* spin--off, this contains three
citation sections -- Subject, Review, and Author -- and is
indexed by subject and author.
HE20.3513/4:Vol./no.

760.   U.S. Public Health Service. National Institutes of Health.
       National Institute of Neurological Disease and Stroke.
       *Epilepsy Abstracts; a Review of Published Literature, 1947--
       67;* ed. by J.F. Mirandolle and L.M. Vencken. 1969. 2 vols.
       *** L.C. Card 70--604019.

       The over 5,600 abstracts included are primarily concerned
       "with the clinical and therapeutic aspects of the epilepsies."
       This includes physiological, biochemical, psychological,
       sociological, and epidemiological aspects of the epileptic.
       Vol. 2 is a computer--based Subject Index and Author
       Index.
       FS2.22/59--2:947--67/pt.1&2

761.   U.S. Public Health Service. National Institutes of Health.
       National Institute of Neurological Disease and Stroke.
       *Epilepsy Bibliography, 1900--50, with Key--word and Author
       Indexes;* edited by J. Kiffin Penry and Richard L. Rapport
       II. 1973. v + 840pp. $7.00* S/N 1749--00036.

       The nearly 12,000 entries cited here are well--indexed by
       subject and author. The preface of this work claims it to
       be a "historical document."
       HE20.3513:Ep5/900--50

762.   U.S. Public Health Service. National Institutes of Health.
       National Institute of Neurological Disease and Stroke.
       *Parkinson's Disease and Related Disorders, Citations from the
       Literature.* V. 1--. 1970--. Monthly. $6.40 a year*,
       $1.60 additional foreign mailing.

       This monthly bibliography continues the cumulative biblio--
       graphy. (See below). Entries are listed by subject in one
       section and by author in another.
       HE20.3511:Vol./no.

763.   U.S. Public Health Service. National Institutes of Health.
       National Institute of Neurological Disease and Stroke.
       *Parkinson's Disease and Related Disorders, Cumulative
       Bibliography 1800--1970.* 1971. 3v. $13.75* per set. L.C.
       Card 79--610736.

       Listed are almost 8500 citations to the international

literature on Parkinson's disease and such related disorders
as Huntington's and Sydenham's chorea, dystonia
muculorum deformans, multiple tics, and torticollis.
Publications listed are primarily clinical in approach or
describe research connected with one of the disorders.
Volume 1 contains the citations; the Author Index (Volume
2) contains secondary, as well as primary authors; and
Volume 3 is the Subject Index.
HE20.3511/3:1800–970/V.1--3

764.   U.S. Public Health Service. National Institutes of Health.
National Library of Medicine. *Clinical Aspects of Chelating
Agents, Therapeutic and Diagnostic Uses, Including Reports
of Their Adverse Effects, January 1967--June 1970;* pre--
pared by William H. Caldwell. 1970. [1] + 31pp.***
(NLM Literature Search Series, no. 70--36).
The 517 citations are listed alphabetically by author. Not
indexed.
HE20.3614/2:70--36

765.   U.S. Public Health Service. National Institutes of Health.
National Library of Medicine. *Current Bibliography of
Epidemiology: a Guide to the Literature of Epidemiology.
Preventive Medicine, and Public Health.* V. 4, no. 1--.
1971--. Monthly, with annual cumulation. $23.20 a year*,
$5.80 additional foreign mailing.
Originally an American Public Health Association
publication, the National Library of Medicine assumed its
publication with Vol. 4, no. 1. The bibliography is prepared
from *Medlars* tapes and is quite complete. The biblio--
graphy is divided into two parts: (1) Selected Subject
Headings -- includes references from Accident Prevention
to Zoonoses; and (2) Diseases, Organisms, and Vaccines.
HE20.3617:Vol./no.

766.   U.S. Public Health Service. National Institutes of Health.
National Library of Medicine. *Monthly Bibliography of
Medical Reviews.* V. 1--. 1968--. $8.15 a year*, $2.05
additional foreign mailing.
This bibliography is designed to provide quick reference to
the latest review in the periodical literature in the bio--
medical fields. Included are articles which are well--
documented surveys of recent biomedical literature. Entries
are given under specific subject headings and under authors'
names.

HE20.3610:Vol./no.

767. U.S. Public Health Service. National Institutes of Health.
National Library of Medicine. *Prostaglandins in Abortion
and Reproductive Physiology, January 1969--December 1972;*
prepared by Geraldine D. Nowak. 1973. [1] + 16pp.***
(NLM Library Search Series, no. 73--1).
Produced by *Medlars,* this bibliography has 226 citations
which are arranged alphabetically by author.
HE20.3614/2:73

768. U.S. Public Health Service. National Institutes of Health.
National Library of Medicine. *Selected References on
Environmental Quality as It Relates to Health.* V. 1--.
1971--. Monthly. $10.50 a year*, $3.55 additional foreign
mailing.
Cited are periodical articles which pertain to the effects
of environmental pollution on human health. Annual
cumulations supersede the monthly issues.
HE20.3616:Vol./no.

769. U.S. Veteran's Administration. *Literature Relating to Neuro--
surgery and Neurologic Sciences;* compiled by John L. Fox.
Rev. 1969. i + 30pp. $.35*.
The bibliography is from 1945--68 with a few earlier classics
in this field.
VA1.20/3:10--4/2

770. U.S. Veteran's Administration. *Notes on Information
Sources in Medical Research;* by Erhard Sanders. 1968.
ii + 17pp.*** (VA Monograph, no. 10--4).
Not strictly a bibliography, computerized and personal
services such as libraries, information centers, and
research centers are discussed in addition to the abstracting
and indexing service.
VA1.48:10--4

771. U.S. Veteran's Administration. *Selected Reading in Techniques
of Sterotaxic Neurosurgery, Bibliography Through 1968;*
compiled by John L. Fox. 1969. ii + 37pp. $.45*
(Bibliography, no. 10--3).
Contained are 714 references to sterotaxic brain surgery
including references to percutaneous cordotomy.
VA1.20/3:10--3

772. U.S. Veteran's Administration. *Spinal Cord Injury, Selected*

Bibliography, Supplement, 1966--70; compiled by Muriel McKenna and Irene Jacobs. 1972. iii + 100pp.*** (Information Bulletin, no. 11--27).
Over 1600 entries comprise this bibliography which is arranged by broad subject categories such as: Neurological Aspects; Internal Medicine; Orthopedic Aspects; Prosthetic Appliances; Pathological. Not indexed.
VA1.22:11--27

Mental Retardation

773.   U.S. Children's Bureau. *Selected Reading Suggestions for Parents of Mentally Retarded Children;* compiled and edited by Eleanor Ernst Timberg in collaboration with Kathryn Arning Gorham. 1968. 29pp.*** L.C. Card HEW 68--17.
Included are the "more easily available and recent books and pamphlets which cover the areas of greatest interest to parents, as well as books and pamphlets which will be found in local libraries." Subject arrangement. Author index.
FS17.121:M52

774.   U.S. Children's Bureau. *Selected Reading Suggestions for Parents of Mentally Retarded Children;* compiled and annotated by Kathryn A. Gorham, Eleanor Ernst Timberg, and Coralie B. Moore. 1970. [3] + 58pp. $.60* L.C. Card 78--608378.
HE21.113:M52/970

775.   U.S. Department of Health, Education, and Welfare. *Mental Retardation Publications of the Department of Health, Education, and Welfare.* Annual.*** L.C. Card HEW 67--35.
Annotated references are arranged under broad subject headings. Subject, Author, Title, and Agency Indexes facilitate the use of this bibliography.
HE1.18:M52/yr.

776.   U.S. Public Health Service. Health Services and Mental Health Administration. Maternal and Child Health Service. *Bibliography on Speech, Hearing, and Language in Relation to Mental Retardation, 1900--1968;* by Maryann Peins. 1970. vii + 156pp.*** L.C. Card 71--606106.
This compilation of references on communication and the mentally retarded is divided into the following categories:

Speech and Language Behavior; Assessment of Speech and Language of the Mentally Retarded; Hearing -- Assessment, Hearing Problems, Rehabilitation and Related Facets; Habilitation Procedures -- Speech, Language, and Oral Communication; Research -- Needs and Trends; Books, Chapters and Research Projects; and Dissertations, Theses, and Unpublished Materials. Author index.
HE20.2759:Sp3/900--68

777.   U.S. Public Health Service. National Institutes of Health. National Institute of Neurological Disease and Stroke. *The Collaborative Study on Cerebral Palsy, Mental Retardation, and Other Neurological and Sensory Disorders of Infancy and Childhood. No. 1, June 1963–1968.* 1968. 1 + v + 27pp.***.,
(See below for annotation).
HE20.3513:C33/no.1

778.   U.S. Public Health Service. National Institutes of Health. National Institute of Neurological Disease and Stroke. *The Collaborative Study on Cerebral Palsy, Mental Retardation, and Other Neurological and Sensory Disorders of Infancy and Childhood. No. 2–.* 1969--. Annual.***.
This is an annual bibliography which covers all manuscripts based on approved systematic sampling methods that were presented at national and international professional conventions or were published in the professional literature.
HE20.3513:C33/no.

779.   U.S. Social and Rehabilitation Service. Rehabilitation Services Administration. *Mental Retardation Abstracts.* V. 1--9. 1964--1972. Quarterly. L.C. Card 66--60248.
Intended as a reference aid for researchers, entries are primarily clinical and arranged by subject. Author and subject indices.
HE17.113:Vol./no.

Psychology and Mental Health

780.   U.S. Children's Bureau. *Research Relating to Emotionally Disturbed Children.* 1968. vi + 182pp.***.
This is a compilation of 842 research reports which appeared in *Research Relating to Children* from 1956 to

171

1968. Subject arrangement.
FS17.212:Em6

781.   U.S. Department of the Air Force. *Response Factors and Selective Attention in Learning from Instructional Materials, Annotated Bibliography*; by Curtis L. Taylor. 1972. iii + 31 + [2]pp.*** (AFHRL--TR 72--63).
D301.45/27:72--63

782.   U.S. Department of the Navy. *Annotated Bibliography of Human Factors Laboratory Reports (1945--68)*; by Albert K. Kurtz and Mary C. Smith. 1969. vi + 369pp.** (Naval Training Device Center, Orlando, Fla.) (Technical Report NAVTRADEVDEN Series, IH--158).
D210.14:IH--158

783.   U.S. Joint Publications Research Service. *Bibliography on Parapsychology (Psychoenergetics) and Related Subjects, USSR.* 1972. a--d + 101pp. NTIS.
A translation from Russian scientific literature.
Y3.J66:13/55557

784.   U.S. Public Health Service. *Annotated Bibliography on Inservice Training for Allied Professionals and Nonprofessionals in Community Mental Health.* 1969. v + 49pp. $.55*
L.C. Card 78--601673.
Annotated references to materials published between 1960 and 1967 deal with aspects of training physicians, nurses, school psychologists, teachers and special educators, welfare workers, police, professional aides, volunteers, etc. for community mental health work. Arrangement is by type of personnel. Subject index.
FS2.24:M52

785.   U.S. Public Health Service. *Annotated Bibliography on In--service Training for Key Professionals in Community Mental Health.* 1969. v + 52pp. $.60* L.C. Card 70--601774.
"This bibliography pertains to inservice training of key professional personnel – psychiatrists, clinical psychologists, psychiatric social workers, and psychiatric nurses – for community mental health programs." It is indexed by types of personnel and by specific training concepts.
FS2.24:M52/3

786.   U.S. Public Health Service. *Annotated Bibliography on In–*

service Training in Mental Health for Staff in Residential Institutions. [1969.] v + 24pp. $.35* L.C. Card 73–601775. Contained are annotated references on training in mental health hospitals, institutions for the mentally retarded, child care residential institutions, and nursing homes. Entries are according to type of personnel – professional, child care workers, aides, attendants, technicians, volunteers -- and by type of training. Subject index.
FS2.24:M52/2

787. U.S. Public Health Service. *Bibliography on Psychotomimetics, 1943--66.* 1968. [3] + 52pp. $2.75*.
FS2.22/13:P95

788. U.S. Public Health Service. *Bibliography on Suicide and Suicide Prevention, 1897–1957, 1958--1967;* by Norman L. Farberow. 1969. iii + 2 + 203pp. $1.75*.
(Revised and updated by no. 803).
FS2.22/13:Su3

789. U.S. Public Health Service. *Comprehensive Community Mental Health Center, Annotated Bibliography;* prepared by Carole Doughton Vacher. 6th ed. [1969]. v + 41pp. $.30*.
This bibliography was prepared for the use of psychiatrists, psychologists, social workers, nurses, and other professionals involved in community mental health centers. Almost 150 selections from the mental–health--related journals from 1957 to 1968 have been briefly annotated and listed by such subject areas as: Consultation and Education; Inpatient; Outpatient; Emergency Services; Diagnosis; Rehabilitation; Aftercare; and Program Evaluation. Author index.
FS2.22/13:M52/8

790. U.S. Public Health Service. *Consultation in Mental Health and Related Fields, Reference Guide;* by; Fortune V. Mannino. 1969. iv + [1] + 105pp. $.50* L.C. Card 70--605768.
Six hundred and forty--six single entries, some of which are listed two or more times, make up this unique biblio--graphy on mental health consultation. At the time it was written, it was to the best of the author's knowledge "the only bibliography on consultation which attempts to classify the entries into categories." Those categories are: (1) Consultation by Fields of Practice; (2) Use of Consul--

tation in Various Settings; (3) Forms of Consultation; (4) Professional Roles in Consultation; (5) The Process of Consultation; (6) Planning Consultation Programs; (7) Consultation Training and Education; (8) Research, Evaluations, Surveys and Reviews. Included is a list of journals consulted and a list of films related to consultation practice. Author index.
FS2.22/13:M52/9

791.   U.S. Public Health Service. *Psychological and Social Aspects of Human Tissue Transplantation, Annotated Bibliography;* by Jacquelyn H. Hall and David O. Swenson. 1968. [Published 1969]. v + 57pp.*.
See no. 792 for notation.
FS2.22/13:T52

792.   U.S. Public Health Service. *Psychological and Social Aspects of Human Tissue Transplantation, Annotated Bibliography, Supplement 1.* 1969. vii + 40pp. $.35*.
Collectively there are nearly 300 annotated items dealing with the psychological, psychiatric, ethical, moral, social, and legal matters in the use of human tissue and in the artificial maintenance of life. This does not include technical reports.
FS2.22/13:T52/2

793.   U.S. Public Health Service. *Research in Individual Psycho-therapy, Bibliography;* prepared by Hans H. Strupp and Allen E. Bergin. 1969. viii + 167pp. $1.50* L.C. Card 70--604225.
Contained are nearly 3,000 entries arranged by author and indexed by 12 content areas, such as Client, Outcome, Therapist, and Prognosis. While there is a fairly complete coverage of the literature, the absence of a good subject index diminishes the usefulness of this bibliography.
FS2.22/12:P95/2

794.   U.S. Public Health Service. *Selected Sources of Inexpensive Mental Health Materials; a Directory for Mental Health Educators.* 1968. xiv + 70pp. $.40* L.C. Card 76--603167.
Though perhaps not a bibliography in the true sense of the word, this annotated list of publishers of educational materials in mental health will assist the mental health educator in gathering inexpensive, and frequently free, information. In addition to listing groups and agencies which publish this type of material, sample titles are also provided.

(No trade or textbook publishers are included.)
FS2.22/13:M52/7

795. U.S. Public Health Service. *Social Aspects of Alienation, Annotated Bibliography;* by Mary H. Lystad. 1969. [7] + 92pp. $1.00* L.C. Card 74--604666.
Covered by the 225 lengthy annotations are various social groups alienated from society -- the worker, student, voter, youth, aged, black, and poor -- and alienation as it relates to social structure, deviant social behavior, culture change, and psychological processes. Author index.
FS2.22/13:A14

796. U.S. Public Health Service. *Volunteer Services in Mental Health, Annotated Bibliography 1955--1959;* prepared by Francine Sobey. 1969. vii + 96pp. $1.00* L.C. Card 75--604082.
Articles, books, workshop and conference proceedings, and reports dealing with volunteer services development in the U.S. are abstracted. Abstracts are arranged by author in the following areas: Philosophy and History of Volunteer Services; Planning and Administration; Institutional Settings; Community Settings; Specialized Services in Multiple Settings. Each of these areas is then further sub--divided and arranged alphabetically by author. Following are annotated lists of research and statistical studies, bibliographies, and directories. Author index.
FS2.22/13:V88

797. U.S. Public Health Service. Health Services and Mental Health Administration. *Consultation Research in Mental Health and Related Fields, a Critical Review of the Lit--erature;* by Fortune V. Mannino and Milton F. Shore. 1971. [v] + [1] + 55pp. $.35* (Public Health Monograph, no. 79). L.C. Card 70--610128.
Seventy--five articles are cited and used in this critical analysis of consultation in mental health.
HE20.2018:79

798. U.S. Public Health Service. Health Services and Mental Health Administration. *An Annotated Bibliography on Mental Health in the Schools, 1970--1973.* 1973. 29pp. $.50* S/N 1724--00322.
"This selected bibliography provides a guide to the professional literature relevant to school mental health

published between 1970 and 1973. The annotations
which accompany each reference are intended to be
factual summaries of the authors methodology and results,
and not evaluative or critical. The list is arranged by subject,
with selected cross references."
HE20.2417:Sch6/970–73

799. U.S. Public Health Service. Health Services and Mental
Health Administration. National Institute of Mental Health.
*Behavior Modification in Child and School Mental Health,
an Annotated Bibliography on Applications with Parents
and Teachers;* by Daniel G. Brown. [1971, reprinted 1972].
viii + 41pp. $.30* S/N 1724--0159.
Over 115 impressive annotations discuss behavioral problems
in school age children. Entries are listed according to
whether they apply primarily to parents, teachers, or a
combination of the two. A good subject index pinpoints
specific behavioral problems such as sibling conflicts, sex
problems, toilet training, eating problems, etc.
HE20.2417:C43

800. U.S. Public Health Service. Health Services and Mental
Health Administration. National Institute of Mental Health.
*Bibliography, Epidemiology of Mental Disorders, 1966--
1968.* 1970. x + 114pp. $1.25* L.C. Card 70--608452.
This bibliography containing 1428 entries is designed for
the specialist in the field. Author, subject, and journal
indexes facilitate its use.
HE20.2417:Ep4

801. U.S. Public Health Service. Health Services and Mental
Health Administration. National Institute of Mental Health.
*Bibliography, Epidemiology of Mental Disorders, 1969–
1970;* compiled by Virginia Hannon. 1973. iii + [2] + 132pp.
$2.10*.
This is a continuation of the above. The more than 1, 600
updated references should help mental health
epidemiologists identify and utilize research related to
their own interests. Subject and author indices.
HE20.2417:Ep4/969--70

802. U.S. Public Health Service. Health Services and Mental
Health Administration. National Institute of Mental Health.
*Bibliography on Human Intelligence, National Clearinghouse
for Mental Health Information, Extensive Bibliography;* by

Logan Wright. 1969. vii + 222pp. $2.50* L.C. Card 79--606037.

Using *Psychological Abstracts* as the primary search source, the author has amassed a total of 6,736 entries to the literature on human intelligence prior to 1966. A lengthy topical outline is intended to provide the researcher with an overview of the publications listed. A topical index rapidly directs researchers with specific topics to particular publications.

HE20.2417:H88

803. U.S. Public Health Service. Health Services and Mental Health Administration. National Institute of Mental Health. *Bibliography on Suicide and Suicide Prevention 1897–1957, 1958--1970;* by Norman L. Farberow [and others]. 1972. [285]pp. $2.00* S/N 1740--0340. L.C. Card 72--602910.

This updates a previous work by the same title (no. 788). Included are 4742 entries on suicide and suicide prevention. Over 2500 of these are from the literature since 1959. This work attempts to include all references on the subject since 1897.

HE20.2417:Su3

804. U.S. Public Health Service. Health Services and Mental Health Administration. National Institute of Mental Health. *Computer Applications in Psychotherapy, Bibliography and Abstracts;* compiled by Kent Taylor. 1970. vii + 92pp. $1.00* L.C. Card 78--607145.

The 176 annotated entries are arranged by six sections according to content. Two of these sections deal with sources and methods of data collection and computer use in interpreting the data. The other sections deal with "more specific types of computer applications in psycho--therapy." Indexed by subject and author.

HE20.2417:C73

805. U.S. Public Health Service. Health Services and Mental Health Administration. National Institute of Mental Health. *Coping and Adaptation, a Behavioral Sciences Bibliography.* 1970. vii + 231pp. $1.75* L.C. Card 75--608850.

This selective bibliography of 425 abstracts represents the first systematic attempt to collect in a single volume contemporary citations to the biological, sociological, and psychological apsects of coping and adapting under stress. An extensive keyword index helps the researcher locate

specific information.
HE20.2417:C79

806. U.S. Public Health Service. Health Services and Mental
Health Administration. National Institute of Mental Health.
*Early Childhood Psychosis: Infantile Autism, Childhood
Schizophrenia and Related Disorders, Annotated Bibliography
1964--69;* prepared by Carolyn Q. Bryson and Joseph N.
Hingten, Clinical Research Center for Early Childhood
Schizophrenia, Indina Univeristy Medical Center, Indianapolis.
1971. vii + 127pp.*** L.C. Card 75--614340.
The 426 entries are arranged by specific subject and are
indexed by author.
HE20.2417:P95/964--69

807. U.S. Public Health Service. Health Services and Mental
Health Administration. National Institute of Mental Health.
Mental Health and Social Change, Annotated Bibliography;
George V. Coelho, ed. 1972. ix + 458pp. $3.00*
S/N 1724--0249.
Seven hundred and thirty informative abstracts are arranged
in the following sections: Biologically--oriented Approaches;
Behavioral and Social Science Approaches; Critical
Episodes; Group Behavioral Disorders; and New Direction
in Human Services. A comprehensive subject index, as
well as an author index, facilitates the use of this impressive
bibliography.
HE20.2417:M52

808. U.S. Public Health Service. Health Services and Mental
Health Administration. National Institute of Mental Health.
*Multi--Ethnic Literature in High School, a Mental Health
Tool* [with Bibliographies] ; by Jean H. Lightfoot. 1973.
vii + 43pp. $.75* S/N 1724--00279.
Discussion is followed by an annotated bibliography of
ethnic literature. Arrangement is by subject, and grade
level is indicated.
HE20.2402:M91

809. U.S. Public Health Service. Health Services and Mental
Health Administration. National Institute of Mental Health.
*Planning for Creative Change in Mental Health Services,
Distillation of Principles on Research Utilization, v. 1 Biblio-
graphy with Annotations.* 1972. vi + 266pp. $2.00*
S/N 1724--0145. L.C. Card 72--600949.

810.   U.S. Public Health Service. Health Services and Mental
       Health Administration. National Institute of Mental Health.
       *Planning for Creative Change in Mental Health Services,
       Distillation of Principles on Research Utilization, v. 2.*
       1972. vi + 252pp. $2.00* S/N 1724–0146.
       Concentrating primarily on the periodical literature, this
       bibliography abstracts mental health literature concerned
       with creative changes in mental health programs. Not
       indexed.
       HE20.2408:Se6/Vol.2

811.   U.S. Public Health Service. Health Services and Mental
       Health Administration. National Institute of Mental Health.
       *Planning for Creative Change in Mental Health Services, Use
       of Program Evaluation.* 1971. v + 110pp. $1.00* S/N 1724–
       0150. L.C. Card 72–600949.
       This bibliography of evaluation research is divided into
       three sections: Conceptual and Methodological Issues;
       Illustrations of Evaluation Studies; and References on
       Design, Measurement, Sampling, and Analysis. Not indexed.
       HE20.2408:Se6/3

812.   U.S. Public Health Service. Health Services and Mental
       Health Administration. National Institute of Mental Health.
       *Television and Social Behavior, Annotated Bibliography of
       Research Focusing on Television's Impact on Children;*
       edited by Charles K. Atkin, John P. Murray, and Oguz B.
       Nayman. 1971. ix + 150pp.*** L.C. Card 70–612410
       The 550 citations, 300 of which are annotated, stress
       research on the impact of television and other visual media
       on the development and behavior of children. Arrangement
       is alphabetical by author within three sections: Television
       Content and Programming; Audience Viewing Patterns
       and General Effects of Television; and The Impact of
       Television and Other Visual Media on Children and Youth.
       Author Index.
       This bibliography compliments a multi–volume work
       entitled *Television and Social Behavior.*
       HE20.2417:T23

813.   U.S. Veterans Administration. *Cooperative Studies in
       Psychiatry, Annotated Bibliography Summarizing Fifteen
       Years of Cooperative Research in Psychiatry, 1956–70.*

1970. [1] + ix + 64pp.*** (IB Series, no. 11-3).
One hundred and fifty lengthy annotations are arranged
by subject. Not indexed.
VA1.22:11–3

Toxicology

814. U.S. Environmental Protection Agency. Air Programs
Office. *Biological Aspects of Lead, Annotated Bibliography,
Literature from 1950--64;* by Irene P. Campbell and Estelle
G. Mergard. 1972. 2Pts. 935pp. $6.75* (set) (AP--104).
L.C. Card 72--602499.
The 4,000 plus annotated entries in this bibliography
represent an extensive search of the literature from 1950--
1964. (This period was chosen because of the developing
advancements and refinements in biochemical and
cytochemical techniques, hence producing more valid
research data.) Indexed by author and subject.
EP4.9:104/Pt.1,2

815. U.S. Public Health Service. Health Services and Mental
Health Administration. Maternal and Child Health Service.
Selected Bibliography on Lead Poisoning in Children;
compiled by Jane S. Lin–Fu. 1971. [5] + 30pp. $.25*
S/N 1730--0014. L.C. Card 74--614983.
"Most papers listed are from pediatric literature on topics
which have been investigated more thoroughly in relation
to adults than to children (such as metabolism, indices of
exposure, and chronic renal complications)." The papers
are grouped under several general headings and are cross--
referenced.
HE20.2759:L46

816. U.S. Public Health Service. National Institutes of Health.
National Library of Medicine. *Drug Interactions, an
Annotated Bibliography with Selected Excerpts, 1967--1970.*
V. 1. 1972. 1821pp. $14.25* S/N 1752–0139.
This major bibliographic effort is designed to provide
physicians and other health professionals with quick access
to reports from the world's published scientific literature
on drug--drug and drug–chemical interactions. In addition
to bibliographic citations, each interaction is briefly
described. This impressive work must be considered a m
major work in the field.
HE20.3614:D84/967--70/vol.1

817.   U.S. Public Health Service. National Institutes of Health.
       National Library of Medicine. *Toxicity Bibliography; a
       Bibliography Covering Reports on Toxicity Studies, Adverse
       Drug Reactions, and Poisoning in Man and Animals.* V. 1–.
       1968–. Quarterly. $25.00 a year*, $6.25 additional foreign
       mailing.
       Approximately 2,300 biomedical journals which are
       indexed on *Medlars* tapes are searched periodically for this
       quarterly selective listing on toxicity. Entries are listed
       under two broad sections: (1) Drugs and Chemicals; and
       (2) Adverse Reactions to Drugs and Chemicals. Section 1
       is indexed by subject and author. Section 2 is not indexed
       but is arranged by subject.
       HE20.3613:Vol./no.

POLITICAL SCIENCE

Domestic

818.   U.S. Bureau of the Budget. *Program Analysis Techniques,
       Selected Bibliography, Revised.* Supplement 2. 1969.
       [3] + 27pp.**.
       This updates the original bibliography (1966). Program
       analysis studies cover (1) community development, (2)
       foreign aid, (3) Health, Education, and Welfare, (4) national
       defense, (5) research and development, (6) resource
       development, (7) transportation, and (8) state and local
       government. Not indexed.
       PrEx2.14:P94/966/supp.2

819.   U.S. Civil Service Commission. *Fifty United States Civil
       Service Commissioners, Biographical Sketch, Biographical
       Sources, Writings.* 1971. [4] + 275pp. Free*** L.C. Card
       78–614566.
       This comprehensive work gives biographical sketches,
       bibliographical references to biographical sources, and a
       list of writings of each of the U.S. Civil Service
       Commissioners. Commissioners are listed chronologically
       by date of tenure. Additionally there are other sources
       of information on Civil Service Commissioners, a biblio–
       graphy of standard reference sources, and a guide to
       organizations and collections listed. Name index.
       CS1.61:C73

820.   U.S. Civil Service Commission. *Federal Civil Service, History,*

Organization, and Activities. 1971. [2] + 55pp. $.60*
S/N 0600--0619. (Personnel Bibliography Series, no. 43).
L.C. Card 72--600592.
  This title was originally published in 1962 and updated in
  1968. This second updating covers material received in
  the Civil Service Library from 1969--1970. Contained are
  abstracts of articles and reports concerning the Federal
  Civil Service, its employees and their attitudes toward
  Federal employment, restriction on employees, and
  contractor--supplied personnel. Subject arrangement. Not
  indexed.
  CS1.61/3:43

820a. U.S. Commission on Civil Rights. *Catalog of Publications.*
       1970. 22pp. Free***.
       CR1.9:970

821.   U.S. Commission on Government Procurement. *Report
       of the Commission on Government Procurement, Index--
       Bibliography--Acronyms.* [1972.] 1973. xii + 144pp.
       $2.10* S/N 5255--00005.
         Seventy--six pages of bibliography accompany the four
         volume *Report.*
       Y3.G74/4:1/972/ind.

822.   U.S. Congress, House. *Resolved: That More Stringent Control
       Should be Imposed Upon Government Agencies Gathering
       Information About United States Citizens: a Collection of
       Excerpts and Bibliography Relating to the Intercollegiate
       Debate Topic, 1971--1972;* compiled by the Congressional
       Research Service, Library of Congress. 1971. v + 265pp.
       $1.00* S/N 5271--0258 (H. Doc. 92--167).

823.   U.S. Congress, Senate. *How Can the Administration of
       Justice Be Improved in the United States? A Collection of
       Excerpts and Bibliography Relating to the High School Debate
       Topic, 1971--72;* compiled by the Congressional Research
       Service, Library of Congress. 1971. v + 122pp. $.55*
       S/N 5271--0240 (S. Doc. 92--10).
         Bibliography and excerpts are divided into three parts
         relating to the following three proposed topics: (1)
         Resolved, That the jury system in the United States should
         by significantly changed; (2) Resolved, That a national
         system of arbitration boards should be established for
         civil cases; (3) Resolved, That mass media coverage of

felony offenses subsequent to arrest should be limited by law to the court record until a verdict is rendered. A selected bibliography follows. Not indexed.

824. U.S. Congress. Senate. *Toward a National Growth Policy: Federal and State Development in 1972;* prepared by the Congressional Research Service, Library of Congress. 1973. vii + 249pp. $1.85* S/N 5271–00369 (S. Doc. 93--19).
While the first portion of this book contains a summary and analysis of Federal legislative and executive actions, innovative Senate legislation, and significant court decisions in 1972 that effect the elements of a national growth policy as defined in the Housing and Urban Development Act of 1970, the greater portion is a bibliography. Contained are "books, government documents, and periodical articles related to the components of national growth policy issued in 1972."
Bibliography follows each of the following chapters: (1) Introduction; (2) Effective Use of Resources on an Areawide Basis; (3) Rural Development and Economic Growth; (4) Renewing Old Communities and Creating New Communities; (5) Good Housing for All Americans; (6) Improving the Environment; and (7) Strengthening the Capacity of Government. Each of these sections is further subdivided as to Federal Policy; State and Local Policies; Bibliographies and Directories. Not indexed.

825. U.S. Congress. Senate. *What Should be the Role of the Federal Government in Extending Public Assistance to All Americans Living in Poverty: a Collection of Excerpts and Bibliography Relating to the High School Debate Topic, 1973--74;* compiled by the Congressional Research Service, Library of Congress. 1973. vii + 247pp. $1.50* S/N 5271–00344 (S. Doc. 93–12).
Bibliography and excerpts are divided into three parts relating to the following proposed topics: (1) Resolved, That the Federal Government should guarantee a minimum annual income for each family unit; (2) Resolved, That the Federal Government should provide a program for the employment of all employable U.S. citizens living in poverty; (3) Resolved, That the Federal Government should enact a program of comprehensive welfare for U.S. citizens living in poverty. A section on how to obtain additional information is provided. Not indexed.

826. U.S. Congress. Joint Economic Committee. *Committee Publications and Policies Governing Their Distribution, 87th--92d Congresses, 1961--1971.* 1971. 27pp. Free***
L.C. Card 78--613786.
Publications are arranged chronologically by Congress.
Availability notation is made for each publication.
Y4.Ec7:P96/961--71

827. U.S. Congress. Senate. Government Operations Committee. *Bibliography of Federal Grants--in--Aid to State and Local Governments, 1964--69.* 1970. vii + 456pp. $1.75*
L.C. Card 76--610490.
Several thousand entries, including books, reports, mono--graphs, hearings, articles, speeches, and films, cover this six year period and exemplify the magnitude of the Federal grant--in--aid programs. Subject arrangement. Not indexed.
Y4.G74/6:G76/6

828. U.S. Department of Agriculture. *Selected Bibliography on Special Districts and Authorities in the United States, Annotated;* by Benjamin Novak. 1968. [2] + 57pp. $.40*
(Miscellaneous Publication, no. 1087).
"The subject of this bibliography is special districts and authorities created under State enabling legislation for the purpose of constructing or operating improvements or for providing services to the inhabitants of an area."
Two hundred and fifty publications are listed according to type -- articles, books, Government publications -- and are indexed by subject, state, and author.
A1.38:1087

829. U.S. Department of Agriculture. *State Water--Rights Laws and Related Subjects, a Supplemental Bibliography 1959--to mid--1967;* compiled by Beatrice H. Holmes, George C. Simons, and Harold H. Ellis. 1972. 268pp. $1.00*
(Miscellaneous Publication, no. 1249).
Citations to legal and general articles dealing with the states water--rights laws are facilitated by subject and geographic indices.
A1.38:1249

830. U.S. Department of the Air Force. Air Force Academy. *The States and Urban Crisis.* 1969. [5] + 46pp.*** (Special Bibliography, no. 43). L.C. Card 73--605758.
A listing of books, periodicals, and documents covers the

following areas: (1) The City; (2) The Problems of the City; (3) The Politics of the City; (4) The Future of the City; (5) Comparative Urbanology. Not indexed. D305.12:43

831. U.S. Department of the Interior. Library. *Public Lands Bibliography, Supplement II;* compiled by the Reference Section. 1968. 37pp.*** (Library List, no. 7).
This supplements the Bureau of Land Management's *Public Lands Bibliography* (1962) and contains a selected list of publications from 1965 through October 1967. "Periodical articles, monographs and theses are arranged in one alphabet. This section is followed by a list of the principal laws enacted during the period 1964–1967, together with the Hearings, House and Senate Reports, and Committee Prints." Not indexed.
I22.9/2:7

832. U.S. Government Printing Office. *Immigration, Naturalization, and Citizenship.* Free* (Price List, no. 67).
Listed are free and for sale publications on immigration, naturalization, and citizenship. This list is revised frequently and all publications listed are supposedly available.
GP3.9:67

833. U.S. Government Printing Office. *Laws, Rules, and Regulations.* Free* (Price List, no. 10).
(Notation is the same as above).
GP3.9:10

834. U.S. Government Printing Office. *Political Science. Government, Crime, District of Columbia.* Free* (Price List, no. 54).
(Notation is the same as above).
GP3.9:54

835. U.S. Library of Congress. Serials Division. *Popular Names of U.S. Government Reports: a Catalog,* Revised and Enlarged; compiled by Bernard A. Bernier, Jr. and Charlotte M. David. 1970. v + 43pp. $.55* L.C. Card 77–608261.
Contained are 753 U.S. Government reports, some of them as early as 1821, arranged alphabetically by the popular report name. The entries are in the form of the L.C.

printed catalog cards.
LC6.2:G74/970

836.   U.S. National Archives and Records Service. *Hearings in the Records of the U.S. Senate and Joint Committees of Congress.* 1972. Free*** (Special List, no. 32). L.C. Card 72–600240.
Arranged by committee. Not indexed.
GS4.7:32

837.   U.S. Social and Rehabilitation Service. *Legal Bibliography for Juvenile and Family Courts, Supplement 2, 1968;* by William H. Sheridan, Alice B. Breer. 1969. 3 + 38pp. $.50*
L.C. Card HEW 66–96.
FS14.112:L52/supp.2

838.   U.S. Social and Rehabilitation Service. *Legal Bibliography for Juvenile and Family Courts, Supplement 3, 1969.* 1970. iii + 36pp. $.45*.
(See no. 839 for notation).
HE17.17:L52/supp.3

839.   U.S. Social and Rehabilitation Service. Youth Development and Delinquency Prevention Administration. *Legal Bibliography for Juvenile and Family Courts, Supplement;* by William H. Sheridan, Alice B. Freer and Eileen A. Hancock. 1973. iv + 18pp. $.40* S/N 1766–0018.
"This publication is a supplement to the *Legal Bibliography for Juvenile and Family Courts.* It is offered as a service to judges, probation officers, law enforcement personnel, counsel, and other professionals in the fields of delinquency, the law, and service for youth." Publications are listed under 23subject categories. Not indexed.
HE17.809:C83/Supp.

Foreign Affairs

840.   U.S. Congress. House. *Resolved That Executive Control of United States Foreign Policy Should Be Significantly Curtailed: a Collection of Excerpts and Bibliography Relating to the National Collegiate Debate Topic, 1968–69.* 1968. v + 266pp. $1.00* (H. Doc. 90–298).

841.   U.S. Congress. Senate. Judiciary Committee. *World Comm–unism, 1964–69, Selected Bibliography, v. 2;* by Arshag O.

Sarkissian and Joseph G. Whelan. 1971. xi + 420 + xxxiipp.***
L.C. Card 71–619015.
This bibliography of nearly 6,000 entries resumes where
the previous bibliography on world communism (Sen. Doc.
88--69 pt. 1, 2) ended. Indexed by name and subject.
Y4.J89/2:C73/59/v.2

842.   U.S. Congress. Senate. Public Works Committee. *Oil
Pollution of the Marine Environment, Legal Bibliography;*
prepared by Carl Q. Christol, (Professor of International Law
and Political Science, USC). 1971. ix + 93pp.**
L.C. Card 77--610749.
This bibliography of articles, books, and documents is
international in scope. Not indexed.
Y4.P96/10:92–1

843.   U.S. Department of the Air Force. Air Force Academy.
The United States and the United Nations. 1972. 38pp.***
(Special Bibliography Series, no. 47).
This references books and articles on the U.N., its main
organs, and the allied agencies. One section specifically
treats the U.S. and its relationship with the U.N. Not
indexed.
D305.12:47

844.   U.S. Department of the Air Force. Air University Library.
The Future: Selected Unclassified References. Pts. 1, 2.
1972. 68pp.*** (Special Bibliography, no. 185).
All parts of the world and selected countries are treated
individually in each part of this bibliography. Part I,
"International Scene," contains selected unclassified
references on the future of the world in general and pays
particular attention to economics, foreign policy, and
politics of various regions and countries. Part II,
"Welfare and Strategy -- Science and Technology,"
contains selected unclassified references on military aspects,
space, and technology of the future in different parts
of the world.
D301.26/11:185/rev.

845.   U.S. Department of the Army. *Nuclear Weapons and NATO,
Analytical Survey of the Literature.* 1970. vii + 450 + [3] pp.
il. 19maps. $7.50* (DA Pamphlet 50–1). L.C. Card 79--
607373.
Over 900 abstracts update a similar survey published in

1965. Contained along with the abstracts are background notes and maps of each NATO member state together with pertinent treaties, etc. A bibliographic supplement covers Communist China's nuclear potential to further emphasize the importance of Western solidarity. D101.22:50--1

846. U.S. Department of State. *Selected Publications and Audio--Visual Materials List.* Quarterly.***. S1.20/2:date

847. U.S. Department of State. External Research Division. *Inter--national Affairs.* 1968. [4] + 104pp.*** (External Research List, no. 7.27).
Contained are listings of research in progress or completed, but not published as of December 1967, on international affairs. Arrangement is by specific area of research. The preface suggests that the research listed will be available on request once the reports have been published. Not indexed. (This annual publication was discontinued with this issue.)
S1.101:7.27

848. U.S. Government Printing Office. *Foreign Relations of the United States.* Free* (Price List, no. 65).
Listed are free and for sale publications on U.S. foreign relations. This list is revised frequently, prices are kept current, and all publications listed are supposedly available.
GP3.9:65

849. U.S. Library of Congress. General Reference and Biblio--graphy Division. *Arms Control and Disarmament.* V. 1--. V. 9, no. 2. 1964--1973. L.C. Card 65--47970.
This was a quarterly bibliography with abstracts and annotations. Cumulative index in each fall quarter issue.
LC2.10:Vol./no.

International Area Studies

Africa

850. U.S. Department of the Air Force. Air University Library. *Africa, Selected References.* Annual Supplements. (Special Bibliography, no. 159 and supplements).

Revised annually with only current literature citations, this bibliography is an excellent guide to recent information on virtually every country in Africa. Specific areas covered are: Communist Penetration; Economics; Military Factors; Politics; Psycho--Social Factors, and Regional Differences. Not indexed.
D301.26/11:159/supp.

851. U.S. Department of State. External Research Division. *Africa.* 1968. ii + 63pp.*** (External Research List, no. 5.27). Contained are listings of research in progress or completed, but not published as of December 1967, on Africa during 1967. The prepace suggests that the research listed will be available on request once the reports have been published. Arrangement is by subject in dealing with Africa in general. Later, each country is treated individually. Not indexed. (This annual publication was discontinued with this issue.)
S1.101:5.27

852. U.S. Library of Congress. General Reference and Bibliography Division. *Botswana, Lesotho, and Swaziland: a Guide to Official Publications, 1868–1968;* compiled by Mildred Grimes Balima. 1971. xvi + 84pp. $1.00* L.C. Card 74--171027.
This guide to the official published records of Botswana (Bechuanaland), Lesotho (Basutoland), and Swaziland from 1868--1968 also includes a number of citations to pertinent British official papers of the period and to documents of the former High Commission of Territories. Publications are listed by country, then chronologically by subject. Indexed by subject and name.
LC2.8:B65/868–968

853. U.S. Library of Congress. General Reference and Bibliography Division. *Ghana: a Guide to the Official Publications, 1872--1968;* compiled by Julian W. Witherell and Sharon B. Lockwood. 1969. xi + 110pp. $1.25* L.C. Card 74--601680.
"This guide to official publications of Ghana lists the published government records from 1872 . . . to 1968. It includes publications of the Gold Coast (1872--1957) and Ghana (1957--1968) and a selection of British Government documents relating specifically to the Gold Coast, Ghana and British Togoland." Authors and subjects

are indexed.
LC2.8:G34/872--968

854.   U.S. Library of Congress. General Reference and Bibliography Division. *Spanish--Speaking Africa, Guide to Official
Publications;* compiled by Susan Knoke Rishworth. 1973.
xii + 66pp. $1.00* L.C. Card 73--10274.
"This guide lists published official records of Spanish--
speaking Africa from the 19th century to the present,
including publications issued by the Spanish Government
about or on behalf of its African territories." Countries
included are Equatorial Guinea, Spanish Sahara, Ifni, and
the Spanish Zone (northern Morocco).
LC2.8:Af8/4

The Americas

855.   U.S. Department of the Air Force. Air Force Academy.
United States in the Caribbean; compiled by Ottie K.
Sutton. 1970. [5] + 34pp.** (Special Bibliography Series,
no. 44).
The books and articles references here pertain not only
to the United States involvement in the Caribbean but
to the countries and people of the island and Central
America. Cuba and the Dominican Republic are treated
separately.
D305.12:44

856.   U.S. Department of the Air Force. Air University Library.
Latin America, Selected References. Annual.***
(Special Bibliography no. 166 and supplements).
Revised annually with only current literature citations,
this bibliography is a superior guide to recent information
on the many aspects of Latin America. Treated specifically
are such topics as Communist Penetration, Conferences
and Alliances, Economics, Education, Politics and
Government, the Military, and Psycho–Social Aspects.
N Not indexed.
D301.26/11:166 and Supp.

857.   U.S. Department of the Army. *Latin America and the
Caribbean, Analytical Survey of the Literature.* 1969.
viii + 319pp. 38 maps. $8.25* (DA Pamphlet 550--7).
L.C. Card 76--603569.
Contained are 900 abstracts and 38 maps dealing not only

with Latin America as a whole but with each country
individually. Each entry is so completely annotated and
seemingly related to those before and after it that the
bibliography reads almost like a documentary. Not indexed.
D101.22:550–7

858.   U.S. Department of State. External Research Office.
       American Republics. 1968. ii + 104pp.*** (External
       Research Series, no. 6.27).
           Contained are listings of research in progress or completed
       as of December 1967, on the American Republics. The
       preface suggests that the research listed will be available
       on request once the reports have been published. Arrange--
       ment is by country and subject of research. Not indexed.
       This annual publication was discontinued with this issue.
       S1.101:6.27

859.   U.S. Department of State. Foreign Service Institute. *Latin
       America, Selected Functional and Country Bibliography; Pt.
       1, Latin American Area.* 1968. [3] + 25pp.***.
       S1.114/3:L34/Pt.1

860.   U.S. Department of State. Foreign Service Institute. *Latin
       America, Selected Functional and Country Bibliography;
       Pt. 2, Countries of Latin America.* 1968. [4] + 46pp.***
           Listed are English language publications about Latin
       America and the individual countries of Latin America.
       Subject arrangement. Not indexed.
       S1.114/3:L34/Pt.2

861.   U.S. Department of State. Foreign Service Institute.
       This Changing World, Reading Guide for the General Sessions.
       1969. [1] + v + 58pp.***.
       S1.114/3:W89

862.   U.S. Library of Congress. *A Revised Guide to the Law and
       Legal Literature of Mexico;* by Helen L. Clagett and David
       M. Valderrana. 1973. xii + 463pp. $6.95* (Latin
       American Series, no. 38). L.C. Card 72–12763.
           This is a complete revision of a 1945 similar guide
       on Mexican law and legal materials. References are listed
       and explained by legal subject groups such as: Constitutional
       Law; Criminal Law; Civil Law; Civil Procedure;
       Commercial Law; Criminal Procedure; Judicial System;
       Aliens; Petroleum; etc. Legal periodicals, dictionaries

and encyclopedias are treated in separate chapters. State codes are covered by an appendix.
LC1.16:38

Asia and the Far East

863. U.S. Department of the Air Force. Air Force Academy.
The United States and Japan; compiled by Ottie K. Sutton.
1972. 5 + 34pp.*** (Special Bibliography Series, no. 45).
L.C. Card 72--601072.
Listed are references to books and articles dealing with the political, economic, social, and cultural relations of Japan and the United States.
D305.12:45

864. U.S. Department of the Air Force. Air University Library.
Asia, Southeastern (Excluding Vietnam), Selected Unclassified References; compiled by Gay Byars. Annual. (Special Bibliography, no. 156 (rev.), supp. no. pt. 1).
This annual supplement covers individually the countries of S.E. Asia, except for Vietnam, -- Burma, Cambodia, Indonesia, Laos, Malaysia, Singapore, Philippines, and Thailand. The publications listed pertain primarily to communism, economics, military aspects, politics and government, psycho–social aspects, and the U.S. policy in the country. Not indexed.
D301.26/11:156(rev.) Supp./pt.1

865. U.S. Department of the Air Force. Air University Library.
Asia, Southeastern (Vietnam), Selected Unclassified Refer--ences; compiled by Gay Gyars. Annual Supplements.*** (Special Bibliography, no. 156 (rev.), supp., pt. 2).
Pt. 2 deals solely with Vietnam. References cover Communism, economic aspects, military aspects, politics and government, and U.S. assistance to Vietnam. Not indexed.
D301.26/11:156(rev.)/supp./pt.2

866. U.S. Department of the Air Force. Air University Library.
Prisoners of War/Southeast Asia, Selected References.
1971.*** (Special Bibliogrraphy, no. 193).
Most references are dated 1969--70.
D301.26/11:193

867. U.S. Department of the Air Force. Air University Library.

South Asia: Selected Unclassified References. 1969.
14pp.*** (Special Bibliography, no. 192, Supp. 1, Pt. 1).
Updating the original bibliography published in 1967, this
listing covers primarily 1967–68 material on the economic
aspects, foreign relations, Communist influence, technology,
military, politics, and psycho--social aspects of and in South
Asia. (Pt. 2 of this bibliography contains classified
document.)
D301.26/11:192/supp.1/pt.1

868. U.S. Department of the Air Force. Pacific Air Force.
China, Taiwan, Hong Kong; prepared by Arlene D.C. Luster.
1969. vi + 231pp.*** (PACAF Basic Bibliographies).
Included are well--annotated publications on all aspects
of China – philosophy, religion, language, literature, drama,
fine arts, foreign relations, history, social life, and customs --
as well as publications on Taiwan, Hong Kong, and
Communist China. Publications are listed by subject
under the country considered. Indexed by author and
title.
D301.62:C44/969

869. U.S. Department of the Air Force. Pacific Air Force.
China, Taiwan, Hong Kong: Supplement 1. 1971. [1] +
v + 76pp.*** (PACAF Basic Bibliographies).
(Notation as above.) Publications listed were issued
during 1969 and 1970.
D301.62:C44/969/supp.1

870. U.S. Department of the Air Force. Pacific Air Force.
Japan and Okinawa, Supplement 1; prepared by M.
Margaret Ono. 1970. [1] + iv + 18pp.*** (PACAF
Basic Bibliographies). L.C. Card 78--607090.
These supplement an existing bibliography dated 1969.
Publications listed cover all aspects of life in Japan and
Okinawa. Entries are annotated and purchase information
is provided. Indexed by author and title.
D301.62:J27/supp.1

871. U.S. Department of the Air Force. Pacific Air Force.
Japan and Okinawa, Supplement 2. 1971. [1] + iv + 35pp.
*** (PACAF Basic Bibliographies).
D302.62:J27/supp.2

872. U.S. Department of the Air Force. Pacific Air Force.

Korea; prepared by Constance R. Johnson. 1970. [1] + iv + 55pp.*** (PACAF Basic Bibliographies). L.C. Card 72--607035.

Life, culture, arts, language and literature, politics and government, religion and philosophy, and war accounts are covered by this annotated bibliography. Indexed by author and title.

D301.62:K84

873.   U.S. Department of the Air Force. Pacific Air Force. *Korea, Supp. 1.* 1971. [1] + iv + 22pp.

D301.62:K84/Supp.1

874.   U.S. Department of the Air Force. Pacific Air Force. *Okinawa;* prepared by Nathalie G. McMahon. 1972. [1] + v + 19pp.*** (PACAF Basic Bibliographies).

This supercedes the Okinawa section of *Japan and Okinawa* (no. 470). Okinawan arts and crafts, literature, history, politics, religion, and social structure are covered by this annotated bibliography. Some attempt is made to place importance on the works mentioned. Indexed by author and title.

D301.62:Ok3

875.   U.S. Department of the Air Force. Pacific Air Force. *Southeast Asia;* prepared by Mollie Lee. 1969. [1] + v + 195pp.*** (PACAF Basic Bibliographies).

Included are books and articles on various aspects of life, history, culture, politics, economics, government, and religion in Southeast Asia, Burma, Cambodia, Indonesia, Laos, Malaysia, the Philippines, Singapore, Thailand, and Vietnam. Publications are arranged alphabetically under the country headings.

D301.62:As4/969

876.   U.S. Department of the Army. *Communist China, Biblio-graphical Survey.* 1971. [1] + x + 253pp. 15pp. 2 maps in picket. $7.50* S/N 0820--0351 (DA Pamphlet 550--9). L.C. Card 72--613755.

The 800 lengthy abstracts cover the current aspects of China's political, social, and economic posture, nuclear threat, global ambitions and objectives, foreign policy and international relations, and cultural revolution. Entries, with full bibliographic information, are listed according to subject. There is no index, but the Table of Contents is

extremely thorough.
D101.22:550–9

877.   U.S. Department of the Army. *Communist North Korea, a Bibliographic Survey.* 1971.* x + 130pp. maps. $3.25* (DA Pamphlet 550–11). L.C. Card 71–614453.
Lengthy annotations of articles, books, and pamphlets present subjects which are basic to understanding North Korea and her people. Material presented is international in origin and pertains to the political, economic, social and strategic aspects of the country. There is no index, but the Table of Contents is thorough.
D101.22:550–11

878.   U.S. Department of the Army. *Japan, an Analytical Bibliography with Supplementary Research Aids and Selected Data on: Okinawa, Republic of China (Taiwan), Republic of Korea.* 1972. x + 371pp. 16 maps. $11.75. S/N 0820–0410. (DA Pamphlet 550–13). L.C. Card 72–603417.
Certainly this has to be one of the most informative and versatile bibliographies covering Japan, Okinawa, Taiwan, and Korea. Virtually every aspect of life -- politics, economics, society, defense, science and technology, culture, and history -- is covered in depth. Thoroughly annotated entries are arranged by specific subject, and the 16 maps, 11 of which are in color, provide a geographic picture of Northeast Asia, Japan, Okinawa, Taiwan, and South Korea. The publication is not indexed, but the Table of Contents is thorough.
D101.22:550–13

879.   U.S. Department of the Army. *South Asia and the Strategic Indian Ocean, a Bibliographic Survey of the Literature.* 1973. xv + 373pp. maps. $10.30* S/N0820–00447 (DA Pamphlet 550–15).
Included are nearly 1,000 abstracts of materials selected from several thousand unclassified books, articles, and documents emphasizing (1) South Asia as a region; (2) individual countries of South Asia; and (3) the strategic aspects of the Indian Ocean. The references cover every aspect of these areas -- military, political, economic, social and cultural. This publication is not indexed, but the Table of Contents is thorough.
D101.22:550–15

880. U.S. Department of State. Agency for International Development. *Vietnam, Bibliography;* prepared by Judith W. Heaney. 1968. [2] leaves + 25pp.*** L.C. Card 70--600671.
Almost every aspect of life in Vietnam is covered by this bibliographical listing. Publications are grouped by the following subjects: General Works; Physical and Cultural Setting; South Vietnam's History Prior to 1954; South Vietnam Between 1954 and 1963; South Vietnam since 1963; Economy; Government and Politics; North Vietnam and Communist Insurgency Warfare; Fiction, the Arts, and Travel. Not indexed.
S18.21/2:V67

881. U.S. Department of State. External Research Office. *Asia.* 1968. 4 + 117pp.*** (External Research Series, no. 2.27).
Contained are unpublished reports (as of December 1967) of research on Asia which was in progress. Material included is from academic institutions or individual scholars. The preface indicates that reports which are listed will be available to those interested. Arrangement is by country and within the country by subject. Not indexed. This annual publication was discontinued with this issue.
S1.101:2.27

882. U.S. Office of Education. *Bibliographical Resources About India: an Annotated List of English--Language Reference Works Published in India, 1965--1970;* compiled by Kiki Skagen. 1972. v + 28pp. $.25* (OE--14171). L.C. Card 72--602895.
Titles covering many aspects of Indian political, economic, social, and cultural life are given.
HE5.214:14171

Eastern Europe and the Soviet Union

883. U.S. Congress. House. *Hungarian in Rumania and Transylvania, Bibliographical List of Publications in Hungarian and West European Languages, Compiled from the Holdings of the Library of Congress;* by Elmer Bako and William Solyom--Feket. 1969. vii + 192pp.*** (H. Doc. 91--134).

883a. U.S. Congress. Senate. Committee on the Judiciary. *Soviet Intelligence and Security Services, 1964--1970: A*

Select Bibliography of Soviet Publications with Some Additional Titles from Other Sources. 1972. v + 289pp.**. Entries cover the following topics: Soviet strategic security; Soviet military intelligence; Partisans and Underground Activity; the 50th anniversary of the State Security Service; warning against Western intelligence; and Soviet Intelligence Activities. Indexed by author.

884. U.S. Department of the Air Force. Air University Library. *Russia -- Foreign Relations -- United States.* 1972. 9pp.*** (Special Bibliography, no. 197).
Books, government documents, and articles pertaining to historical and current aspects of Russian foreign policy affecting the United States are cited. Not indexed.
D301.26/11:197

885. U.S. Department of the Air Force. Air University Library. *Sino--Soviet Conflict: Selected References.* 1971. 13pp.*** (Special Bibliography, no. 194).
Books, articles, and documents concerning Sino--Soviet problems are cited. Though the bibliography addresses itself to the Sino--Soviet relations, references are made to United States relations with both countries and to the political implications of the conflict in each country.
D301.26/11:194

886. U.S. Department of the Army. *Communist Eastern Europe, an Analytical Survey of the Literature.* 1971. xi + 367pp. maps. $8.00* S/N0820-0352. (DA Pamphlet 550--8). L.C. Card 78--611513.
The lengthy annotations cover in some detail the social, political, and economic aspects and events of Eastern Europe. Besides each country in the Communist Bloc being treated individually, the following areas are singled out for special consideration: (1) Communist Eastern Europe and International Communism; (2) Communist Eastern Europe and USSR; (3) USSR and the Communist Bloc; and (4) Invasion of Czechoslovakia. This publication is not indexed, but the contents table is explicit.
D101.22:550--8

887. U.S. Department of the Army. *USSR: Strategic Survey Bibliography.* 1969. ix + 238pp. 9 maps in pocket. $5.00*

(DA Pamphlet 550–6). L.C. Card 77–601689.
Contained are 1000 abstracts of unclassified literature
from 1963 through August 1968 on all aspects of life in
the USSR. Publications are divided into five major sections:
(1) Introduction: Fifty Years of Soviet Power; (2) An
Overview; (3) National Policy, Strategy and Objectives;
(4) The Soviet Nation; The spectrum of Politics,
Sociology and Economics; and (5) Aids to Further
Research on the Soviet Union. These major areas are
extensively subdivided, and the annotations are so lengthy
that the bibliography itself reads like a documentary. The
publication is not indexed, but the Table of Contents is
explicit.
D101.22:550–6

888. U.S. Department of State. External Research Office.
USSR and Eastern Europe. 1968. ii + 60pp.***
(External Research Series, no. 1.27).
This bibliography contains listings of research in progress
or completed, but not published as of December 1967, on
the USSR and Eastern Europe. The preface suggests that
the research listed will be available on request once the
reports have been published. Arrangement is by subject.
Not indexed. This annual publication was discontinued
with this issue.
S1.101:1.27

889. U.S. Library of Congress. Slavic and Central European
Division. *Czechoslovakia, Bibliographic Guide;* by
Rudolf Sturm. 1967. (Published in 1968). xii + 157pp.
$1.00* L.C. 68–60019.
This is primarily a selection guide for "libraries building
their collections relating to Czechoslovakia, specialists
dealing with the area in depth; and . . . general readers
with only occasional and less specialized interests.
LC35.1:C99/2

Near and Middle East

890. U.S. Department of the Air Force. Air University Library.
The Arab–Israeli Conflict. 1972. 46pp. (Special Bibliography
no. 203).
Hundreds of periodical and book entries cover the many
aspects of the Arab–Israeli conflict. Some of the headings
under which entries are listed are: Background/Causes;

The Six Day War, June 1967; The Palestine Problem;
Guerrillas; Suez Canal; Sinai Peninsula; Jerusalem;
and the Current Situation and Future Prospects. Not
indexed.
D301.26/11:203

891. U.S. Department of the Air Force. Air University Library.
The Middle East: Selected References; by Mary Ward.
1972. 41pp.*** (Special Bibliography, no. 162, supp. 7).
With few exceptions, this bibliography contains entries
to books, documents, and articles dated 1968--1971.
Special subjects on the Middle East include the following:
(1) Economic Aspects; (2) Foregin Relations, (3) Military
Aspects; (4) Political Aspects; (5) Psycho–Social Aspects,
(6) Arab–Israeli Conflict; (7) Jerusalem; and (8) General
Information on the Arab States and the Persian Gulf
Area. Not indexed.
D301.26/11:162/supp.7

892. U.S. Department of the Army. *Middle East, Tricontinental I
Hub, Bibliographic Survey, Vol. 2.* 1968. x + 266pp.
27 maps.** (DA Pamphlet 550–2--1).
Supplementing Vol. 1 published in 1965, this bibliography
presents unclassified selected publications through 1967.
Lengthy annotated listings are organized so as to present
a comprehensive commentary of the Middle East, its history,
law, people, foreign relations, and current inflammatory
situation. Each country is treated individually, as well
as with the while of the region. Background notes on each
country, statistical tables, and maps form useful appendices
to this thorough work. This publication is not indexed, but
the contents table is detailed.
D101.22:550--2--1

893. U.S. Department of State. External Research Office.
Middle East. 1968. [3] + 25pp.*** (External Research
Series, no. 4.27).
Contained are listings of research in progress or completed,
but not published as of December 1967, on the Middle
East. Arrangement is by country and subject of research.
Not indexed. This annual publication was discontinued
with this issue.
S1.101:4.27

894. U.S. Department of State. Foreign Affairs Documentation

Center. *Foreign Affairs Research, Special Papers Available: Near East and South Asia; a List of Papers Accessioned Between 1964--70 in the Foreign Affairs Research Documentation Center.* 1970. 3 + 72pp.***.
General works are listed by subject with material on specific countries listed separately. Not indexed.
S1.126/2:Ea7/2

895. U.S. Department of State. Foreign Service Institute. *Near East and North Africa, Selected Functional and Country Bibliography.* [1968] [2] + 43pp.*** L.C. Card 68--60921.
This is a mimeographed list of English language publications arranged by subject and pertaining to the Near East and North Africa.
S1.114/3:N27

896. U.S. Library of Congress. *American Doctoral Dissertations on the Arab World, 1883--1968;* compiled by George Dimitri Selim. 1970. xvii + 103pp. $.55* L.C. Card 79--607590.
Over 1000 dissertations "on all subjects related to the Arab world" which have been accepted by U.S. and Canadian universities from 1883 through 1967--68 are listed alphabetically by author. In addition to standard bibliographic information, each entry contains the name of the university where the work was submitted and the year of acceptance. A good subject index leads the searcher to the proper dissertation.
LC1.12/2:Ar1/883--968

Oceana

897. U.S. Department of the Air Force. Pacific Air Forces. *Micro-- nesia, Polynesia, and Australasia;* prepared by Helen M. Williams. 1970. (PACAF Basic Bibliography).
All phases of life, from plant life to government and economy, are included in this bibliography. Hawaii, Australia, and New Zealand are treated separately in addition to being treated with the islands as a whole. Indexed by author and title
D301.62:M58/970

898. U.S. Department of the Air Force. Pacific Air Forces. *Micro-- nesia, Polynesia, and Australasia, Supp. 1.* 1971. [1] + v + 33pp.***

D301.62:M58/970/Supp.1

899. U.S. Department of the Army. *Insular Southeast Asia, Australia, Indonesia, Malaysia, New Zealand, Philippines, Singapore, Bibliographic Survey;* compiled by the Army Library. 1971. xi + 419pp. maps. $9.25* S/N 0820–0394 (DA Pamphlet 550–12). L.C. Card 72–602663. Contained are lengthy annotations concerned with the economic, social, political, and cultural development of Australia, Indonesia, Malaysia, New Zealand, the Philippines, Singapore, and insular Southeast Asia as a whole. The area is treated as a whole and then individually. Appendices comprised of texts, charts, statistical tables, and maps support the annotated bibliographical contents. This publication is not indexed, but the contents table is explicit.
D101.22:550–12

900. U.S. Department of the Army. *Pacific Islands and Trust Territories, Select Bibliography.* 1971. vii + 171pp. maps. $5.00* (DA Pamphlet 550–10). L.C. Card 75–612338. The materials selected for this thoroughly annotated biblio-graphy are reflective of the strategic, political, economic, and sociological aspects of the Pacific Islands and are supported by 26 appendices consisting of pertinent data and maps. Entries are divided according to the following chapter headings: (1) The Pacific: The Shifting Strategic Picture; (2) The Pacific Islands: An Overview; (3) The Pacific History in Perspective; (4) Micronesia, Melanesia and Polynesia: Political, Economic and Sociological Patterns; and (5) Source Materials for Further Research and Reference. This publication is not indexed, but the contents table is thorough.
D101.22:550–10

Western Europe and the Mediterranean

901. U.S. Department of Air Force. Air University Library. *Europe, Western: Selected References, 1969–1971.* 1972. 44pp.*** (Special Bibliography, no. 188). Contained are unclassified references to books, articles, and documents on the political, social, and economic aspects of Western Europe. All entries are post–1968. Not indexed.
D301.26/11:188/Supp.5, pt.1

902. U.S. Department of Air Force. Air University Library.
Malta: Selected References. 1971. 10pp.*** (Special
Bibliography, no. 196).
Bibliographic citations are of contemporary books and
articles dealing with the historic, economic, political, and
defensive aspects of Malta. Not indexed.
D301.26/11:196

903. U.S. Department of Air Force. Air University Library.
Western Europe: Selected References; compiled by Melrose
Byrant. 1968. 124pp.*** (Special Bibliography, no. 188).
Listed by subject areas are citations to books and articles
dealing with the various aspects of Western Europe,
especially the European Free Trade Association, the
European Common Market, and relations between the U.S.
and Western Europe. Not indexed.
(More current supplements may be available
upon request.)
D301.26/11:188/Supp.4, pt.1

904. U.S. Department of State. External Research Office.
Western Europe, Great Britain and Canada. 1968. [4] + 105pp.
*** (External Research Series, no. 3.27).
Contained are listings of research in progress or completed,
but not published as of December 1967, on Western
Europe, Great Britain, and Canada. The preface suggests
that the research listed here will be available on request
once the reports have been published. Arrangement is by
country and subject of research. Not indexed. This
annual publication was discontinued with this issue.
S1.101:3.27

905. U.S. Department of State. Foreign Affairs Documentation
Center. *Foreign Affairs Research, Special Papers
Available: Western Europe, Great Britain, and Canada; a
List of Papers Accessioned Between 1964--1970 in the
Foreign Affairs Research Documentation Center.* 1970.
72pp.***.
General works are listed by subject with material on
specific countries listed separately. Not indexed.
S1.126/2:W52

906. U.S. Library of Congress. Slavic and Central European
Division. *Federal Republic of Germany, Selected Biblio--
graphy of English--Language Publications with Emphasis*

on Social Sciences; compiled by Arnold H. Price. 1972.
ix + 63pp. $.70* S/N 3020--0010. L.C. Card 72--677.
Contained are 690 references which are well--indexed.
LC35.2:G31/3

Military Affairs

907. U.S. Department of the Air Force. Air Force Academy.
The Military and Society. 1972. 83pp.** (Special
Bibliography Series, no. 46).
References to books and articles are divided into the
following categories: (1) The Military and the Economy;
(2) The Military and Education, Propaganda, and Public
Opinion; (3) The Military and Foreign Policy; (4) The
Military and Science and Technology; (5) Minorities in
the Military; and (6) Raising Armies. Not indexed.
D305.12:46

908. U.S. Department of the Air Force. Air University Library.
Strategic TRIAD: Selected References; compiled by Melrose
Bryant. 1972. 26pp.*** (Special Bibliography, no. 204.
References are to numerous articles and books which
pertain to missile systems, Strategic Arms Limitation
Talks and the balance of powers, the Soviet threat, and
strategic target planning. Not indexed.
D301.26/11:204

909. U.S. Department of the Air Force. Air University Library.
*Volunteer Force, Zero Draft, and the Selective Service:
Selected References.* 1971. 11pp.*** (Special Biblio--
graphy, no. 195).
This bibliography, with its supplements, includes current
reports, articles, books, and government documents on
the draft, Selective Service, and the all volunteer armed
force. Not indexed.
D301.26/11:195

910. U.S. Department of the Air Force. Air University Library.
*Volunteer Force, Zero Draft, and the Selective Service:
Selected References, Supp. 1.* 972. 10pp.*** (Special
Bibliography, no. 195).
D301.26/11:195/Supp.1

911. U.S. Department of the Air Force. Air University Library.
War, Selected Reference; compiled by Mary Louise Pitts.

1970. 78pp.*** (Special Bibliography, no. 190).
The various aspects of war -- its causes, principles,
alliances, etc. -- are treated by this lengthy bibliography.
Other topics included are: War in Historical Perspective;
U.S. Treaties After WWII; Development of Aerospace
Power; Military Geography; Psychological War; Limited
War; Nuclear War; Wars of National Liberation;
Guerrilla Warfare; and Impact of War on Society, Arts,
Sciences, Cultures. Not indexed.
D301.26/11:190/Rev. 1970

912.   U.S. Department of the Air Force. Pacific Air Forces.
Arms and Armaments, Supp. II; prepared by Duane A.
Johnson. 1969. iv + 16pp.*** (PACAF Basic Bibliographies).
Included are publications dated 1967–1969. (Supplements
may be available).
D301.62:Ar5/969/Supp.2

913.   U.S. Department of the Air Force. Pacific Air Forces.
Intelligence; prepared by James H. Harlan. 1969. iv + 98pp.
*** (PACAF Basic Bibliographies). L.C. Card 58–61792.
The various phases of military intelligence are included in
this annotated bibliography. Some of the topics treated
individually are: Protest Movement; Espionage and
Counterespionage; Guerrila Tactics; Prisoners and Prisons;
Propaganda and Psychological Warfare; Survival, Escape
and Rescue. Indexed by title and author.
D301.62:In8/969

914.   U.S. Department of the Air Force. Pacific Air Forces.
Intelligence, Supp. 1. 1971. [1] + iv + 64pp.*** (PACAF
Basic Bibliographies).
D301.62:In8/969/Supp.1

915.   U.S. Department of the Army. Army Command and General
Staff College. *Military Justice.* 1972. [1] + 28pp.**
(Special Bibliography, no. 26).
D101.76:26

916.   U.S. Department of the Army. Army Command and General
Staff College. *Principles of War (Supplement).* 1973.
5pp.** (Special Bibliography, no. 29).
D101.76:29

917.   U.S. Department of the Army. Army Command and General
Staff College. *Race Relations, Armed Forces, 1960--72.*

1972. 22pp.** (Special Bibliography, no. 27).
D101.76:27

918. U.S. Department of the Army. Army Command and General
Staff College. *Stragegy and Tactics, 1000 A.D. -- 1970.*
1971. [1] + 4pp.** (Special Bibliography, no. 21).
D101.76:21

919. U.S. Government Printing Office. Army. *Field Manuals and
Technical Manuals.* Free* (Price List, no. 19).
Listed are Army field manuals and technical manuals which
are currently for sale by the GPO. This list is revised
frequently, and prices and availability are supposedly
current.
GP3.9:19

920. U.S. Government Printing Office. *Defense. Veterans' Affairs.*
Free* (Price List, no. 85).
Listed are free and for sale publications on all aspects of
veterans' affairs. This list is revised frequently; prices
are kept current; and all publications listed are
supposedly available.
GP3.9:85

921. U.S. Government Printing Office. *Navy, Marine Corps and
Coast Guard.* Free* (Price List, no. 63).
Listed are selected for sale and free publications on the
Navy, Marine Corps and Coast Guard. This list is revised
frequently, and all publications listed are supposedly
available from the GPO.
GP3.9:63

922. U.S. Marine Corps. *Annotated Bibliography of Naval Gunfire
Support;* compiled by Harold A. Vivins. 1971. [1] + ii +
10pp.** (Marine Corps Historical Bibliography).
D214.15:G95

923. U.S. Marine Corps. *Annotated Bibliography of United
State Marine Corps' Concept of Close Air Support;* by
James S. Santelli. 1968. [3] leaves + 24pp.*** (Marine
Corps Historical Bibliography).
The 130 briefly annotated references deal in whole or in
part with the development and employment of close air
support by the Marine Corps. "The scope of the biblio-
graphy covers a period of time which begins with the first

real combat employment of the technique of close air support in Nicaragua in 1927 through the war in Vietnam." D214.15:Ai1

RECREATION AND LEISURE

924. U.S. Department of Agriculutre. Economic Research Service. *Outdoor Recreation, Publications and Articles by the Economic Research Service, 1962–69;* compiled by Hugh A. Johnson. 1970. 2 + 8pp.*** (ERS–442). L.C. Card 74--609323.
A93.21:442

925. U.S. Department of the Air Force. Pacific Air Forces. *Community Recreation;* prepared by Edith Jensen. 1971. iv + 193pp.*** (PACAF Basic Bibliographies).
All phases of recreation from camping to the individual sports are covered by subject in this annotated bibliography. Book are analyzed critically and certain ones are recommended as essential to library collections. Indexed by author and title.
D301.62:R24/2/971

926. U.S. Department of the Interior. Bureau of Outdoor Recreation. *Developing America's Recreation Opportunities: Campgrounds.* 1972. [3] + 22pp.***.
Provided are references to organizations and literature which can assist in the successful development of campgrounds. Arrangement is by specific aspect of planning and develop-ment. Not indexed.
I66.2:C15

927. U.S. Department of the Interior. Bureau of Outdoor Recreation. *Guides to Outdoor Recreation Areas and Facilities.* 1968. 1 + 116pp. $.40*.
Listed with purchase information are national, regional, and state guides to outdoor recreational areas and camping facilities. Separate sections list guides to camping, canoeing, fishing, hiking, and hunting.
I66.15:G94/968

928–931. These indexes reference to articles, books, dissertations, directories, conference proceedings, documents, reports, speeches, and bibliographies dealing with outdoor recreation and environmental quality. The first three volumes contained abstracts of citations, but in volume four items are described only by keywords. Indexed by subject, name, and geographic area.

928. U.S. Department of the Interior. Bureau of Outdoor Recreation. *Index to Selected Outdoor Recreation Literature: Vol. 1, Citation item no. 60001–60091, Calendar Year 1966.* 1967. [i] + ii + 151pp. $.75* L.C. Card 68--60814. I66.15:L71/v.1

929. U.S. Department of the Interior. Bureau of Outdoor Recreation. *Index to Selected Outdoor Recreation Literature: Vol. 2, Citation Item nos. 7000–70847, Winter 1966–Spring 1967.* 1968. [2] leaves + ii + 239pp. $1.25*. L.C. Card 68--60814 I66.15:L71/v.2

930. U.S. Department of the Interior. Bureau of Outdoor Recreation. *Index to Selected Outdoor Recreation Literature: Vol. 3, Citation Item nos. 70848--71686.* 1969. [2] leaves + i + 232pp. $1.75*. L.C. Card 68--60814. I66.15:L71/v.3

931. U.S. Department of the Interior. Bureau of Outdoor Recreation. *Index to Selected Outdoor Recreation Literature: Vol. 4, Citation Item nos. 80001--81113.* 1969. [2] leaves + i + 224pp. $1.75*. L.C. Card 68--60814. I66.15:L71/v.4

932. U.S. Forest Service. *Forest Recreation Research Publications.* 1973. 5pp.***.
This is the sixth annual supplement to the *Bibliography of Forest Service Outdoor Recreation Research Publications, 1942--1966.* Publications are listed by author. Addresses for obtaining the publications listed are given.
A13.11/2:R24/Supp.6

933. U.S. Forest Service. Pacific Northwest Forest and Range Experiment Station. *Questionnaires for Research, Annotated Bibliography on Design, Construction, and Use;* by Dale R. Potter and others. 1972. [3] + 80 + [1]pp. Free*** (PNW Research Paper, no. 140). L.C. Card 72--603779.
"Questionnaires as social science tools are used increasingly to study people aspects of outdoor recreation and other natural resources fields. An annotated bibliography including subjective evaluations of each article and a key-- word list is presented for 193 references to aid researchers and managers in the design, construction, and use of mail questionnaires."

A13.78:PNW--140

SAFETY OF LIFE

General

934. U.S. Department of the Air Force. Pacific Air Forces.
Accident Prevention; by Louise St. John. 1971. v + 57pp.***
(PACAF Basic Bibliographies).
The highly specialized aspects of accident prevention
are the topics of this bibliography. Entries are divided into
the following categories: Atomic Defense; Aviation
Safety; Chemicals and Explosives; Fire Prevention;
Industrial Safety; Safe Driving Education; and Safety
Education. Indexed by author and title.
D301.62:Ac2/971

935. U.S. Department of the Army. Office of Civil Defense.
Fallout Shelters, Guide to Informative Literature; prepared
by McGuaghan and Johnson, Architects. 1968. 15pp.***
(Leaflets, L–45).
Listed are free publications from the Office of Civil Defense
which describe fallout shelter programs and shelter design
principles.
D119.13:45

936. U.S. Department of the Army. Office of Civil Defense.
Publications Catalog. 1972. x + 63pp.*** (MP–20).
Listed and briefly described are Office of Civil Defense
publications. They are arranged according to broad
subject categories and indexed by title and key words in
the title. Information is given on how to obtain these titles,
most of which are free. (1974 *Catalog* supercedes this).
D119.11:20/972

937. U.S. Government Printing Office. *Atomic Energy and
Civil Defense.* Free* (Price List, no. 84).
Listed are for sale and free publications concerned with
many aspects of civil defense and atomic energy. This
list is revised frequently; prices are kept current; and
publications listed are supposedly available.
GP3.9:84

938. U.S. Public Health Service. Bureau of Radiological Health.
Regulations, Standards, and Guides for Microwaves, Ultra–

violet Radiation, and Radiation from Lasers and Television Receivers, Annotated Bibliography; by Lloyd R. Setter [and others]. 1969. xii + 77pp.*** (Environmental Health Series, RH--35). L.C. Card 78--601117.

"This report is an annotated bibliography of guidelines, standards, and regulations pertaining to public health protection against electromagnetic radiation from television receivers, lasers, ultraviolet radiation, and micro-- waves. Each category of radiation is treated in a separate section. . . . Annotations include identification of the document, type of standard, intended complier, intended benefitter, limits and specifications, and general guidance. FS2.300:RH--35

939.   U.S. Public Health Service. Bureau of Radiological Health. *Regulations, Standards, and Guides Pertaining to Medical and Dental Radiation Protection, Annotated Bibliography;* by David R. Snavely and others. [1969.] x + 73pp.*** (Environmental Health Series, RH--37).

"Included are annotations of general standards, guides and recommendations; standards on the safe operation, handling, and design of radiation equipment and sources; and standards and guides pertaining to radiation measure-- ment. . . . Annotations include identification of the document, type of standard, intended complier, intended benefitter, limits and specifications, and general guidance." FS2.300:RH--37

Fire

940.   U.S. Department of the Interior. Library. *Fire in the Far Northern Regions, Bibliography;* compiled by Signe M. Larson. 1969. [11] + 36pp. NTIS (PB 189 099) (Bibliography Series, no. 14). L.C. Card 70--608865.

Contained are 198 entries from 1950 to June 1969 on forest and tundra fires in high latitutdes. The arrangement is alphabetical by main entry. Indexed by subject and name. I22.9/2:14

941.   U.S. Forest Service. Southeastern Forest Experiment Station. *Fire, a Summary of Literature in the United States from Mid-- 1920's to 1966;* by Charles T. Cushwa. 1969. [1] + ii + 117pp.***.

Over 800 entries cover the "Literature concerning properties, uses and effects of controlled and uncontrolled

209

fire." Entries are placed into sixteen subject categories, among which are: Forestry; Insects; Disease; Genetics; Range; Soil; and Wildlife.
A13.63/13--2:F51

942. U.S. National Bureau of Standards. *Bibliographies on Fabric Flammability: Part 1, Wearing Apparel; Part 2, Fabrics Used on Beds; Part 3, Carpets and Rugs;* by Sidney H. Greenfeld, Elizabeth R. Warner, and Hilda W. Reinhart. 1970. v + 36pp. $.40* (NBS Technical Note, no. 498). L.C. 79--606550.
This bibliographical series was iniated to facilitate research and development in the development of new standards and test methods for faric flammability, these being necessitated by the 1967 Amendment to the Flammable Fabrics Act of 1953. This first bibliography of the series deals specifically with wearing apparel, bedding, and carpets and rugs. Subject and author indices facilitate its use.
C13.46:498

943. U.S. National Bureau of Standards. *Bibliographies on Fabric Flammability: Part 4, Interior Furnishing;* by Sidney H. Greenfeld, Elizabeth⟩ ⟨ Warner, and Hilda W. Reinhart. 1970. iv + 18pp. $.30* (NBS Technical Note, no. 498--1). L.C. Card 79--606550.
Included here are all of the entries on beds, and carpets and rugs which appeared in parts 2 and 3, along with additional publications on upholstered furniture, draperies, curtains, and materials that are used in interior furnishings. Indexed by subject and author.
C13.46:498-1

944. U.S. National Bureau of Standards. *Bibliographies on Fabric Flammability: Part 5, Testing and Test Methods;* by Sidney H. Greenfeld, Elizabeth R. Warner, and Hilda W. Reinhart. 1970. vi + 33pp. $.45* (NBS Technical Note, no. 498--2). L.C. Card 79--606550.
Approximately 300 citations relate to test methods and the testing of fabrics and products made from fabrics and related materials. Covered are all products whithin the ranges defined in the 1967 Amendment ot the Flammable Fabrics Act. Indexed by subject and author.
C13.46:498-2

945. U.S. National Bureau of Standards. *Bibliography on Motor Vehicle and Traffic Safety.* 1971. iv + 220pp.***. L.C. Card 78--613735.
Listed by subject are all the publications acquired by the Office of Vehicle Systems Research since its establishment in 1967. Not indexed.
C13.37/4:M85

946. U.S. National Highway Safety Bureau. *Contract Research Reports, July 1, 1970.* 1970. [1] + iii + 43pp.**.
TD8.13:C76

947. U.S. National Highway Safety Bureau. *Drug Use and High--way Safety: a Review of the Literature;* by James L. Nichols. 1971. 110pp. $1.25* S/N 5003--0050.
Reviewed is the research literature concerning several aspects of drug use as it relates to traffic safety. Some of the topics include the following: The Effects of Drugs; Types of Drug Users; Research Problems in Assessing Risk; Laboratory Findings Concerning the Effects of Drugs; Survey Findings; Toxicological Investigations; and a disucssion of the legal aspects of drug--driving laws.
TD8.2:D84

948. U.S. National Highway Safety Bureau. *Highway Safety Literature: an Announcement of Recent Acquisitions.* 1969--. Biweekly beginning with 71--13.***.
Listed by subject are the recent acquisitions of the NHSB Annual author and subject indices.
TD8.10:yr.–no.

949--953. The below are the annual cumulative subject bibliographies compiled from the weekly citations in *Highway Safety Literature.* Each entry contains thorough bibliographic information and a detailed abstract.

949. U.S. National Highway Safety Bureau. *Highway Safety Literature, Annual Cumulation (Year): Accident Biblio--graphy.* 1969--. Annual.***.
TD6.10/3:yr./ab

950. U.S. National Highway Safety Bureau. *Highway Safety Literature: Highway Safety Bibliography.* 1969--.

Annual.***.
TD8.10/3:yr./hs

951. U.S. National Highway Safety Bureau. *Highway Safety Literature, Annual Cumulation (Year): Human Factors Bibliography.* 1969--. Annual.***.
TD8.10/3:yr./hf

952. U.S. National Highway Safety Bureau. *Highway Safety Literature, Annual Cumulation (Year): Related Areas Bibliography.* 1969--. Annual.***
TD8.10/3:yr./ra

953. U.S. National Highway Safety Bureau. *Highway Safety Literature, Annual Cumulation (Year): Vehicle Safety Bibliography.* 1969--. Annual.***.
TD8.10/3:yr./vs

954. U.S. National Highway Traffic Safety Administration. *Annotated Bibliography: The Relationship Between Vehicle Defects and Vehicle Crashes;* prepared by the Baylor College of Medicine. 1970. 59pp. NTIS. (DOT HS 007--369).
TD8.11:007--369

955. U.S. National Highway Traffic Safety Administration. *Research Reports of the National Highway Traffic Safety Administration, a Bibliography, 1967--70.* 1971. [1] + ii + 138 + 7pp.**.
TD8.13:R31/967--70

956. U.S. National Transportation Safety Board. *National Transportation Safety Board List of Publications.* 1969--. Annual. Free*** L.C. Card 76--603270.
TD1.115:yr.

SCIENCE AND TECHNOLOGY

General

957. U.S. Air Force Cambridge Research Laboratories. *Bibliography, with Abstracts, of AFCRL Publications from (date to date).* Quarterly.*** (AFCRL Special Reports Series, no.)
Listed are all AFCRL in--house reports, journal articles, and contractors reports issued each quarter.

D301.45/42:no.

958. U.S. Air Force Office of Scientific Research. *Air Force Scientific Research Bibliography: v. 6, 1962;* by Thomas C. Goodwin [and others]. 1968. xviii + 940pp. $8.50* L.C. Card 61--60038.
Subject and author indices lead to several thousand Air Force research publications published annually.
D301.45/19--2:700/v.6

959. U.S. Air Force Office of Scientific Research. *Air Force Scientific Research Bibliography: v. 7, 1963–1964.* 1970. xvi + 734pp. $7.25.* L.C. Card 61--60038.
D301.45/19--2:700/v.7

960. U.S. Air Force Office of Scientific Research. *Air Force Scientific Research Bibliography: v 8, 1965.* 1969. xvi + 939pp. $8.75*. L.C. Card 61--60038.
D301.45/19--2:700/v.8

961. U.S. Army Natick Laboratories. *Bibliography of Technical Publications and Papers, July 1967–June 1968.* iv + 48 + 3 + [2] pp.** (Technical Report, no. 69–1).
D106.21:69--1

962. U.S. Atomic Energy Commission. *Nuclear Science Abstracts.* 1948-- . Semi--monthly. $75.50 a year*, $19.00 additional foreign mail. L.C. Card 50–4390.
See no. 963 for notation.
Y3.At7:16/vol./no.

963. U.S. Atomic Energy Commission. *Nuclear Science Abstracts Index.* 1948--. Semi--annual. $35.70 a year, $9.40 addition foreign mail. L.C. Card 50--4390.
Nuclear Science Abstracts provides the only comprehensive abstracting and indexing coverage of international nuclear science literature. It covers scientific and technical reports of the U.S. Atomic Energy Commission and its contractors, other U.S. Government Agencies, other governments, universities, international conferences and symposia, and industrial and research organizations. Abstracted are reports, articles, and books, which may in some way be related to nuclear science, on chemistry, engineering, environmental and earth sciences, instrumentation, isotope and radiation source technology, life sciences, materials, nuclear materials and waste management, particle

accelerators, physics (astrophysics and cosmology), physics (atmospheric), physics (atomic and molecular), physics (electrofluid and magnetofluid), physics (high--energy), physics (low--temperature), physics (nuclear), physics (plasma and thermo--nuclear), physics (radiation and shielding), physics (thoretical), reactor technology and regulation, civil defense, and some general publications.

In addition to accompanying indexes, cumulative indexes are issued quarterly, semi--annually, and annually. Y3.At7:16--5/vol./no.

964.   U.S. Atomic Energy Commission. *Science and Society, Bibliography, 1965–67;* prepared by the staff of the AEC Library with subject index by Hugh E. Voress. 1968. [2] + 87pp. NTIS (TID--3916).
Y3.At7:22/TID--3916

965.   U.S. Atomic Energy Commission. *Science and Society, Bibliography;* compiled by Hugh E. Voress. 1971. 3 + 21pp. $.35* S/N5210–0272 (WASH--1182).
These bibliographies attempt to bring under a single cover varied sources that discuss the relationships and effects of science and technology on society. In this most recent publication, there are 410 entries to all types of literature on the subject published during 1968 through March 1971. Indexed by author.
Y3.At7:22/WASH--1182

966.   U.S. Congress. House. Committee on Science and Astronautics. *Technology Assessment, Annotated Bibliography and Inventory of Congressional Organizations for Science and Technology.* 1970. vii + 92pp.** (Committee Print, no. 91--Q). L.C. Card 73--608323.
Y4.Sci2:91–1/Q

967.   U.S. Congress. Senate. Committee on Government Operations. *Inventory of Congressional Concern with Research and Development, 91st Congress, 1969–1970: Part 5, Biblio--graphy;* prepared by Barbara A. Luxenberg. 1971. ix + 251 – 315pp.***.
See no. 969 for notation.
Y4.G74/6:R31/2/pt.5

968.   U.S. Congress. Senate. Committee on Government Operations. *Inventory of Congressional Concern with Research and Development, 92nd Congress, 1971: Part 6, Bibliography;*

by Claire Riley Geier. 1972. ix + 317 -- 343pp.***.
See no. 969 for notation.
Y4.G74/6:R31/2/pt.7

969.   U.S. Congress. Senate. Committee on Government Operations.
*Inventory of Congressional Concern with Research and
Development, 92nd Congress, 1972: Part 7, Bibliography;*
by Claire Riley Geier. 1973. ix + 345 -- 358pp.***.
Included in these bibliographies "are publications that
show Congressional interest in science and technology and
other documents showing the mutual concerns of govern--
ment and science. . . . This bibliography is arranged in five
sections: Public Laws, Conference Committee Reports,
Senate Publications, Joint Committee Publications, and
House Publications." A subject index cross--references
all publications.
Y4.G74/6:R31/2/pt.7

970.   U.S. Forest Service. Forest Products Laboratory. *List of
Publications on Glue, Glued Products, and Veneer.* 1968.
ii + 32pp. Free***.
Publications cover the many aspects of glue and its use.
Some of the specific topics under which publications are
listed are: Gluing of Wood; Gluing of Materials Other
Than Wood; Durability of Glues; Veneer; and
Fundamentals of Adhesion. Entries contain full biblio--
graphic information. Not indexed.
A13.27/7:G52/2/968

971.   U.S. Government Printing Office. *Scientific Tests, Standards
Mathematics, Physics.* Free* (Price List, no. 64).
Listed are free and for sale publications dealing with
scientific tests, mathematics, standards, and physics. This
list is revised frequently; prices are kept current; and all
publications selected for inclusion are supposedly available.
GP3.9:64

972.   U.S. Joint Publications Research Service. *People's Republic
of China Scientific Abstracts.* Irregular. Price upon request. NTIS.

973.   U.S. Joint Publications Research Service. *Reference Aid,
Directory of JPRS Ad Hoc Publications, Jan--Dec. 1973.*
1974. NTIS. (JPRS--61363).
Y3.J66:13/JPRS--61363

974.   U.S. Military Academy. *Landmarks in Science, Great*

Rare Books for the United States Military Academy Library Collections; by Edward P. Rich and Marie T. Capps. 1969. 12pp.** (USMA Library Bulletin, no. 8). D109.10:8

975. U.S. National Aeronautics and Space Administration. *NASA Patent Abstracts Bibliography: a Continuing Bibliography.* No. 1--. 1972--. Semi–annual. NTIS (SP--7039 [no.]). Each entry is placed into one of 34 subject categories (same as the *STAR Index,* see below) and is accompanied by an abstract, a STAR citation, and a key illustrations taken from the patent or application for patent drawing. Patents are indexed by accession number, source, number, subject, and inventor. NAS1.21:7039(no.)

976. U.S. National Aeronautics and Space Administration. *Scientific and Technical Aerospace Reports, a Semi--Monthly Abstract Journal with Indexes.* 1963--. Semi--monthly. $76.50 a year*, $19.15 additional foreign mail. L.C. Card 64--39060. Provided by this major abstracting service is virtually complete coverage of all unclassified reports dealing with almost any aspect of aerospace which has been issued by NASA or its contractors, other government agencies, universities, and research organizations. Abstracts are grouped under the following categories: Aerodynamics; Aircraft; Auxiliary Systems (includes fuel cells, etc.); Biosciences; Biotechnology; Chemistry; Communications; Computers; Electronic Equipment; Electronics; Facilities, Research and Support; Fluid Mechanics; Geophysics; Instrumentation and Photography; Machine Elements and Processes; Masers; Materials, Metallic; Materials, Non--metallic; Mathematics; Meteorology; Navigation; Nuclear Engineering; Physics, General; Physics, Atomic, Molecular, and Nuclear; Physics, Plasma; Physics, Solid–State; Propellants; Propulsion Systems; Space Radiation; Space Sciences; Space Vehicles; Structural Mechanics; Thermodynamics and Combustion; and General.
Abstracts are indexed by author, corporate author, subject, contract number, and accession/report number. Cumulative annual indexes. NAS1.9/4:vol./no.

977. U.S. National Bureau of Standards. *National Bureau of Standards Films.* Revised. 1974. 32pp. Free***.

Listed are NBS Films on science, weights and measures, dental research and techniques, safety, and the environment. All are available for free viewing by educational and non-profit and noncommercial groups.
C13.2:F48/974

978--982. These annual supplements provide complete citations to all NBS papers published during the year in National Bureau of Standards and non–NBS media. Entries are separated into NBS publications and other publications by NBS personnel. Indexed by author and key word.

978.   U.S. National Bureau of Standards. *Publications of the National Bureau of Standards, 1966--67;* by Betty L. Oberholtzer. 1969. 213pp. $2.00* (NBS SP--305). L.C. Card 48--47112.
C13.10:305

979.   U.S. National Bureau of Standards. *Publications of the National Bureau of Standards, 1968--69: a Compilation of Abstracts and Key Word and Author Indexes;* by Betty L. Oberholtzer. 1970. 497pp. $4.50* (NBS SP--305/supp.1).
C13.10:305/supp.1

980.   U.S. National Bureau of Standards. *Publications of the National Bureau of Standards, 1970.* 1971. 378pp. $3.25* (NBS SP–305/supp.2).
C13.10:305/supp.2

981.   U.S. National Bureau of Standards. *Publications of the National Bureau of Standards, 1971.* 1972. 338pp. $3.00* (NBS SP–305/supp.3).
C13.10:305/supp.3

982.   U.S. National Bureau of Standards. *Publications of the National Bureau of Standards, 1972.* 1973. 449pp. $3.75* (NBS SP–305/supp.4).
C13.10:305/supp.4

983.   U.S. National Bureau of Standards. *Some References on Metric Information with Charts on All You Need to Know About Metric, Metric Conversion Factors.* 1973. [3] + 8pp. $.25* S/N 0303–01219 (NBS SP–389). L.C. Card 73--600344.
"Included is a list of publications produced by the National Bureau of Standards and available from the Superintendent

of Documents. Also included is a list assembled by the National Council of Teachers of Mathematics, of organizations that market metric materials for educators, and a list of additional sources of metric information."
C13.10:389

983a. U.S. National Bureau of Standards. *Toward a Metric America, a Brief Bibliography and Other References.* 1973. 9pp.***
C13.37:67

984. U.S. National Technical Information Service. *Government Reports Announcements.* 1946 -- . Semi--monthly. (Title has varied) $52.50 a year*, $15.00 additional foreign mailing. NTIS. L.C. Card 46--2794.
See no. 985 for notation.
C51.9/3:vol./no.

985. U.S. National Technical Information Service. *Government Reports Announcements Index.* Semi--monthly. $57.50 a year* $15.00 additional foreign mailing. NTIS. (Annual cumulative indexes are sold separately). L.C. Card 46--2794.
Government Reports Announcements (GRA) is the most comprehensive bibliographic periodical published by the U.S. Government. It abstracts unclassified business, economic, scientific, and technical published reports done by the Government or under contract to the govern–ment. It even announces NASA and AEC reports, which are abstracted through *Scientific and Technical and Aero–space Reports* (no. 976) and *Nuclear Science Abstracts* (no. 962--3). Except for NASA and AEC reports, which are abstracted in their respective journals, all other publications are abstracted at length, and have complete bibliographic and availability information.
Abstracts are listed according to the following categories: Aeronautics; Agriculture; Astronomy and Astrophysics; Atmospheric Sciences; Behavioral and Social Sciences; Biological and Medical Sciences; Chemistry; Earth Sciences and Oceanography; Electronics and Electrical Engineering; Energy Conversion (Non–Propulsive); Materials; Mathematical Sciences; Mechanical, Industrial, Civil, and Marine Engineering; Methods and Equipment; Military Sciences; Missile Technology; Navigation, Communications, Detection, and Counter--measures; Nuclear Science and Technology; Ordnance; Physics; Propulsion and Fuels; and Space Technology. This subject

arrangement makes scanning for publications possible. The separate index thoroughly indexes by subject, personal author, corporate author, contract number, and accession/report number. ,

Most publications are available on microfiche or in paper copy from the NTIS. A few, which are available from the Government Printing Office, are so indicated, and the Superintendent of Documents Classification number is provided.

C51.9:vol./no.

Aerospace

986.   U.S. Air Force Cambridge Research Laboratory. *AFCRL Space Science Research During 1967;* A. McIntyre, ed. 1968. v + 34 + [16]pp. NTIS. (Special Report, no. 70). D301.45/42:70

987.   U.S. Air Force Cambridge Research Laboratory. *Lunar and Planetary Research, Supp. 4.* 1968. 337pp. NTIS (Special Report, no. 92). D301.45/42:92

988.   U.S. Air Force Office of Scientific Research. *UFOs and Related Subjects, Annotated Bibliography;* by Lynn Catoe. 1969. [2] + xi + 401pp. $3.50* (AFOSR Series, no. 68--1656). L.C. Card 68--62196.
More than 1600 items on UFOs and related subjects such as the occult, extraterrestrial life, and the solar system, make this what is thought to be "the most comprehensive biblio-- graphy published" on this subject. Arrangement is by subject with an author index.
D301.45/19--2:68--1656

989.   U.S. Department of the Air Force. Advanced Systems Division. *Annotated Bibliography of Advanced Systems Division Reports* (1950--72); by Horace H. Valverde, Helen E. Lebkisher, Arlene Reynolds. 1973. v + 248 + [2]pp.**

990.   U.S. Department of the Air Force. Pacific Air Forces. *Aeronautics;* prepared by Mary Kay Briggs. 1971. vi + 76pp. *** (PACAF Basic Bibliographies). L.C. Card 58--61784. D301.62:Ae8/971

991. U.S. Department of the Navy. Medicine and Surgery
      Bureau. *Annotated Bibliography of Reports Issued by the
      Naval Aerospace Institute, Pensacola, Fla., January 1, 1964--
      July 1, 1968;* compiled by Catherin F. Kasparek and
      Christine E. Turner. 1969. 112 + 2pp.**.
      D206.20:N22/964--68

992. U.S. Department of Transportation. *Aircraft Noise and Sonic
      Boom, Selected References;* compiled by Maria R. Haywood.
      1969. [1] + iii + 41pp. NTIS (Bibliographic List, no. 2).
      L.C. Card 75--605946.
      Listed are 255 partially annotated references to journal
      articles, reports, and papers dealing with aircraft noise
      and sonic boom. Source and availability are given for each
      entry. Indexed by author.
      TD1.15:2

993. U.S. Federal Aviation Administration. *Altimetry, Literature
      Review and Bibliography, Final Report, Phase 1;* by Jack
      J. Sharager. 1970. iii + 102pp. NTIS. L.C. Card 73--609418.
      TD4.509:70--59

994. U.S. Federal Aviation Administration. *Listing of Aircraft
      Development Service Reports, March 1968--March 1969.*
      1969.**
      TD4.609:R29/968--969

995. U.S. Government Printing Office. *Space, Missiles, the Moon,
      NASA, and Satellites: Space Education, Exploration,
      Research, and Technology.* Free* (Price List, no. 79A).
      Listed are selected free and for sale publications on
      the above. This publication is revised frequently; prices
      are kept current; and all publications listed are supposedly
      available.
      GP3.9:79A

996. U.S. Joint Publications Research Service. *Bibliography of
      Soviet Literature on Aviation, Alpine and Space Biology
      and Medicine;* by A.A. Sergeyev. 1971. 440pp. NTIS.
      (JPRS--53329).
      Y3.J66:13/53329

997. U.S. Joint Publications Research Service. *Bibliography of
      Soviet Upper Atmosphere and Outer Space Studies, USSR.*
      1968. 2p + 5[leaves]. NTIS. (JPRS--44343).

998.   U.S. Library of Congress. Science and Technology Division. *Wilbur & Orville Wright, a Bibliography Commemorating the 100th Anniversary of the Birth of Wilbur Wright, April 16, 1967;* compiled by Arthur G. Renstrom. 1968. vi + [1] + 187pp. $.55* L.C. Card 68--60013.

> Issued jointly as a research tool in the history of aeronautics and as a centennial tribute to the Wright Brothers, this bibiliography contains "2,055 entries to books, articles, pamphlets, patents, government documents, and court records in English and eight foreign languages." References are grouped accordingly: Published Writings of Wilbur and Orville Wright; Interviews, Speeches, Statements; Biographical References – Wright Brothers; Biographical References – Wilbur Wright; Biographical References – Orville Wright; Wind Tunnel; Aeroplanes and Flights; Powerplant; Automatic Stabilizer; Control Devices; Patents and Patent Suits; Wright Companies and School; Wright -- Smithsonian Institution Controversy; Monuments and Museums; Memorials; Medals and Honors; Memorabilia; Art; Poetry; Music; Motion Pictures and Film Strips; and Juvenile Publications. An index is provided to authors, persons, and institutions.

LC33.2:W93

999.   U.S. National Aeronautics and Space Administration. *Aero--nautical Engineering, Special Bibliography with Indexes.* 1970--. Monthly. NTIS (NASA SP--7037[no.]). L.C. Card 71--613578.

> Contained is a selection of annotated references to un--classified reports and journal articles that were intro--duced into the NASA scientific and technical information system and announced in *Scientific and Technical Aerospace Reports* and *International Aerospace Abstracts.* Indexed by subject, author, and contract number.

NAS1.21:7037(no.)

1000. U.S. National Aeronautics and Space Administration.*Aero--space Bibliography.* 6th ed. 1973. 116pp. $1.25* S/N 3300--460 (NAS EP--48). L.C. Card 66--61596.

> Presented is a current guide for general adult readers and elementary and secondary school teachers to books, references, periodicals, and other educational materials related to space flight and space science. Entries are

annotated and graded. Indexed by subject.
NAS1.19:48/6

1001. U.S. National Aeronautics and Space Administration. *Aero-- space Engineering: a Special Bibliography with Indexes.* 1970. 1145pp. NTIS (NASA SP–7037). This was the first in a new series (see no. 999) now being published monthly.
NAS1.21:7037

1002. U.S. National Aeronautics and Space Administration. *Biblio-- graphies on Aerospace Science, Continuing Bibliography with Indexes, Selection of Annotated References to Unclassified Bibliographies Introduced into the NASA Information System (Date).* 1967--. NTIS (NAS SP–7006). Abstracted are bibliographies, literature searches, abstract compilations, literature reviews and surveys, and report listings. Indexed by author and subject.
NAS1.21:7006(no.)

1003. U.S. National Aeronautics and Space Administration. *Effect of the Space Environment on Man's Response to Infection, Review of the Literature and Annotated Bibliography;* by Harold V. Ellingson and others. 1969. iii + 58pp. NTIS (NAS CR–1487). L.C. Card 70–605106. Contained are annotated selected references to the effect that the space environment has on man's ability to combat infection. In thinking about man's response to infection, the following are specifically considered: radiation, changes in atmospheric composition and pressure, space foods, weightlessness, confinement with minimal hygiene, and a combination of factors. Not indexed.
NAS 1.26:1487

1004. U.S. National Aeronautics and Space Administration. *Lunar Surface Studies, a Continuing Bibliography with Indexes, a Selection of Annotated References to the Un-- classified Reports and Journal Articles Introduced into the NASA Information System, (Date).* NTIS (NAS SP–7003– no.). Included in this continuing bibliography, which comes out at irregular intervals, are abstracts for such various aspects of lunar surface studies as (1) the theory of lunar origin, (2) the lunar atmosphere, and (3) the physical

characteristics of the lunar surface. Indexed by subject
and author.
NAS1.21:7003(no.)

1005. U.S. National Aeronautics and Space Administration.
OGO Program Bibliography. 1969. viii + 135pp.**
(National Space Science Data Center (NSSDC) Report, no.
68–14). L.C. Card 68–67204.
Contained are references, frequently with abstracts, to
published and unpublished scientific and technical reports,
papers, and articles having to do with the Orbiting Geophysical Observatory (OGO).
NAS1.37:68–14

1006. U.S. National Aeronautics and Space Administration.
OGO Program Bibliography, Supp. 3; compiled by David
T. Kohnhorst. 1970. vii + 80pp.** (NSSDC Report, no.
70–01).
Contained are all new citations collected since the 1968
cumulative edition.
NAS1.37:70–01

1007. U.S. National Aeronautics and Space Administration.
*Planetary Atmospheres, a Continuing Bibliography with
Indexes, a Selection of Annotated References to Un-
classified Reports and Journal Articles That Were Intro-
duced into the NASA Information System During the Period
June 1966 Through December 1967.* 1968. 58 + 58pp.
NTIS (NAS SP–7017/02).
Included are 357 references on the atmospheres of Mars,
Venus, Jupiter, Mercury, and Saturn. Additionally there
are references on extraterrestrial environments, planetary
observation techniques, and theories of planetary origin.
Indexed by author and subject.
NAS1.21:7017(02)

1008–1010. This massive three volume work comprehensively covers
the published materials of NACA and NASA regarding
the many and detailed aspects of light aircraft design. Some
entries have lengthy annotations while others have none.
Publications are listed by NACA and NASA series and are
not annotated.

1008. U.S. National Aeronautics and Space Administration.
*Study of NACA and NASA Published Information of
Pertinence in Design of Light Aircraft: Vol. 1, Structures;*

by Frederick O. Smeana. 1970. 5 + 434pp. NTIS (NASA CR--1484). L.C. Card 606543.
NAS1.26:1484

1009. U.S. National Aeronautics and Space Administration. *Study of NACA and NASA Published Information of Pertinence in Design of Light Aircraft: Vol. 2, Aerodynamics and Aerodynamic Loads;* by James C. Williams, 3d, Delbert C. Summey, and John N. Perkins. 1970. v + 705pp. NTIS (NASA CR--1485).
NAS1.26:1485

1010. U.S. National Aeronautics and Space Administration. *Study of NACA and NASA Published Information of Pertinence in Design of Light Aircraft: Vol. 3, Propulsion Subsystems, Performance, Stability and Control, Propellers, and Flight Safety;* by Clifford J. Moore and Dennis M. Phillips. 1970. iv + 484pp. NTIS (NASA CR--1486).
NAS1.26:1480

Biological Science and Natural History

1011. U.S. Agricultural Research Service. *Bibliography on Chagas' Disease (1909–69);* by Margaret C. Olivier, Louis J. Olivier and Dorothy B. Segal. 1972. vii + 633pp. $5.50* S/N 0111--0086 (Index–Catalogue of Medical and Veterinary Zoology, Special Publication, no. 2).
A77.219/4:2

1012. U.S. Atomic Energy Commission. *Contributions to the Bibliography of the Raccoon (Procyon Lotor)*; by Glen C. Sanderson and others. 1971. 82pp. NTIS. (COO–1332--26). L.C. Card 70–616042.
Y3.At7:22/COO–1332--26

1013. U.S. Department of the Interior. Fish and Wildlife Service. *Annotated Bibliography of Helminths of Waterfowl (Ana--tidae);* by Malcolm E. McDonald. 1969. ii + 333pp.**
(Bear River Research Station, Denver Wildlife Research Center, Division of Wildlife Research). (Special Scientific Report – Wildlife, no. 125).
"This bibliography is an attempt to list all the publications dealing with helminths of waterfowl (Anatidae) -- reports of their occurrences, description, classification, life history, and pathological effects." Included are almost

2900 references which are international in scope. Not
indexed.
I49.15/3:125

1014. U.S. Department of the Interior. Library. *American Ivory--
Billed Woodpecker (Campephilus p. Principalis): a Biblio-
graphy;* by Ruth Rehfus. 1969. NTIS (PB 185 558)
(Library, Bibliography Series, no. 12).
I22.9/2:12

1015. U.S. Department of the Interior. Library. *California Condor
(Gymongyps Californianus), Literature Since 1900;* compiled
by Ruth Rehfus. 1968. [2] + 16pp.*** (Library, Bibliography Series, no. 7A).
Listed alphabetically by author are full bibliographic
citations to the literature on the California condor since
1900. (Earlier literature is in: "The Annals of Gymnops
to 1900", by H. Harris. *Condor* 43(1):3--55, January/
February 1941).
I22.9/2:7A

1016. U.S. Government Printing Office. *Insects, Worms and Insects
Harmful to Man, Animals, and Plants.* Free* (Price List,
no. 41).
Listed are selected for sale and free publications on the
above. This list is revised frequently; prices are kept
current; and all publications listed are supposedly available.
GP3.9:41

1017. U.S. National Institutes of Health. National Institute of
Allergy and Infectious Diseases. *Selected Readings in Micro-
biology.* 1971. 6pp. Free***.
This is a short reading list of some of the popular books
dealing with microbiology.
HE20.3259:M58

1018. U.S. National Museum. *Bibliography and Index to Scientific
Contributions of Carl J. Drake for the Years 1914--67;* by
Florence A. Ruhoff. 1968. vii + 81pp. $.45* (Bulletin,
no. 267). L.C. Card 68--60954.
Arranged chronologically by publication date are all of
the works of Carl J. Drake, renowned entomologist.
Publications are indexed by order, family, genus, and
species.
SI3.3:267

1019. U.S. Smithsonian Institution. *Second Supplement to the Annotated, Subject--Heading Bibliography of Termites, 1961-- 1965;* by Thomas E. Snyder. 1968.*** (Smithsonian Miscellaneous Collections, Vol. 152, no. 3).
In 1961 "a Supplement 1955--1060 to an 'Annotated Subject--Heading Bibliography of Termites 1350B.C. to A.D. 1954' by Thomas E. Snyder was published as Publication 4463, Smithsonian Miscellaneous Collections, Vol. 143, no. 3." This second supplement covers from 1961--1965 and includes 1135 annotated references. Arrangement is by subject, with an extensive subject index for cross--referencing.
SI1.7:152/3

Chemistry

1020. U.S. Atomic Energy Commission. *Bibliography of Mass Spectroscopy Literature for (date) Compiled by Computer Method.* Semi--Annual. NTIS (IS--nos.).
Nuclear Science Abstracts or *Government Reports Announcements* should be consulted for current order information and publication numbers.
Y3.At7:22/IS--no.

1021. U.S. Atomic Energy Commission. *Sodium Technology, 1962-- 1971.* 1972. vi + 1052pp. NTIS (TID--3334, pt. 2).
Y3.At7:22/TID--3334, pt. 2

1022--1026. This continuing bibliography, which has thousands of entries per year, is arranged by 36 major classifications -- 23 for helium and 13 for alpha--particles. "The purpose of this bibliography is to facilitate and stimulate research on helium, thereby contributing to the wise and effective use of this limited natural resource." Indexed by author and subject.

1022. U.S. Bureau of Mines. *Helium Bibliography of Technical and Scientific Literature, Jan. 1, 1947--Jan. 1, 1962, Supplement to the Bureau of Mines Bulletin 484;* compiled by Harold Lipper and Carla W. Cherry. 1968. [2] + iii + 525pp. $2.75* (Information Circular, no. 8373).
I28.27:8373

1023. U.S. Bureau of Mines. *Helium Bibliography of Technical and Scientific Literature, 1962, Including Papers on Alpha-- Particles;* by Phillip C. Tully and Lowell Stroud. 1969.

[2] + vi + 357pp. $3.25* (Information Circular, no. 8398). L.C. Card 70--601446.
I28.27:9398

1024. U.S. Bureau of Mines. *Helium Bibliography of Technical and Scientific Literature, 1963, Including Papers on Alpha Particles;* by Phillip C. Tully, Billy Joe King, and Emily Dowdy. 1970. 2 + xxvi + 831pp. $7.00 (Information Circular, no. 8467). I28.27:8467

1025. U.S. Bureau of Mines. *Helium Bibliography of Technical and Scientific Literature, 1964, Including Papers on Alpha Particles;* by Phillip C. Tully, Emily Dowdy, and Betty G. Noe. 1970. [2] + xxxix + 946pp. $7.50* (Information Circular, no. 8489). I28.27:8489

1026. U.S. Bureau of Mines. *Helium Bibliography of Technical and Scientific Literature, 1965, Including Papers on Alpha Particles;* by Phillip Tully, Emily Dowdy and Betty G. Noe. 1971. [2] + xxxi + 760pp. $6.25* S/N 2404--0968 (Information Circular, no. 8523). I28.27:8523

1027. U.S. Bureau of Mines. *Helium--4 Experimental PVT References, 1895--1968;* by Robert E. Barleua. 1968. 3 + 24pp.*** (Information Circular, no. 8388).
Arranged alphabetically by author are 163 references to original experimental PVT data on helium. This bibliography purports to be complete from 1895 through 1968.
I28.27:8388

1028. U.S. Department of Defense. *Literature Search, Injection Molding Processing Parameters [with Bibliography];* by Nicholas T. Baldanza. 1969. iii + 32 + [1] pp. NTIS (PLASTEC Note, no. 21).
"This study is concerned with the relationship between processing parameters and the physical and mechanical properties of injection molded parts thus produced. Subjects of primary interest were: injection pressure and temperature; mold temperature; and molding cycle; flow rate, shear rate, melt viscosity and elastic shear stresses of plastic in the mold; internal stresses in the molded part; and instrumentation for measurement of these parameters. A total of 164 references are cited. The high--lights of these various pieces of information are discussed."

227

D4.11/2:21

1029. U.S. Department of Defense. *Literature Survey on Thermal Degradation, Thermal Oxidation, and Thermal Analysis of High Polymers, 3:* by Dorothy A. Teetsel, David W. Levi. 1969. ii + 192N + [1]pp. NTIS (PLASTEC Note, no. 20). D4.11/2:20

1030. U.S. Department of Defense. *Literature Survey on Thermal Degradation, Thermal Oxidation, and Thermal Analysis of High Polymers, 4;* by Eleanor C. Schramm and David W. Levi. 1972. Issued with perforations. NTIS (PLASTEC Note, no. 23). D4.11/2:23

1031. U.S. Department of Defense. *Reverse Osmosis Bibliography, Abstracted and Indexed;* by Joan B. Titus. 1973. iii + 178 + [3]pp. NTIS (AD 769 208) (PLASTEC Report, no. 45). "More than 650 significant works on reverse osmosis published over the past five years (1968--1972) are described. Subject and author indexes are provided as well as a glossary of relevant terms and a list of companies and government agencies in the field." D4.11:45

1032. U.S. Department of Defense. *Subject Index, Bibliography, and Code Description of Technical Conference Papers on Plastics, May 19, 1967--May 10, 1968;* by Joan B. Titus and Arnold Molzon. 1968. [1] + iv + 167 + [3]pp. NTIS (PLASTEC Report, no. 35). L.C. Card 62–61556. D4.11:35

1033. U.S. Department of Defense. *Subject Index, Bibliography, and Code Description of Technical Conference Papers on Plastics, May 15, 1968–May 8, 1969.* 1969. [1] + iii + 130pp. NTIS (PLASTEC Report, no. 39). The papers presented at technical conferences on plastic materials and related technology (which were available to PLASTEC) have been listed, indexed by subject, material, type of data and author. Hundreds of papers from numerous conferences have been listed. D4.11:39

1034. U.S. National Aeronautics and Space Administration. *Annotated Bibliography of Pyrrone and BBB Publications;*

by Harold D. Burks. 1972. iii + 64pp. NTIS (NASA TM X--2641).

"This annotated bibliography covers the research and development of two closely related classes of high– temperature polymers, polyimidazo--benzophenanthrolines (BBB), from their inception in 1965 through 1971. This compilation of available reference information is not inclusive, but it is sufficiently complete to aid the polymer chemist and materials engineer in the research and development of these two high--temperature stable polymeric systems."

NAS1.15:2641

1035. U.S. National Aeronautics and Space Administration. *High Energy Propellants, Continuing Bibliography with Indexes, Selection of Annotated References to Unclassified Reports and Journal Articles Introduced into NASA Information System During the Period (date).* NTIS. (NASA SP–7002 [no.]).

Scientific and Technical Aerospace Reports or *Government Reports Announcements* should be consulted for current order information and publication numbers.

NAS1.21:7002(no.)

1036. U.S. National Aeronautics and Space Administration. *Secondary Aerospace Batteries and Battery Materials, Bibliography;* by G. Halpert and W.H. Webster, Jr. 1969. [2] + iii + 151pp. NTIS (NASA SP–7027).

Over 370 items from the foreign and domestic literature are abstracted here. "This bibliography encompasses subjects ranging from metallurgical process and inorganic preparations to electrochemical and analytical measure– ments as applied to these systems." Entries are indexed by (1) system and component; (2) Techniques and processes used in the investigations, e.g., analytical, thermal, metallurgical, and kinetic; and (3) author.

NAS1.21:7027

1037. U.S. National Bureau of Standards. *Activation Analysis: a Bibliography Through 1971;* edited by G.J. Lutz, R.J. Boreni, R.S. Maddock, and J. Wing. 1972. 92pp. $7.00* S/N 0303–0999 (Technical Note, no. 467).

Superceding previous issues, this bibliography which utilizes a computer storage and retrieval system is a single volume arranged in two parts. Part I gives a complete

readout of the bibliographic information in the file
arranged according to accession numbers. Part 2 contains
three indices on the three categories which describe
activation analysis – Element Determined, Matrix Analyzed
and Technique Used. A fourth index is the Author Index.
This bibliography will be periodically updated.
C13.46:467/4

1038. U.S. National Bureau of Standards. *Bibliography of Ion--Molecule
Reaction Rate Data (January 1950 -- October 1971);* by
George A. Sinnott. 1973. vi + 66pp. $1.00* S/N 0303–
01126. (Special Publication, no. 381).
"A bibliography is presented of papers in the open literature
that contain original experimental data on ion--molecule
reaction rates or cross sections. Positive and negative ion--
molecule and ion–ion reactions are included but not
electron impact processes. For papers to be included, the
reactants must have been identified and data for kinetic
energies below 10 electron volts must have been presented."
C13.10:381

1039. U.S. National Bureau of Standards. *Bibliography of Temperature
Measurement, January 1953 -- December 1969;* by Paul
D. Freeze and Leslie P. Parker. 1972. iv + 70pp. $2.00*
(Special Publication, no. 373). L.C. Card 72--600291.
"There are presented more than 500 references to the field
of temperature measurement. . . . The period covered is
from 1953 to June 1960. References are divided into a
number of categories based on the type of instrument
used.
C13.10:373

1040. U.S. National Bureau of Standards. *Bibliography of Thermo--
physical Properties of Air from 0 to 300 degrees K;* by
L.A. Hall. 1969. iii + 121pp. $1.25* (Technical Note, no.
383). L.C. Card 75–604598.
Over 600 "references together with an abbreviated abstract
are presented for mechanical, thermodynamic, and transport
properties of air from 0 to 300 degrees K published up to
December 1968. Each article has been reviewed and
coded with regard to properties studied, type of article
(i.e., experimental, theorectical, etc.), and method of
presentation of data. The temperature and pressure
ranges for each property with four sub–categories: solid,
liquid, gas up to 200 degrees K, and gas above 200 degrees

K."
C13.46:383

1041. U.S. National Bureau of Standards. *Bibliography of Thermo-- physical Properties of Methane from 0 to 300 degrees K;* by L.A. Hall. 1968. iii + 119pp. $.60* (Technical Note, no. 367). Included are 660 articles which are abstracted and indexed. The index is according to property with four sub--categories -- solid, liquid, gas up to 200 degrees K, and gas above 200 degrees K.
C13.46:367

1042. U.S. National Bureau of Standards. *Bibliography on High Temperature Chemistry and Physics of Materials, (date).* 1968--. Quarterly.*** (Special Publication, no. 315--no.). L.C. Card 77--600413.
This is a recurring bibliography of references to research involving temperatures above 1000 degrees C and their effects on various materials.
C13.10:315--issue

1043. U.S. National Bureau of Standards. *Chemical Kinetics in C--O--S and H--N--O--S Systems, Bibliography 1889 -- June 1971;* by Francis Westley. 1972. x + 62 + [1]pp. $.70* (Special Publication, no. 362).
"A bibliography, a reaction oriented list of references, is provided for published papers and reports containing rate data reactions for COS, COS_2, CS, CS_2, CS_3, D_2S, H_2S, S_2S_2, HSO_2, S, SH, SO, SO_2, SO_3, SO_4, S_2, S_2O_2, S_4, and S_6 with each other and with CO, CO_2, D, D_2, H, H_2, H_2O, N, N_2, N_2O, N_2O_5, NO, NO_2, NO_3, NOS, O, OH, O_2, O_3, R and RH. Three lists of critical reviews dealing with the above reactions are included. 317 papers covering 240 reactions are listed."
C13.10:362

1044. U.S. National Bureau of Standards. *Cryongenic Data Center Current Awareness Service, Publications and Reports of Cryogenic Interest Noted, List.* Weekly. $20.00*** a year, U.S. and Canada, $25.00 elsewhere (air mail). (Cryogenic Data Center, NBS, Boulder, Colorado 80302).
C13.51:nos.

1045. U.S. National Bureau of Standards. *Determination of Light Elements in Metals, Bibliography of Activation Analysis Papers;*

G.J. Lutz, ed. 1970. 77pp. $.75* (Technical Note, no. 524). L.C. Card 72–607244.

Entries are listed alphabetically by author with full biblio--graphic description and accession number. They "are indexed according to the elements boron, carbon, nitrogen, oxygen, phosphorous, silicon, and sulfur. The indexes are arranged by Element Determined and subdivided according to Matrices and Nuclear Reactions involved." Also indexed by author.

C13.46:524

1046. U.S. National Bureau of Standards. *Equilibrium Critical Phenom--ena in Fluids and Mixtures, Comprehensive Bibliography with Key--Word Descriptors;* by Stella Michaels [and others]. 1970. iv + 231 + [2] pp. $4.00* (Special Publication, no. 327). L.C. Card 70–606320.

"This bibliography of 1088 citations comprehensively covers research conducted throughout the world between Jan. 1, 1950 through December 31, 1967. Each entry is characterized by speciric key--word descriptors, of which there are approximately 1500, and is indexed by subject and author."

C13.10:327

1047. U.S. National Bureau of Standards. *Forensic Science, A Biblio--graphy of Activiation Analysis Papers;* G.J. Lutz, ed. 1970. iii + [1] + 26 + [15] pp. $.50* (Technical Note, no. 519). L.C. Card 71--606934.

References are indexed by 32 categories for precise literature searching by the forensic scientist. Indexed by author.

C13.46:519

1048. U.S. National Bureau of Standards. *Heavy--Atom Kinetic Isotope Effects, an Indexed Bibliography;* by Martin J. Stern and Max Wolfsberg. 1972. iv + 34 + [1] pp. $.45* S/N 0303--0844 (Special Publication, no. 349). L.C. Card 70--611342.

"The complete literature from the earliest entry found (1911) through 1965" is compiled in this bibliography. There is a list of review articles and theoretical papers through 1968. The subject index has been annotated to describe briefly the type of reaction being observed. Also indexed by author.

C13.10:349

1049. U.S. National Bureau of Standards. *Pollution Analysis, Biblio-graphy of Literature of Activation Analysis;* G.J. Lutz, ed. 1970. vii + 12 + [21]pp. $.45* (Technical Note, no. 532). Entries are of reports and articles reporting the results of activation analysis applied to pollution samples. The areas tested for trace elements are air atmosphere, water, foodstuffs, pesticides, particles, dusts, drugs, and soils. Publications are indexed according to "the broad categories of Element Determined, Matrix Analyzed and Technique Used."
C13.46:532

1050. U.S. National Bureau of Standards. *Publications and Services of the National Bureau of Standards Cryogenics Division, Institute for Basic Standards, Boulder, Colorado, 1953–1972;* by J.R. Mendenhall, V.J. Johnson, and N.A. Olien. 1973. vii + 75 + [1]pp. $.75* (Technical Notes, no. 639) L.C. Card 73--602866.
Besides cataloging the publications of the Cryogenics Division of the NBS for the period 1953 through 1972, this publication contains a listing of available thermodynamic properties charts, bibliographies, and miscellaneous reports of cryogenic interest. The approximately 800 entries are indexed by subject and author. In addition, there is a resume of the services and activities of the Cryogenics Division.
C13.46:639

1051. U.S. National Bureau of Standards. *Supplementary Biblio-graphy of Kinetic Data on Gas Phase Reactions of Nitrogren, Oxygen, and Nitrogen Oxides;* by Francis Westley. 1973. xii + 80pp. $1.25* (Special Publication, no. 371). L.C. Card 72--600272.
C13.10:371

1052. U.S. Tennessee Valley Authority. *Fertilizer Abstracts.* V. 1–. 1968--. Monthly. $25.00*** a year, $15.00 additional foreign mailing (Fertilizer Center, Tennessee Valley Authority, Muscle Shoals, Alabama 35660). L.C. Card 71--11106.
This bibliography, which is international in scope, provides sources of information on fertilizer technology, marketing and use.
Y3.T25:36/Vol. & no.

1053. U.S. Congress. Joint Committee on Printing. *Bibliography on Electronic Composition.* 1970. iii + 58pp.*** L.C. Card 79--609465.
Y4.P93/1:E1 2/2

1054. U.S. Department of the Air Force. Pacific Air Forces. *Communications and Electronics;* prepared by Harry W. McAnallen. 1969. [1] + iv + 111pp. Free*** (PACAF Basic Bibliographies). L.C. Card 58--61785.
Popular and technical books and articles on all phases of radar, television, radio electronics, computers, transistors, and sound reproduction are included. All references are completely annotated. Indexed by author and title.
D301.62:C73/969

1055. U.S. Department of the Air Force. Pacific Air Forces. *Communications and Electronics, Supp. I.* 1971. iv + 51pp. Free***.
D301.62:C73/969/Supp.1

1056. U.S. Department of Commerce. Office of Technical Services. *Computers, Selected Bibliographic Citations Announced in U.S. Government Research and Developments Reports, 1966.* 1968. ii + 86pp.***.
(U.S. Government Research and Developments Reports is now U.S. Government Reports Announcements.).
C1.54:C73

1057. U.S. Department of Commerce. Office of Technical Services. *Electronic and Electrical Engineering, Selected Bibliographic Citations Announced in U.S. Government Research and Development Reports, 1966.* 1968. iii + 35pp.***.
(See previous notation).
C1.54:E12

1058. U.S. Department of Commerce. Office of Telecommunications. *Bibliography on Propagation Effects from 10GH$_z$ to 1000TH;* by L.E. Vogler, S.F. Van Horn. 1972. 85pp. $.75* (OT/ITS Research Report, no. 30).
"A bibliography is presented on the subject of electro--magnetic wave propagation over line--of--sight paths through the troposphere at frequencies above 10GH$_z$. The references are divided into three main categories

covering the areas of propagation through nonturbulent clear atmosphere, turbulent clear atmosphere, and pre--cipitation."
C1.60:30

1059. U.S. Department of Commerce. Office of Telecommunications. *Survey of Technical Requirements for Broadband Cable Teleservices: V. 7, Selected Bibliography;* by N. Holmberg, E. Gray, P. McManamon. 1973. viii + 133 + [1] pp. $1.55*.
Entries are concerned with "cable television of Community Antenna Television (CATV) and broadband cable systems which offer or have proposed to offer various teleservices in addition to one--way distribution of present television channels. The bibliography includes publications related to technical teleservices, system management system economics, and legal, social, privacy and security aspects of the system." Organization is by subject. Not indexed.
C1.60/3.73–13/v.7

1060. U.S. Government Printing Office. *Radio and Electricity. Electronics, Radar, and Communications.* Free* (Price List, no. 82).
Listed are selected free and for sale publications on electricity and communications. This list is revised frequently; prices are kept current; and all publications listed are supposedly available.
GP3.9:82

1061. U.S. National Aeronautics and Space Administration. *Annotated Bibliography of Computer--Aided Circuit Analysis and Design;* by Charles W. Meissner, jr. 1968. v + 41pp. NTIS (NASA SP–7023).
One.hundred and fifty–six annotated entries "cover the literature peculiar to computer--aided circuit analysis" which include enough background material to provide a good overview of the subject since its infancy. Author index.
NAS1.21:7023

1062. U.S. National Aeronautics and Space Administration. *Communications Satellites, Continuing Bibliography with Indexes, Selection of Annotated References to Unclassified Reports and Journal Articles That Were Introduced into NASA Information System During the Period (quarter).* NTIS. (NASA SP--7004[no.]).

Included in this continuing bibliography are references with abstracts to all aspects of communications satellite theory and technology. Following are some of the topics included: television broadcasting, telemetry, and multi-station systems. Indexed by subject and author. NAS1.21:7004 (no.)

1063. U.S. National Aeronautics and Space Administration. *Technology Transfer, Selected Bibliography;* by Terry Sovel Heller, John S. Gilmore, and Theodore D. Browne. Rev. Ed. 1971. vii + 175pp. NTIS (NASA CR--1724). L.C. Card 71--6114000.
This revised bibliography updates and expands a similar 1968 publication. "The bibliography is concerned with technology transfer in the following sense: Technology is considered to be technical information and capability, including scientific knowledge, making possible the conception, development, design production, and distribution of goods and services. 'Transfer' here means the movement of science and technology (in either an em--bodied form or as information only) from one known place to another." Contained are 564 citations and 65 abstracts of important technology transfer literature which is indexed by author and key--word--in--context.
NAS1.26:1724

1064. U.S. National Bureau of Standards. *Annotated Bibliography of the Literature on Resource Sharing Computer Networks;* by R.P. Blanc and others. 1973. iv + 90pp. $1.25* (Special Publication, no. 384). L.C. Card 73--600268.
"This bibliography consists of references with critical annotations to the literature on computer networks. A classification scheme has been developed to place each annotation in a category reflective of its content. Five indexes to the bibiliography are included: author index, corporate author index, network index, key word out of context index, and report number index."
C13.10:384

1065. U.S. National Bureau of Standards. *Bibliography on Methods for Measurement of Inhomogeneities in Semiconductors, 1953--67;* by Harry A. Schafft and Susan Gayle Needham. 1968. ii + 45pp. $.35* (Technical Note, no. 445).
"About 130 papers which deal with the measurement techniques useful in detecting the type and location of

various inhomogeneities, primarily in germanium and silicon, are listed with key words."
C13.46:445

1066. U.S. National Bureau of Standards. *Computer Literature Bibliography, v. 2, 1964--67;* by W.W. Youden. 1968. [1] + iv + 381 + [3]pp. $5.00* (Special Publication, no. 309). L.C. Card 68–62478.
Contained are approximately 5,200 references to computer literature published from 1964--1967. This continues *Computer Literature Bibliography, 1946–1963* (NBS Miscellaneous Series, no. 266). Author and Key--Word--In–Context indices facilitate in locating information rapidly.
C13.10:309

1067. U.S. National Bureau of Standards. *Controlled Accessibiblity Bibliography;* by Susan K. Reed and Martha M. Gray. 1973. 2 + 11 + 1pp. il. $.35* (Technical Note, no. 780).
"A bibliography of 96 references on controlled accessibility has been compiled. The purpose in compiling this limited bibliography was to free the effort to solve problems of controlled accessibility from domination by discussion of the issues of privacy. Insofar as possible, except when the two subjects are referred to in the same work or for overriding historical considerations, references dealing with privacy have not been included."
C13.46:780

1068. U.S. National Bureau of Standards. *Measurement of Carrier Lifetime in Semiconductors, Annotated Bibliography Covering the Period 1949--67;* by W. Murray Bullis. 1968. ii + 62pp. $.60* (Technical Note, no. 465).
"About 300 papers concerned with the measurement and interpretation of carrier lifetime in semiconductors are listed together with key words and a brief comment for each. Eight types of entries are included: Description of Methods, Analysis of Results, Standard Methods, Experi--mental Results, Theoretical Models, Auxiliary Procedures and Data, Reviews, and Books. Emphasis is placed on methods of carrying out measurements of carrier lifetime. . . . Two indexes, a Key Word Index and an Author Index, are provided together with the various methods for measuring carrier lifetime."
C13.46:465

1069. U.S. National Bureau of Standards. *Research and Development in Computer and Information Sciences: Vol. 1, Information Acquisition, Sensing, and Input, Selective Literature Review* [with bibliography] ; by Mary Elizabeth Stevens. 1970. vi + 165pp. $1.50* (Monograph, no. 113). L.C. Card 70--603263. C13.44:113/v.1

1070. U.S. National Bureau of Standards. *Research and Development in Computer and Information Sciences: Vol. 2, Processing Storage, and Output Requirement in Information-Processing Systems, Selective Literature Review* [with bibliography; by] Mary Elizabeth Stevens. 1970. vi + 125pp. $1.25* (Monographe, no. 113). C13.44:113/v.2

1071. U.S. National Bureau of Standards. *Research and Development in Computer and Information Sciences: Vol. 3, Overall System Design Considerations, Selective Literature* [with bibliography; by] Mary Elizabeth Stevens. 1970. v + 143pp. $1.25* (Monographe, no. 113).
Though the titles indicate that these volumes are primarily bibliographic sources, they are actually reviews and analyses of the literature. Each volume, however, concludes with a good bibliography.
C13.44:113/v.3

1072. U.S. National Bureau of Standards. *Superconducting Devices and Materials, Literature Survey.* Quarterly. $20.00 a yr. NTIS.
Contained are publications and reports pertaining to superconducting devices and to theory and experiment related to such devices.
C13.37/5:no

1073. U.S. National Bureau of Standards. *Wire--Bond Electrical Connection, Testing Fabrication and Degradation, Bibliography 1957--71;* by Harry A. Schafft. 1972. iii + 54 + [1]pp. $.60* (Technical Note, no. 593).
"More than 245 papers relevant to wire--bond type electrical interconnections used in microelectronics and low--power discrete and hybrid devices are listed together with key--words. . . . The selection of papers is generally limited to those that are pertinent to wire bonds where the wire diameter is less than about 50 um (2 mils) and where the wire is bonded by either thermocompressive or

ultrasonic means." Author and key word indexes.
C13.46:593

1074. U.S. Public Health Service. *Annotated Bibliography of Biomedical Computer Applications;* compiled by Ruth Allen. 1969. [6] + 216pp.*** L.C. Card 76–602281.
Articles and reports annotated here present the varied use of the computer in the biomedical fields. An author and subject index guide to specific areas of interest.
FS2.209:B52/2

Engineering

1075. U.S. Army Corps of Engineers. *Annotated Bibliography of BEB and CERC Publications;* compiled by R.H. Allen and E.L. Spooner. 1968. iii + 141 + 3pp.*** (Coastal Engineering Research Center: Miscellaneous Paper, no. 1–68).
Beach Erosion Board publications from 1940–1963 and Coastal Engineering Research Center publications from 1963–1967 are listed in numerical sequence by series. A summary or abstract accompanies each title. Subject, author, and title indexes facilitate its use.
D103.42/2:1–68

1076. U.S. Army Corps of Engineers. *Annotated Bibliography of Explosive Excavation Related Research.* 1972. v + 220 + [2]pp. NTIS.
Described are all reports prepared from fiscal years 1962–1972.
D103.24/2:E–72–32

1077. U.S. Army Corps of Engineers. *Bibliography of Winter Construction, 1940–67;* by Charles W. Fulwider and Jay H. Stearman. Rev. Ed. 1968. iii + 84 + [2]pp.*** (Cold Regions Research and Engineering Laboratory, Hanover, N.H., Research Report, no. 83).
D103.33/2:83/2

1078. U.S. Army Corps of Engineers. *Groins: an Annotated Biblio-- graphy;* by J.H. Balsillie and R.O. Bruno. 1972. v + 24pp. *** (Army Coastal Engineering Research Center, CE, Washington, D.C.) (Miscellaneous Paper, 1–72).
"About 460 articles published since 1900 on groins and groin type structures are presented in this bibliography. Annotations accompany each bibliographic entry where

possible." Indexed by author, title, and subject. Un-- available literature such as foreign articles, although not annotated, are included as entries.
D103.42/2:1--72

1079. U.S. Army Corps of Engineers. *List of Publications of the U.S. Army Waterways Experiment Station, Including Hydraulic Reports of Other Corps of Engineers Laboratories and Reports of Hydraulic Model Investigations Sponsored by Other Corps of Engineers Offices.* 1973. 309pp.***.
Publications are listed chronologically by series. Indexed by subject.
D103.24:973

1080. U.S. Army Corps of Engineers. *Literature Review of Dusting Technology in Deicing [with bibliographies];* by Bruce P. Cavan. 1969. 52pp.*** (Lake Survey District, Corps of Engineers, 630 Federal Bldg. and Courthouse, Detroit, Mich. 48226). (Lake Survey Research Report, no. 5--7). L.C. Card 75--607400.
D103.209:5--7

1081. U.S. Army Corps of Engineers. *Publications Available for Purchase, U.S. Army Engineer Waterways Experiment Station and Other Corps of Engineers Agencies.* 1971. 60pp. Free*** (Director, Army Engineer Waterways Experiment Station, P.O. Box 631, Vicksburg, Miss. 39180).
Revised frequently, this lists by series, publications which may be purchased from the Corps of Engineers.
D103.39:P96/971

1082. U.S. Bureau of Mines. *Bibliography of Investment and Operating Costs for Chemical and Petroleum Plants, January-- December 1967;* by Sidney Katell and William C. Morel. 1968. [2] + 125pp. $1.00* (Information Circular, no. 8386).
See notation for no. 1083.
I28.27:8386

1083. U.S. Bureau of Mines. *Bibliography of Investment and Operating Costs for Chemical and Petroleum Plants, January -- December 1968.* 1969. 3 + 132pp. $1.25* (Information Circular, no. 8415).
This series, which began with Information Circular no. 7516 in October 1949, is concerned with all phases of cost engineering in chemical and petroleum plants. Most

abstracts deal with "construction and operating costs, though other subjects include cost--estimating methods and theory, reports on construction projects in the United States and abroad, and developments in petroleum pro-- duction and refining and in the nuclear field." Entries are easily approached through subject and author indices.
I28.27:8415

1084. U.S. Department of the Interior. *Sprinkler Irrigation, Bibliography Selected from Foreign Literature, 1964–69;* compiled by Ludmilla Floss. 1970. [5] + 54pp. NTIS (PB 190 403) (Library, Bibliography Series, no. 15). L.C. Card 74--608866.
The material included in this bibliography refers to the technological aspects of sprinkler irrigation systems and does not attempt to cover agricultural aspects. Author index.
I22.9/2:15

1085. U.S. Department of the Interior. Bureau of Reclamation. *Draft Tube Surges, Review of Present Knowledge and Annotated Bibliography*; by H.T. Falvey. 1971. [1] + i + 25 + [4]pp. NTIS (REC--ERC Series, no. 71--42).
I27.60:71--42

1086. U.S. Department of the Interior. Bureau of Reclamation. *List of Bureau of Reclamation Bibliographies;* compiled by Janet B. Talbot. 1970. [5] + 39pp. $.80*** (Office of Engineering Reference, Library Branch, Denver, Colo. 80225). L.C. Card 75–609350.
I27.10/5:246

1087. U.S. Environmental Protection Agency. *A Literature Search and Critical Analysis of Biological Trickling Filter Studies, V. 1.* 1972. vii + 341 + [1]pp. $2.50* (Water Pollution Research Control Research Series 17050 DDY 12/71).
EP1.16:17050 DDY 12/71/v.1

1088. U.S. Environmental Protection Agency. *A Literature Search and Critical Analysis of Biological Trickling Filter Studies, V. 2.* 1972. v + 361pp. $2.75*.
Contained are 5665 entries with good citations to the literature which is international in scope. Entries are arranged alphabetically by author, but are not indexed. Vol. 1 is the critical analysis of the literature. Vol. 2 is the

bibliography.
EP1.16:17050 DDY 12/71/v.2

1089. U.S. Government Printing Office. *Maps. Engineering, Surveying.* Free* (Price List, no. 53).
Listed are selected for sale and free publications on civil engineering and maps. This list is revised frequently; prices are kept current; and publications listed are supposedly available.
GP3.9:53

1090. U.S. National Aeronautics and Space Administration. *Lubrication Corrosion and Wear, Continuing Bibliography with Indexes, Selection of Annotated References to Unclassified Reports and Journal Articles Introduced into NASA Information System, (Date).* NTIS (NASA SP--7020[no.]).
"References are included for topics such as lubricating systems, design and performance of bearings; special applications of lubricants, e.g., as heat transfer and anti-corrosion agents; stress corrosion and fatigue cracking in metals and alloys; friction and wear characteristics of materials; and corrosion types and techniques for corrosion preventions. In addition, references describing the instrumentation and methods for the testing of lubricants are included." Indexed by subject and author.
NAS1.21:7020

1091. U.S. National Bureau of Standards. *Hydraulic Research in the United States, 1968, Including Contributions from Canadian Laboratories; edited by Gersho Kulin.* 1969. 331pp. $2.50* (Special Publication, no. 316). L.C. Card 34--3323.
C13.10:316

1092. U.S. National Bureau of Standards. *Hydraulic Research in the United States, 1970, Including Contributions from Canadian Laboratories;* edited by Gershon Kulin and Pauline E. Gurewitz. 1971. 346pp. $2.50* (Special Publication, no. 346).
C13.10:346

1093. U.S. National Bureau of Standards. *Hydraulic Research in the United States, 1972, Including Contributions from Canadian Laboratories;* edited by Gershon Kulin and Pauline H. Gurewitz. 1974. xiv + 325pp. $3.00* S/N 0303--

1176. (Special Publication, no. 382). L.C. Card 73--60019. This publication which was annual through 1966 is now biennial. Listed are current and recently concluded research projects in hydraulics and hydrodynamics for the biennial period. Projects are reported from more than 250 university, industrial, state and federal government laboratories in the U.S. and Canada.
C13.10:382

1094. U.S. Tennessee Valley Authority. *Flood Damage Prevention, Indexed Bibliography*. 7th ed. 1973. [2] + 56pp.***
(TVA, Technical Library, Knoxville, Tennessee 37902).
Nearly 500 entries are in this new and expanded edition. Indexed by subject.
Y3.T25:31F65/973

Nuclear Science and Physics

1095. U.S. Atomic Energy Commission. *Bibliographies of Atomic Energy Literature Issued or in Progress*. 1964--. Bi--monthly. NTIS (TID–3700's).
Y3.At7:22/TID--3700's

1096. U.S. Atomic Energy Commission. *Bibliography of the Division of Isotopes Development and Contractor Publications;* compiled by P.S. Baker. 1972. v + 216pp. NTIS (ORNL--11C–33).
Y3.At7:22/ORNL 11C--33

1097. U.S. Atomic Energy Commission. *Bibliographies of Interest to the Atomic Energy Program, 1962–66;* compiled by Theodore F. Davis and others. 1968. vi + 250pp. NTIS (TID--3350).
"References with abstracts are given for 2001 bibliographies and literature surveys compiled from 1962 through 1966 that are related to atomic energy. Entries are categorized by subject, and appropriate cross references are provided. A report number index showing availability is included together with a corporate author index."
Y3.At7:22/TID--3350

1098. U.S. Atomic Energy Commission. *Bibliography of Mass Spectroscopy Literature for 1971*. 1973. xv + 607pp. NTIS (IS–3032).
Y3.At7:22/IS3032

1099.   U.S. Atomic Energy Commission. *Bibliography of Non--Destructive Assay Methods for Nuclear Material Safeguards;* compiled by Raymond E. Edwards, G. Vance Gritton and W.A. Higinbotham. 1972. [7] + 87pp. $1.00* (WASH–1170). Y3.At7:22/WASH--1170

1100.   U.S. Atomic Energy Commission. *Controlled Fusion and Plasma Research, Literature Search;* compiled by Milton O. Whitson. 1971. vii + 344 + 129pp. NTIS (TID--3557/1970 supp.). Y3.At7:22/TID–3557(1970 supp.)

1101.   U.S. Atomic Energy Commission. *Controlled Fusion and Plasma Research, Literature Search.* 1972. vii + 339 + 145pp. NTIS (TID–3557/1972 supp.). Y3.At7:22/TID--3557(1972 supp.)

1102.   U.S. Atomic Energy Commission. *Ecological Techniques Utilizing Radionuclides and Ionizing Radiation, Selected Bibliography;* by Vincent Schultz. 1969. [1] + 21pp. NTIS (RLO--2213--1). Y3.At7:22/RLO--2213--1

1103.   U.S. Atomic Energy Commission. *Ecological Techniques Utilizing Radionuclides and Ionizing Radiation, Selected Bibliography, Supp. 1.* 1972. [1] + i + 129pp. NTIS (RLO--2213--1/supp.). Y3.At7:22/RLO–2213–1/supp.

1104.   U.S. Atomic Energy Commission. *Marine Radioecology, Selected Bibliography of Non--Russian Literature;* by Eledon Edmundson, Jr., Vincent Schultz, and Alfred W. Klement, Jr. 1969. [1] + i + 127pp. NTIS (TID–3917). Y3.At7:22/TID–3917

1105.   U.S. Atomic Energy Commission. *Marine Radioecology, Selected Bibliography of Non–Russian Literature, Supp. 1.* 1972. [1] + i + 76pp. NTIS (TID–3917/Supp.1). Y3.At7:22/TID–3917(Supp.1)

1106.   U.S. Atomic Energy Commission. *Nuclear Rockets, Bibliography, 1966–67;* compiled by Hugh E. Voress. 1968. vi + 39pp. NTIS (TID–3586). Y3.At7:22/TID--3586

1107. U.S. Atomic Energy Commission. *Plowshare, Selected Annotated Bibliography of Civil, Industrial, and Scientific Uses of Nuclear Exposives;* compiled by Robert G. West, Robert G. Kelly. 1971. vii + 359pp. NTIS (TID--3522/rev.9).
Y3.At7:22/TID--3522(Rev.9)

1108. U.S. Atomic Energy Commission. *Pulsars, Bibliography;* by William D. Matheny. 1970. 76pp. NTIS (TID--3320).
Y3.At7:22/TID--3320

1109. U.S. Atomic Energy Commission. *Pulsars, Bibliography, Supp. 1.* 1971. iii + 40 + 24pp. NTIS (TID--3320/Supp.1).
Y3.At7:22/TID--3320 (supp.1)

1110. U.S. Atomic Energy Commission. *Pulsars, Bibliography, Supp. 2.* 1972. iii + 31pp. NTIS (TID--3320/Supp. 2).
Y3.At7:22/TID--3320(supp.2)

1111. U.S. Atomic Energy Commission. *Pulsars, Bibliography, Supp. 3.* 1973. iii + 91 + [38] pp. $5.45 NTIS (TID--3320/Supp.3).
Y3.At7:22/TID--3320(Supp.3)

Abstracts for this series are draw from *Nuclear Science Abstracts.*

1112. U.S. Atomic Energy Commission. *Radioactive Waste Processing and Disposal.* 1972. [5] + 592pp. NTIS (TID--3311/Supp.3).
Y3.At7:22/TID--3311(Supp.3)

1113. U.S. Atomic Energy Commission. *Reactor Fuel Burnup Calculations, Annotated Bibliography of Selected Literature;* compiled by Guy M. Inman. 1969. iii + [3] + 32pp. NTIS (WASH–1142).
Y3.At7:22/WASH--1142

1114. U.S. Atomic Energy Commission. *Reactor Safety, Literature Search.* (Revised and supplemented frequently). NTIS (TID--3525).
Y3.At7:22/TID–3525

1115. U.S. Atomic Energy Commission. *Reading Resources in Atomic Energy.* 1968. iv + 20pp.*** (AEC, P.O. Box 62,

Oak Ridge, Tenn. 37830). (Understanding the Atom
Series). L.C. Card 68–60542.
Two lists of general reading materials on atomic energy are
presented -- one for children and one for adults. Author
index.
Y3.At7:54At7/3

1116. U.S. Atomic Energy Commission. *Russian Radioecology,
Bibliography of Soviet Publications with Citations of
English Translations and Abstracts;* by Alfred W. Klement,
Jr., Charles F. Lytle, Vincent Schultz. 1968. iv + 131pp.
NTIS (TID–3915).
Y3.At7:22/TID–3915

1117. U.S. Atomic Energy Commission. *Russian Radioecology,
Bibliography of Soviet Publications with Citations of
English Translations and Abstracts, Supp. 1.* 1972. [1] + iii +
66pp. NTIS (TID--3915/Supp.1).
Y3.At7:22/TID--3915(supp.1)

1118. U.S. Atomic Energy Commission. *Safeguards and Nuclear
Materials Management, Annotated Bibliography of
Selected Literature;* compiled by Guy M. Inman. 1969.
iv + 44pp. NTIS (WASH--1141).
Y3.At7:22/WASH--1141

1119. U.S. Atomic Energy Commission. *Seismology, Aftershocks,
and Related Phenomena Associated with Underground Nuclear
Explosions, Bibliography of Selected Papers with Abstracts.*
1971. [1] + vii + 36pp. NTIS (NVO--87). L.C. Card 77–
614677.
Y3.At7:22/NVO–87

1120. U.S. Atomic Energy Commission. *Selected Annotated
Bibliography of Civil, Industrial, and Scientific Uses for
Nuclear Explosions;* compiled by Robert C. Kelly. 1972.
iv + 52pp. NTIS (TID--3522/9th rev./supp.1).
Y3.At7:22/TID--3522(Rev.9, Supp.1)

1121. U.S. Atomic Energy Commission. *Selected Bibliography of
Terrestrial, Freshwater and Marine Radiation Ecology;* by
Vincent Schultz and F. Ward Whicker. 1971. [1] + iv + 185pp.
NTIS (TID--25650). L.C. Card 71–612361.
Y3.At7:22/TID–25650

1122. U.S. Atomic Energy Commission. *Selected Bibliography on Radio–Active Occurrences in the United States;* by J. Victoria Krusiewski. 1970. 136pp. $1.25* (RME–4110). Y3.At7:22/RME–4110

1123. U.S. Atomic Energy Commission. *Technical Books and Mono-- graph Sponsored by the Atomic Energy Commission.* 6th ed. 1968. 92pp.*** (AEC, P.O. Box 62, Oak Ridge, Tenn. 37830). L.C. Card 62–60273.
    Listed are more than 200 books by the AEC and nearly 50 books in preparation which were prepared for researchers. Each publication is described in detail, and purchase price and availability are noted. Those publications "in prep-- aration" are listed separately. Indexed by author and title.
    Y3.At7:44T22/968

1124. U.S. Atomic Energy Commission. *Terrestrial and Freshwater Radioecology, Selected Bibliography, Supp. 5.* 1968. 1 + i + 75pp. NTIS (TID–3910/Supp.5). Y3.At7:22/TID--3910(Supp.5)

1125. U.S. Atomic Energy Commission. *Terrestrial and Freshwater Radioecology, Selected Bibliography, Supp. 6.* 1970. [1] + ii + 201pp. NTIS (TID--3910/Supp.6). Y3.At7:22/TID--3910(Supp.6)

1126. U.S. Atomic Energy Commission. *Terrestrial and Freshwater Radioecology, Selected Bibliography, Supp. 7.* 1971. [1] + ii + 219pp. NTIS (TID–3910/Supp.7). Y3.At7:22/TID--3910(Supp.7)

1127. U.S. Atomic Energy Commission. *Terrestrial and Freshwater Radioecology, Selected Bibliography, Supp. 8.* 1972. [1] + ii + 146pp. NTIS (TID–3910/Supp. 8). Y3.At7:22/TID--3910(Supp.8)

1128. U.S. Atomic Energy Commission. *Transplutonium Elements, Bibliography, Supp. 1.* 1969. v + 33pp. NTIS (TID--3317/ Supp.1). Y3.At7:22/TID--3317(Supp. 1)

1129. U.S. Atomic Energy Commission. *Transplutonium Elements Bibliography, Supp. 2;* prepared by Charles E. Stuber. [1970] v + 90pp. il. NTIS

(TID–3317/Supp.2).
Y3.At7:22/TID--3317(Supp.2)

1130. U.S. Atomic Energy Commission. *Transplutonium Elements Bibliography: Supp. 3;* prepared by Charles E. Stuber. 1972. iv + 90 + 34pp. NTIS (TID--3317/ Supp.3).
Y3.At7:22/TID--3317(Supp.3)

1131. U.S. Atomic Energy Commission. *Transplutonium Elements, Bibliography: Pt. 1, 95<Z<101; Pt. 2, Z>102.* 1968. NTIS (TID--3525).
Y3.At7:22/TID--3525

1132. U.S. Library of Congress. Science and Technology Division. *Nuclear Science in Mainland China, Selected Bibliography;* by Chi Wang. 1968. vi + 70pp. $.70* L.C. Card 68–62146. Contained are 615 titles of research reports, studies, articles, etc. on nuclear science in mainland China from 1958 through 1966. Each item listed is in the Library of Congress. Subject and author indexes.
LC33.2:C44/4

1133. U.S. National Aeronautics and Space Administration. *Properties of Selected Radioisotopes, Bibliography; Pt. 1, Unclassified Literature, Selection of Annotated References to Technical Papers, Journal Articles and Books;* compiled and edited by Dale Harris and Joseph Epstein. 1968. vii + 182pp. NTIS (NASA SP--7031).
Compiled here is the best available information on the nuclear, chemical, and physical properties of Sr--90, Cs--134, Cs--137, Ce--144, Pm--147, Po--210, Pu--238, Cm--242, and Cm--244. Eighteen different properties are reviewed for each of the above followed by an annotated bibliography.
NAS1.21:7031

1134. U.S. National Bureau of Standards. *Annotated Accession List of Data Compilations of the Office of Standard Reference Data;* by Herman M. Weisman and Gertrude B. Sherwood. 1970. iii + 193pp. $1.50* (Technical Note, no. 554). L.C. Card 74--609410.
Annotated at length are all the significant reference data compilations throughout the world. "The documents are organized in the following categories: General Collections, Nuclear Properties (including Fundamental Particles

Properties), Atomic and Molecular Properties, Solid State
Properties, Chemical Kinetics, Colloid and Surface
Properties, Mechanical Properties, and Thermodynamic
and Transport Properties. Sources of availability for the
listed publications are also provided." This is an out--
standing reference sourcebook for locating data.
C13.46:554

1135. U.S. National Bureau of Standards. *Bibliography of Ion--*
Molecules Reaction Data, January 1950–October 1971; by
George A. Sinnot. 1973. vi + 66 + [1] pp. $1.00* S/N 0303--
01126 (Special Publication, no. 381). L.C. Card 73--
600085.
"A bibliography is presented of papers in the open literature
that contain original experimental data on ion--molecule
reaction rates or cross sections. Positive and negative ion--
molecule and ion--ion reactions are included but not
electron impact processes. For papers to be included, the
reactants must have been identified and data for kinetic
energies below 10 electron volts must have been presented."
The bibliography is accompanied by a section of
"Reactions Equations" and an Author Index.
C13.10:381

1136. U.S. National Bureau of Standards. *Bibliography on*
Analyses of Optical Atomic Spectra: Sec. 1 [H1--V23];
by Charlotte E. Moore. 1968. vii + 80pp. $1.00*
(Special Publication, no. 306--1).
This bibliography and the three following update volumes
one through three of *Atomic Energy Levels as Derived*
from Analyses of Atomic Spectra (1949--) (NBS
Circular, no. 467). Literature references are given for each
spectrum of the following elements: Hydrogen; Helium;
Lithium; Beryllium; Boron; Carbon; Nitrogen; Oxygen;
Fluorine; Neon; Socium; Magnesium; Aluminum;
Silicon; Phosphorus; Sulfur; Chlorine; Argon;
Potassium; Calcium; Scandium; Titanium; and Vanadium.
C13.10:306–1

1137. U.S. National Bureau of Standards. *Bibliography on*
Analyses of Optical Atomic Spectra: Sec. 2 [Cr24--Nb41].
1969. vi + 57pp. $.60* (Special Publication, no. 306--2).
This section covers the following elements: Chromium,
Manganese; Iron; Cobalt; Nickel; Copper; Zinc; Callium;
Germanium; Arsenic; Selenium; Bromine; Krypton;

Rubidium; Strontium; Yttrium; Zirconium; and
Niobium.
C13.10:306–2

1138. U.S. National Bureau of Standards. *Bibliography on Analyses of Optical Atomic Spectra: Sec. 3 [42Mo--57La, 89Ac].*
1969. vi + 37pp. $.50* (Special Publication, no. 306–3).
This section covers the following elements: Molybdenum;
Technetium; Ruthenium; Rhodium; Palladium; Silver;
Cadmium; Indium; Tin; Antimony; Tellurium; Iodine;
Zenon; Cesium; Barium; Lanthanum; Hafnium;
Tantalum; Tungsten; Rehenium; Osmium; Iridium;
Platinum; Gold; Mercury; Thallium; Lead; Bismuth;
Polonium; Astatine; Radium; and Actinium.
C13.10:306–3

1139. U.S. National Bureau of Standards. *Bibliography on Analyses of Optical Atomic Spectra: Sec. 4 [57La–89Ac--99Es].*
1969. viii + 48pp. $.55* (Special Publication, no. 306--4).
This last section covers two groups of rare–earth spectra,
the lanthanides and the actinides. The Spectra of
Lanthanum are: Cerium, Praseodymium, Neodymium,
Promethium, Samarium, Europium, Gadolinium, Terbium,
Dysprosium, Holmium, Erbium, Thulium, Ytterbium,
Lutetium. The Spectra of Actinium are: Thorium,
Protactinium, Uranium, Neptunium, Plutomium,
Americium Curium, Berkelium, Californium, and Einsteinium.
C13.10:306--4

1140. U.S. National Bureau of Standards. *Bibliography on Atomic Energy Levels and Spectre, July 1968 through June 1971;*
by Lucy Hagan and W.C. Martin. 1972. iv + 102pp. $1.00*
(Special Publication, no. 363).
Contained are approximately 1100 references classified
by subject for individual atoms and atomic ions. A
number index identifies the references. "References
included contain data on energy levels, classified lines, wave
lengths, Zeeman Effect, Stark Effect, hyperfine structure,
isotope shift, ionization potentials, or theory which gives
results for specific atoms or atomic ions."
C13.10:363

1141. U.S. National Bureau of Standards. *Bibliography on Atomic Line Shapes and Shifts (1889 through March 1972) [with List of References];* by J.R. Ruhr, W.L. Wiese, and L.J.

Roszman. 1972. x + 154 + [1]pp. $1.75* (Special
Publication, no. 366).
Referenced are about 1400 separate publications from
1889 through March of 1972 which cover exhaustively
the atomic spectral line broadening literature.
C13.10:366

1142. U.S. National Bureau of Standards. *Bibliography on Atomic
Transition Probabilities, January 1916 -- June 1969;* by
B.M. Miles and W.L. Wiese. 1970. viii + 104pp. $1.25*
(Special Publication, no. 320). L.C. Card 76--604227.
Entries are arranged according to elements and stages of
ionization. The method employed and the classification of
transitions are indicated for each reference. Supplements
keep the information current.
C13.10:320

1143. U.S. National Bureau of Standards. *14--MeV Neutron
Generators in Activation Analysis, Bibliography;* G.J. Lutz,
Editor. 1970. 98pp. $1.00* (Special Publication, no. 533).
L.C. Card 72--608312.
C13.46:533

1144. U.S. National Bureau of Standards. *Photonuclear Reaction
Data, 1973 [with List of References];* by E.G. Fuller and
Others. 1973. iv + 125 + [1]pp. il. $2.10* (NBS
Special Publication, no. 380).
Though containing textual material, a primary portion of
this book is a comprehensive, annotated data index and
bibliography which cover experimental data for the field of
photonuclear reactions published in the scientific and
technical journals from 1955--1972.
C13.10:380

1145. U.S. National Bureau of Standards. *Time and Frequency,
Bibliography of NBS Literature Published July 1955 --
December 1970;* by B.E. Blair. 1971. 50pp. $.55*
S/N 0303--0871 (Special Publication, no. 350). L.C.
Card 73--611327.
This bibliography gives reference to papers and
publications of the past 15 years. It documents past
progress, aids access to available literature, and gives present
direction, scope, and status of NBS time and frequency
research.
C13.10:350

SOCIOLOGY

General

1146. U.S. Department of the Army. *Planning for Retirement, a Bibliography.* 1973. iii + 53 + [1] pp.*** (DA Pamphlet, no. 28--4).

Though designed for military personnel, this bibliography is good for anyone approaching or planning retirement. Publications are listed in the following broad subject categories: Education; A Second Career; Financial Planning; Health and Medical Care; Your Retirement Home; Leisure Time; Travel; Periodicals; Sources of Additional Information; and State Agencies on Aging. Not indexed.
D101.22:28--4

1147. U.S. Government Printing Office. *Social Services, Aging, Family Planning, Handicapped, Medicare, Nursing Homes, Pensions and Retirement, Poverty, Social Security and Social Welfare.* Free* (Price List, no. 78).

Listed are selected for sale and free publications on the topics mentioned in the title. This list is frequently revised; prices are current; and the publications listed are supposedly available.
GP3.9:78

1148. U.S. Social and Rehabilitation Service. *Publications of the Social and Rehabilitation Service, July, 1973.* 1973. ii + 37pp. Free***.

Publications are listed alphabetically by title under the issuing agency. Some of the primary subjects of these publications are: aging, delinquency, health services, mental retardation, and the disadvantaged and disabled. Subject and author indices assist in locating a desired publication. Most items included are free or inexpensive.
HE17.17:P96/973

1149. U.S. Social Security Administration. *Basic Readings in Social Security.* 1970. [5] + 181pp. $.75* L.C. Card 61--61469.

Entries are listed according to subject -- public assistance, poverty, unemployment insurance, poverty and minimum income proposals, Social Security programs in other nations, etc. There are separate listings for statistical publications and bibliographies dealing with the various Social Security programs. Author index. HE3.38:R22

Children

1150. U.S. Children's Bureau. *Bibliography on the Battered Child.* 1969. 22pp. L.C. Card 76–605031.
This publication is revised through 1968 to include publications and reports on the many aspects of child abuse. Entries are arranged by type -- articles and editorials, theses and dissertations, newspaper articles and editorials, and studies. Not indexed. (See no. 1156 for a continuation of this topic.)
FS17.212:B22

1151. U.S. Children's Bureau. *Good References on Day Care.* 1968. [3] leaves + 22pp.*** L.C. Card HEW 68–119.
Books and articles are listed under the following subject headings: Day Care Guides and Standards; Environmental Standards; Education and Child Development; Social Services; Health and Nutrition; Training of Staff; Parent Involvement; Administration and Coordination; and Evaluation. Availability and purchase information are indicated. Not indexed.
FS17.212:D33

1152. U.S. Government Printing Office. *Child Development, and Other Publications Relating to Children and Youth.* Free* (Price List, no. 71).
Listed are selected free and for sale publications relating to children and youth. This list is revised frequently; prices are kept current; and publications listed are supposedly available.
GP3.9:71

1153. U.S. Office of Child Development. *Bibliography: Home--Based Child Development Program Resources.* 1973. [3] + 27pp.***.
Seventy--five annotated entries, including periodical articles, will acquaint the reader with a number of recent, readily available resource materials to assist in planning and carrying out a home--based child development program emphasizing parent involvement.
HE21.211:H75

1154. U.S. Office of Child Development. *Bibliography on Early Childhood.* 1970. [1] + 16pp.** L.C. Card 78--610516. This is apparently a reprint of a 1969 memeographed publication by the same title (FS1.18:C43). The books and pamphlets listed deal with such topics as Book Selection for Children to Classroom Disorders. Arrangement is alphabetical by author. Not indexed. HE21.211:Ea7

1155. U.S. Office of Child Development. *Research Relating to Children.* No. 1-- 32. 1950--1973.* (NO. 32, the last issue, cost $1.75*). Entries are to on--going and recently completely research on children. Lengthy abstracts are grouped accordingly: Long--Term Research; Growth and Develop-- ment; Special Groups of Children; The Child in the Family; Socioeconomic and Cultural Factors; Educational Factors and Services; Social Services; and Health Services. Indexed by subject and researcher. HE21.112:no.

1156. U.S. Public Health Service. Health Services and Mental Health Administration. National Institute of Mental Health. *Selected References on the Abused and Battered Child.* [1972.] 11pp. $.20* L.C. Card 73--601389. Articles and books are arranged alphabetically by main entry according to the year of publication. Since similar bibliographies (no. 1150) cover prior years, this one includes only those references since 1968. HE20.2417:C43/2

1157. U.S. White House Conference on Children. *An Annotated Bibliography on Children.* 1970. 75pp. $.75* L.C. Card 71--610411. Included are publications on children which are well--known and generally available and those which are very current. Y3.W58/3--2:9C43

1158. U.S. White House Conference on Children. *World of Children: Films from the 1970 White House Conference on Children;* compiled by Victor Margolin. 1970. 18pp. $.40*. The films annotated here represent some of the best video available on topics related to children. They are an excellent resource for anyone working with children --

parents, teachers, the medical profession, and law
enforcement officers.
Y3.W58/3--2:2W89

Criminology

1159. U.S. Children's Bureau. *Prevention of Juvenile Delinquency,
a Selected Annotated Bibliography.* 1968. [1] + 15pp.
$.30*.
Listed alphabetically by author are 29 books and journals
published since 1960 which were selected and annotated
"to introduce concerned citizens, students, and others to
recent thinking and developments in the field.
FS17.212:J98

1160. U.S. Department of the Air Force. Pacific Air Forces.
Criminology; prepared by Frances D. Fetz. 1969. iv + 51pp.
*** (PACAF Basic Bibliographies).
D301.62:C86/969

1161. U.S. Department of the Air Force. Pacific Air Forces.
Criminology: Supp. 1. 1970. [1] + iv + 33pp.***.
Kept current with frequent supplements, this annotated
bibliography covers many aspects of criminology --
Crime and Criminals, Criminal Investigation, Criminal
Law, and Penology.
D301.62:C86/969/supp.1

1162. U.S. Department of the Air Force. Pacific Air Forces.
Criminology: Supp. 2. 1971. [1] + iv + 33pp.***.
D301.62:C86/969/supp.2

1163. U.S. Department of Justice. *Corrections, a Bibliography.*
1971. 14pp.***.
J16.10:C81

1164. U.S. Department of Justice. Law Enforcement Assistance
Administration. *LEAA Reference List of Publications.* 1971.
19pp. $.20* S/N 2700--0078.
The subtitle reads "selected listings on law enforcement,
criminal justice, federal grants, crime problems, research
and delinquency, collective violence, organized crime,
drugs and drug abuse, commission reports, committee
reports. Publications are listed according to their source --
American Medical Association, Federal Bureau of Prisons,

LEAA, American Correctional Association, etc. Prices are given for all publications, and U.S. Government Printing Office publications are identified with the SuDoc call number.
J1.20/2:L41

1165--1170. More than a bibliography, these volumes and their supple-- ments give the complete holdings of the Law Enforcement Assistance Administration. Each catalog -- Author, Periodicals, Subject, and Title -- gives complete bibliographic citations to the materials. The bulk of the material will deal with the varied aspects of law enforcement and criminal justice -- drugs, delinquency, felons, probation, trial, statistics, etc. -- but there are also titles of a general nature.

1165. U.S. Department of Justice. Law Enforcement Assistance Administration. *Library Book Catalog of the Law Enforcement Assistance Administration; Author Catalog.* 1972. [2] + 465pp. $5.00* S/N 2700--00170. J1.20/3:Au8/972--2

1166. U.S. Department of Justice. Law Enforcement Assistance Administration. *Library Book Catalog of the Law Enforcement Assistance Administration: Periodicals Catalog.* 1972. [1] + 25pp. $.55* S/N 2700--00171. J1.20/3:P41

1167. U.S. Department of Justice. Law Enforcement Assistance Administration. *Library Book Catalog of the Law Enforcement Assistance Administration: Subject Catalog.* 1972. [2] + 812pp. $8.25*. J1.20/3:Su1

1168. U.S. Department of Justice. Law Enforcement Assistance Administration. *Library Book Catalog of the Law Enforcement Assistance Administration: Subject Catalog. Supplement June 1973.* 1973. [2] + 199pp. $2.05* S/N 2700--00211. J1.20/3:Su1/supp.

1169. U.S. Department of Justice. Law Enforcement Assistance Administration. *Library Book Catalog of the Law Enforcement Assistance Administration: Title Catalog.* 1972. [2] + 473pp. $2.25* S/N 2700--0153.

J1.20/3:T53/972--2

1170.   U.S. Department of Justice. Law Enforcement Assistance
Administration. *Library Book Catalog of the Law
Enforcement Assistance Administration: Title Catalog.
Supplement June 1973.* 1973. [2] + 136pp. $1.50*
S/N 2700--00213.
J1.20/3:T53/972--2/supp.

1171.   U.S. Public Health Service. Health Services and Mental Health
Administration. National Institute of Mental Health. *Crime
and Delinquency Abstracts.* Vol. 1--8. 1966--1972. Bimonthly.
The lengthy abstracts on current published research and
of on--going research are facilitated by author and subject
indices. Included is a list of journals from which articles
were abstracted.
This was formerly entitled *International Bibliography
on Crime and Delinquency* and was classified FS2.22/13--
4:Vol./no.
HE20.2420:Vol./no.

1172.   U.S. Social and Rehabilitation Service. Youth Development
and Delinquency Prevention Administration. *Publications
and Films.* 1970. 15pp.***.
Publications and films are described briefly. Running
time for film is noted.
HE17.809:P96/970

Population Studies and Family Planning

1173.   U.S. Air Force Academy. *The Malthusian Spectre,
Challenges of Food and Population;* compiled by Ottie
K. Sutton with assistance of Louis Bassetti. 1969. [5] +
33pp.** (AF Academy Library, Special Bibliography, no. 42).
L.C. Card 72--606141.
A listing of books, periodicals, and documents covers the
following: (1) world poverty and hunger; (2) agricultural
perspectives; (3) Malthusianism -- and the opposition;
(4) population pressures; (5) population: fetility and
control; and (6) the third world predicament. Not
indexed.
The SuDoc number is indicated for U.S. Government
publications
D305.12:42

1174. U.S. Bureau of the Census. *Bureau of the Census Catalog.* Quarterly, cumulative to annual volume. $10.90* for 4 consecutive issues and 12 monthly supplements. L.C. 47--46253.

This is a bibliographic listing with price and SuDoc call number of current Census Bureau publications. Infor-- mation available through the Data User Services Office only is listed separately. Indexed by subject and geographic area.

(Formerly classed C3.163/3:date.)
C56.222:date

1175--1181. Included in the following are staff papers and publi-- cations of the Census Bureau on methodological research. Publications are arranged alphabetically by author within such subject categories as Statistical Theory and Sampling Methods; Measurement of Coverage and Response Error; and Data Processing. Availability is noted for most titles. See no. 1182

See no. 1182 for index.

1175. U.S. Bureau of the Census. *Census Bureau Methodological Re-- search, 1963--66, Annotated List of Papers and Reports.* 1968. [4] + 32pp. $.25* L.C. Card A68--7966.
C3.163/4:M56/963--66

1176. U.S. Bureau of the Census. *Census Bureau Methodological Re-- search, 1967.* 1969. [4] + 15pp. $.30*.
C3.163/4:M56/967

1177. U.S. Bureau of the Census. *Census Bureau Methodological Research, 1968.* 1970. [4] + 17pp. $.30*.
C3.163/4:M56/968

1178. U.S. Bureau of the Census. *Census Bureau Methodological Research, 1969.* 1970. [4] + 17pp. $.30*.
C3.163/4:M56/969

1179. U.S. Bureau of the Census. *Census Bureau Methodological Research, 1970.* 1971. [4] + 15pp. $.30*.
C3.163/4:M56/970

1180. U.S. Bureau of the Census. *Census Bureau Methodological Research, 1971.* 1972. [4] + 15pp. $.30*.
C56.222/3:M56/971

1181. U.S. Bureau of the Census. *Census Bureau Methodological Research, 1972.* 1973. [4] + 22 + [2] pp. $.60*.
C56.222/3:M56/972

1182. U.S. Census Bureau. *Census Bureau Methodological Research, 1963--71 Key Word Subject Index.* 1973. 230pp.***
(Data User Services Office).
This indexes the research in the seven above entries.
C56.222/3:M56/963--71/Ind.

1183. U.S. Children's Bureau. *Selected References for Social Workers on Family Planning, Annotated List;* compiled by Mary Watts. 1968. [3] + 23pp. $.25* L.C. Card HEW68–41.
Annotated entries for books and journal articles are listed under the following headings: General; Studies of Attitudes About Family Planning; Examples of Family Planning Services, Social Work References; and Others. Not indexed.
(See also no. 1186).
FS17.212:F21

1184. U.S. National Archives and Records Service. *Federal Population Censuses, 1790–1890: Catalog of Microfilm Copies of the Schedules.* 1971. 90pp.*** L.C. Card 72–610891.
Listings are chronological by census, followed alpha--betically by state or territory and country. The following is given for each microfilm: photocopy number, total number of rolls, price, and price for each state or territory.
GS4.2:P81/2/790--890--5

1185. U.S. Public Health Service. *International Family Planning, Bibliography;* by David L. Kasdon. 1969. v + 62pp. $.35* L.C. Card 73--604079.
Contained are 217 abstracts of books and journal articles which are listed alphabetically by author. Sub--ject and geographic indices facilitate its use. Included separately is a list of journals fully covered by this bibliography.
FS2.22/13:F21/2

1186. U.S. Public Health Service. Health Services and Mental

Health Administration. Federal Health Program Service. *Selected References of Social Workers on Family Planning, Annotated List;* compiled by Mary E. Watts. 1971. 3 + 38pp. $.50* L.C. Card 78--611907.

In addition to the topics mentioned in the previous entry, this most current bibliography includes selected references on Contraceptives and Abortion. Not indexed. HE20.2759:So1

1187.   U.S. Public Health Service.Health Services and Mental Health Administration. National Center for Health Statistics. *Marriage and Divorce, Bibliography of Statistical Studies.* Rev. 1969. 1969. [1] + 9pp. L.C. Card 79--604103.

"Compiled to provide a guide to quantative research studies on marriage and divorce" this bibliography includes only publications which utilize marriage and divorce statistics; publications which include theories and findings that could be tested by analyses of quantative data; publications which are bibliographies of reports; or publications which are statistical treatments of marriage and divorce. Arrangement is by subject. Not indexed. FS2.121:M34/969

Poverty

1188.   U.S. Department of Agriculture. *The Poor, Select Biblio-- graphy;* by Peter R. Maida and John L. McCoy. 1969. 1 + ii + 56pp. $.60* (Miscellaneous Publication, no. 1145). L.C. Card 70--602234.

Six hundred and sixty–two citations cover all aspects of poverty in the United States from its historical perspective to alternative solutions to the problem. Entries are grouped by such subjects as: Poverty in Contrast with Affluence; The Elderly; Family Types and Behavior; Cultural Milieu; and Welfare and Dependency. Author index. A1.38:1145

1189.   U.S. Social and Rehabilitation Service. *Poor People at Work, Annotated Bibliography on Semi--Professionals in Education, Health, and Welfare Services;* by Linda I. Millman and Catherine Chilman. 1969. [1] + 40pp.*** L.C. Card 79--602342.

Included is most of what has been written . . . in the professional literature and official reports in the five

years prior to 1969 on poor people employed as semi--professionals in human service occupations. Arrangement is alphabetical by author under subject category.
FS17.17:P79

1190. U.S. Social Security Administration. *Poverty Studies in the Sixties: a Selected, Annotated Bibliography;* compiled by James S. Parker. 1970. [5] + 126pp. $.60. L.C. Card 78--605471.
Represented by this bibliography is a broad view of the general field of poverty and its related programs, such as housing, unemployment, and education. Entries are arranged by subject. Indexed by author.
HE3.38:P86

TRANSPORTATION

General

1191. U.S. President. Committee on Employment of the Handi--capped. *Guidebooks for Handicapped Travelers.* 1968. 16pp.***.
Guidebooks which are available to handicapped travelers are listed according to state and/or city. Addresses given for obtaining guidebooks.
PrEx1.10/8:T69

1192. U.S. Department of Transportation. *Department of Trans--portation Selected Readings.* 1970. v + 15pp.** (Biblio-graphic List, no. 3). L.C. Card 78--608319.
TD1.15:3

1193. U.S. Department of Transportation. *Transportation for the Handicapped, Selected References.* 1969. v + 26pp. NTIS (Bibliographic List, no. 1).
Almost 200 entries cover the transportation of the handicapped by air and automobile. Special attention is given to special equipment for the blind and handicapped and the accessibility of travel facilities to them. Subject arrangement. Author index.
TD1.15:1

1194. U.S. Department of Transportation. *Urban Mass Transpor--tation, Bibliography;* compiled by Dawn E. Willis. 1971.

[7] + 140pp. NTIS (Bibliographic List, no. 6).
Includes 900 selected references from 1960 through June
1971. Indexed by author and subject.
TD1.15:6

1195. U.S. Department of Transportation. Safety Office. *Published
Reports by the Office of High Speed Ground Transportation
and the Northeast Corridor Transportation Project,
Department of Transportation.* 1969. [2] + 17 + [6] pp.**
TD3.12:H53/2

1196. U.S. Department of Transportation. Safety Office. *Published
Reports by the Office of High Speed Ground Transportation
and the Northeast Corridor Transportation Project,
Department of Transportation.* October 1969. [2] + 30pp.***.
TD3.12:H53/2/969–2

1197. U.S. Department of Transportation. Urban Mass Transporation
Administration. *Urban Transportation Bibliography.* 1971.
110pp. NTIS (PB 199031).
TD7.10:Ur1

Air

1198. U.S. Civil Aeronautics Board. *List of Publications.* 1971.
16pp.***.
C31.255:971

1199. U.S. Department of the Air Force. Air University Library.
Pilot Training. 1972. 15pp.*** (Special Bibliography,
no. 201).
Included are documents, books, and articles on requirements,
training, and proficiency of pilots.
D301.26/11:201

1200. U.S. Department of Defense. Defense Documentation Center.
Supersonic Transports. 1973. 169pp. NTIS (AD-755600).
(Report No. DDC-TAS 72-72).
Citations from October 1961 to December 1971 are
arranged under 13 major headings and indexed by subject,
author, monitoring agency, contractor, and report number.

1201. U.S. Department of Transportation. *Hijacking, Selected
Readings.* 1971. vi + 53pp. NTIS (Bibliographic List,
no. 5). L.C. Card 73–614747.
Supplements a 1969 document (no. 1205), chronologically
listing 268 entries, many annotated, for the period February

1969 through December 1970. Indexed by subject.
TD1.15:5

1202.   U.S. Department of Transportation. *Airport Problems,*
Access and Air Traffic Congestion, Selected Readings.
1971. v + 34pp. NTIS (Bibliographic List, no. 4). L.C.
Card 75--611968.
This listing of 191 journal articles, reports and papers on
airport access and air traffic delays updates other biblio--
graphic lists on similar subjects by the FAA. Availability
and sources for obtaining the publications listed are given.
Author index.
TD1.15:4

1203.   U.S. Federal Aviation Administration. *Air Traffic and*
Airport Congestion, Selected References; compiled by Nancy
B. Nelsen. 1969. iii + 39pp. NTIS. L.C. Card 78--601787.
This is a selected, partially annotated bibliography of 224
newspaper and journal articles, and papers and technical
reports on the subject of congestion at airports.
TD4.17/3:17

1204.   U.S. Federal Aviation Administration. *FAA Publications.*
Semi--Annual. Free***.
This "catalog of selected printed materials which may be
of interest to the public, to pilots and to the aviation
industry" is arranged by subject. Instructions for
ordering are provided.
TD4.17:yr.

1205.   U.S. Federal Aviation Administration. *Hijacking, Selected*
References; compiled by Ann O'Brien. 1969. i + 22pp.
NTIS.
Listed chronologically from 1961 through 1968 are 206
articles in periodicals and newspapers which deal with air
piracy.
TD4.17/3:18

1206.   U.S. Government Printing Office. *Air Force, Aviation, Civil*
Aviation, Naval Aviation, and Federal Aviation Administration.
Free*   (Price List, no. 79).
Listed are selected free and for sale publications on
aviation. This lists is revised frequently; prices are kept
current; and publications listed are supposedly available.
GP3.9:79

Roads and Highways

1207. U.S. Bureau of Public Roads. *Literature References to High-ways and Their Environmental Considerations.* 1969. xiv + 80pp.**. L.C. Card 71–603293.
TD2.123:L71

1208. U.S. Bureau of Public Roads. *New Developments in Highways, Design, Economics, Environment, Hydraulics, Maintenance, Management, Materials, Right–of–Way, Structures, Traffic, Newsbriefs for Highway Managers and Practicing Engineers.* 1969. [7]p.**.
TD2.124:969

1209. U.S. Federal Highway Administration. *Federal Highway Administration Publications.* 1969.**.
TD2.10:P96/969

1210. U.S. Government Printing Office. *Transportation, Highways, Roads, and Postal Service.* Free* (Price List, no. 25).
Listed are selected free and for sale publications. This list is revised frequently; prices are kept current; and all publications listed are supposedly available.
GP3.9:25

Water

1211. U.S. Coast Guard. *Coast Guard Auxiliary, Bibliography of Publications.* 1971. iii + 59pp.** L.C. Card 74–611965.
Listed with price information are government and non-government publications concerned with boating, boating skills, and boating safety. A source directory follows.
TD5.21/2:971

1211a. U.S. Coast Guard. *United States Coast Guard Annotated Bibliography;* compiled by Truman R. Strobridge. 1972. 35pp.***.
Listed with brief annotations are books, monographs, booklets, and pamphlets about the U.S. Coast Guard. Materials included are more scholarly than popular in nature, which makes this bibliography useful to researchers and historians.

1212. U.S. Maritime Administration. *Port Information Sources.*

1972. 4 + 24pp.*** (Office of Ports and Intermodel Systems).
C39.227:P83

1213. U.S. Maritime Administration. *Publications of the Maritime Administration.* 1973. 11pp. Free***.
Price and source availability are given for the numerous Maritime Administration technical, statistical, and informational publications dealing with shipping, containerization, seamen, ports, and personnel and training. Available charts are also listed.
C39.227:P96/973

MISCELLANY

1214. U.S. Census Bureau. *Foreign Statistical Publications, Accession List.* Quarterly.** L.C. Card 49--3797.
Included are important foreign statistical publications. Arrangement is by country publishing the material.
C56.238:date

1215. U.S. Department of Agriculture. Information Office. *Popular Publications for the Farmer, Suburbanite, Home--maker, Consumer.* Rev. 1972. 1972. vi + 20pp. Free***.
Numerous free "how to" and informational bulletins and pamphlets are listed. Topics cover everything from cooking and canning and freezing to weed control and poisonous plants. This free booklet provides one with access to popular, handy and free publications.
A21.9/8:5/20

1215a. U.S. Department of Agriculture. Library. *Non--Urban Patterns of Land Utilization, 1963--68;* compiled by Betty Baxtresser. 1968. iv + 39pp.*** (Library List, no. 93).
Contained are 576 references on "current and projected patterns of rural growth, transportation, land values, public lands, forest resources, natural resource conservation, and regional planning." Items are listed under broad categories such as: Rural Growth; Transportation; Conservation; and Regional Planning. Indexed by subject and author.
A17.17:93

1216. U.S. Department of the Interior. Bureau of Reclamation.

Publications for Sale. 1973. [2] + 29pp. Free*** (Denver Federal Center, Denver, Colorado 80225).

1217--1223. The following are selected free and for sale publications on the topics mentioned in the title. Lists are revised frequently; prices are kept current; and all publications are supposedly available.

1217. U.S. Government Printing Office. *Census Publications, Statistics of Agriculture, Business, Governments, Housing, Manufactures, Minerals, Population, and Maps.* Free* (Price List, no. 70).
GP3.9:70

1218. U.S. Government Printing Office. *Library of Congress.* Free* (Price List, no. 83).
GP3.9:83

1219. U.S. Government Printing Office. *National Parks, Historic Sites, National Monuments.* Free* (Price List, no. 35).
GP3.9:35

1220. U.S. Government Printing Office. *Posters and Charts.* Free* (Price List, no. 81).
GP3.9:81

1221. U.S. Government Printing Office. *Tariff and Taxation.* Free* (Price List, no. 37).
GP3.9:37

1222. U.S. Government Printing Office. *Smithsonian Institution, National Museum and Indians.* Free* (Price List, no. 55).
GP3.9:55

1223. U.S. Government Printing Office. *States and Territories of the United States and Their Resources, Including Beautification, Public Buildings and Lands, and Recreational Resources.* Free* (Price List, no. 87).
GP3.9:87

1224. U.S. Library of Congress. *Federal Libraries, Select List of Documents Available Through Educational Resources Information Center;* compiled by Frank Kurt Cylke. 1972. [5] + 26pp.
This is an annotated listed of materials about Federal

Libraries which are available from ERIC.
LC1.32/2:F31

1225. U.S. Library of Congress. *Copyright Office. Selected Biblio–graphy on Copyright.* Revised frequently. 2pp. Free***.
Listed are the primary books and periodicals dealing with
United States, British and Canadian, and International
copyright.
LC3.4/2:2B

1226. U.S. National Museum. *Publications of the United States National Museum (1947–1970).* 1971. 77pp. $.60*
(National Museum Bulletin, no. 298).
As the last issue in this Bulletin series, this publication
supplements Bulletin 193, *A List and Index of the Publi–cations of the United States National Museum (1875–1948).*
Publications are indexed by subject, author, and place.
SI3.3:298

1227. U.S. Tennessee Valley Authority. *Bibliography of the TVA Program.* 1968. [1] + 77pp.*** (TVA, Technical Library,
Knoxville, Tennessee 37902).
Besides the development of a hydroelectric system, the
TVA has been active in archeological investigations,
fertilizer technology, forestry programs, and recreational
development. The publications listed here cover the many
aspects of the TVA program.
Y3.T25:31 T25/968

1228. U.S. Tennessee Valley Authority. *Indexed Bibliography of the Tennessee Valley Authority, Cumulative Supplement, January – December (Year).* Annual.*** (TVA, Technical
Library, Knoxville, Tennessee 37902). L.C. Card 36–26628.
Listed are journal articles about the TVA. Indexed by
subject and author.
Y3.T25:31/T25/2/yr.

APPENDIX A

Purchase and Availability Infomation

Price and availability were indicated for a bibliography when known. However, *all prices are subject to change without notice.* The following designate availability:

*   U.S. Government Printing Office
**   Limited use. Not generally available.
***   Available from issuing agency.
NTIS   National Technical Information Service

Ordering from the Government Printing Office

If ordering from the Government Printing Office, remit check, postal money order, express order, or GPO coupons. *Prices are subject to change without notice.* Address order to:
> Superintendent of Documents
> U.S. Government Printing Office
> Washington, D.C. 20402   Tel. (202) 541–2081

Although the following retail Government Printing Office Bookstores have in stock only about 1,000 of the most popular GPO titles, one might prefer ordering from one of them.

Government Printing Office
710 North Capitol Street
Washington, D.C. 20402
Telephone: Area code 202–783--3238

Forrestal Bookstore
Room 1--J--001
James Forrestal Building
1000 Independence Ave.
(L'Enfant Plaza)
Washington, D.C. 20407
Telephone: Area code 202–426--7937

Department of Commerce, Lobby
14th and Constitution Avenue NW.
Washington, D.C. 20230
Telephone: Area code 202–967–3527

Atlanta Bookstore
Room 100, Federal Building

275 Peachtree Street NE.
Atlanta, Georgia 30303
Telephone: Area code 404–526–6947

Birmingham Bookstore
Room 102A, 2121 Building
2121 Eighth Avenue North
Birmingham, Alabama 35203
Telephone: Area code 205–325–6056

Boston Bookstore
Room G25, John F. Kennedy Federal Building
Sudbury Street
Boston, Massachusetts 02203
Telephone: Area code 617–223–6071

Canton, Ohio Bookstore
Federal Office Building
201 Cleveland Avenue SW.
Canton, Ohio 44702
Telephone: Area code 216–455–8971

Chicago Bookstore
Room 1463 – 14th floor
Everett McKinley Dirksen Building
219 South Dearborn Street
Chicago, Illinois 60604

Dallas Bookstore
Room 1C46
Federal Building – U.S. Courthouse
1100 Commerce Street
Dallas, Texas 75202
Telephone: Area code 214–749–1541

Detroit Bookstore
Room 229, Federal Building
231 W. Lafayette Blvd.
Detroit, Michigan 48226
Telephone: Area code 313–226–7816

Denver Bookstore
Room 1421
Federal Building – U.S. Courthouse
1961 Stout Street

Denver, Colorado 80202
Telephone: Area code 303--837--3965

Kansas City Bookstore
Room 135, Federal Office Building
601 East 12th Street
Kansas City, Missouri 64106
Telephone: Area code 816--374--2160

Los Angeles Bookstore
Room 1015, Federal Office Building
300 North Los Angeles Street
Los Angeles, California 90012
Telephone: Area code 213--688--5841

New York Bookstore
Room 110
26 Federal Plaza
New York, New York 10007
Telephone: Area code 212--264--3826

Philadelphia Bookstore
U.S. Post Office and Courthouse
Main Lobby
Ninth and Chestnut Streets
Philadelphia, Pennsylvania 19107
Telephone: Area code 215--597--0677

San Francisco Bookstore
Room 1023, Federal Office Building
450 Golden Gate Avenue
San Francisco, California 94102

A telephone call to one of the above, especially the Washington Office (202--541--2081) should result in current price and availability information.

Requesting Material from Issuing Agencies

If a bibliography is designated as being available from the issuing agency (***), request the publication directly from that Office. Since government offices frequently change name or are moved about in the governmental structure, reference is given from the agency as it was called when it produced a particular bibliography to its current title and address as of 1974.

Directory of Issuing Agencies

Agency for International Development
U.S. Department of State
Washington, D.C. 20523
Tel. 202--632--9318

Agricultural Marketing Service
U.S. Department of Agriculture
Washington, D.C. 20250
Tel. 202--447--6766

Agricultural Research Service
U.S. Department of Agriculture
Washington, D.C. 20250
Tel. 202--447--4433

Agriculture Department
Information Department
Washington, D.C. 20250
Tel. 202--447--2791

Air Force Academy Library
U.S. Air Force Academy
Colorado, 80840
Tel. 303--472--2590

Air Force Cambridge Research Laboratories
L.G. Hanscon Field
Bedford, Mass. 01730
Tel. 617--861--4895 (Library)

Air Force Department
The Pentagon
Washington, D.C. 20330
Tel. 202--545--6700

Air Force Systems Command
Andrews Air Force Base
Washington, D.C. 20331

Air Programs Office
now

Air and Water Programs Office
Environmental Protection Agency
Office of Public Affiars
Communications Services Division
401 M St. SW
Washington, D.C. 20460
Tel. 202--755--0707

Air University Library
Maxwell Air Force Base, Ala. 36112

Army Cold Regions Research and Engineering Laboratory
P.O. Box 282
Hanover, N.H. 03755
Tel. 603–643–3200

Army Command and General Staff College
Fort Leavenworth, Kansas 66027
Tel. 913–684–4358

Army Chief of Engineers
U.S. Department of the Army
Washington, D.C. 20314
Tel. 202–693–6136

Army Corps of Engineers
Office of the Chief of Engineers
Publications Depot
890 Picket Street
Alexandria, Va. 22304

Army Corps of Engineers
U.S. Coastal Engineering Research Center
5201 Little Falls Road NW.
Washington, D.C. 20016
Tel. 282–2592

Army Engineer Waterways Experiment Station
P.O. Box 631
Vicksburg, Miss. 39180
Tel. 601--636–311

Army Medical Service
U.S. Army Health Services Command
The Pentagon

Washington, D.C. 20310

Army Natick Laboratories
Natick, Mass. 01760
Tel. 617–653–1000

Blind and Physically Handicapped Division
Library of Congress
Taylor St. Annex
1291 Taylor Street
Washington, D.C. 20542
Tel. 202–426–5100
202–882–5500

Budget Bureau
now
Office of Management and Budget
Executive Office Building
Washington, D.C. 20503
Tel. 202–395–300

Cabinet Committee on Opportunity for the Spanish Speaking
in the United States
1707 H. Street NW.
Washington, D.C. 20006
Tel. 202–382–6651

Catalog Publication Division
Library of Congress
10th First Street SE.
Washington, D.C. 20540
Tel. 202–426–6120

Census Bureau
Social and Economic Statistics Administration
U.S. Department of Commerce
Washington, D.C. 20233
Tel. 301–763–7273

Center for Disease Control
U.S. Public Health Service
1600 Clifton Road NE.
Atlanta, Ga. 30333
Tel. 404–633–3311

Children's Bureau
Office of Child Development
Washington, D.C. 20201
Tel. 202–755–7725

Civil Defense Office
now
Defense Civil Preparedness Agency
The Pentagon
Washington, D.C. 20301
Tel. 202–695–9441

Civil Rights Commission
1121 Vermont Avenue NW
Washington, D.C. 20425
Tel. 202–254–6758

Civil Service Commission
1900 E Street NW
Washington, D.C. 20415
Tel. 202–655–4000

Coast Guard
400 Seventh Street SW
Washington, D.C. 20590
Tel. 202–426–2158

Community Health Service
Health Services Administration
5600 Fishers Lane
Rockville, Md. 20852
Tel. 301–443–1070

Congress
see
United States Congress

Copyright Office
Washington, D.C. 20559
Tel. 703–557–8700

Corps of Engineers
see
Army Corps of Engineers

Defense Civil Preparedness Agency
The Pentagon
Washington, D.C. 20301
Tel. 202-695-9441

Domestic Commerce Bureau
now
Domestic and International Business Administration
Washington, D.C. 20230
Tel. 202-967-3808

Earth Sciences Laboratory
U.S. Army Natick Laboratories
Natick, Mass. 01760
Tel. 617-653-1000

Economic Opportunity Office
1200 Nineteenth St. NW.
Washington, D.C. 20506
Tel. 202-254-5000

Economic Research Service
U.S. Department of Agriculutre
500 Twelfth Street SW.
Washington, D.C. 20250
Tel. 202-447-8104

Education Office
400 Maryland Avenue SW.
Washington, D.C. 20202
Tel. 202-962-7223

Emergency Health Service
Health Services Administration
5600 Fishers Lane
Rockville, Md. 20852

Employment Security Bureau
now
Manpower Administration
Fourteenth Street and Constitution Avenue NW.
Washington, D.C. 20210
Tel. 202-961-2822

Environmental Data Service
National Oceanic Atmospheric Administration
3300 Whitehaven Street
Washington, D.C. 20235
Tel. 202--343--6812
202--343--6282

Environmental Protection Agency
401 M Street SW.
Washington, D.C. 20460
Tel. 202--755--707

Environmental Science Services Administration
now
National Oceanic Atmospheric Administration
Office of Public Affairs
Department of Commerce
Rockville, Md. 20852
Tel. 301--496--8243

External Research Division
now
External Research Office
Bureau of Intelligence and Research
U.S. Department of State
·2201 C Street NW.
Washington, D.C. 20520
Tel. 202--632--1342

Farmer Cooperative Service
U.S. Department of Agriculture
Washington, D.C. 20250
Tel. 202--447--8870

Federal Aviation Administration
U.S. Department of Transportation
800 Independence Avenue
Washington, D.C. 20591
Tel. 202--426--3883

Federal Highway Administration
U.S. Department of Transportation
400 Seventh Street
Washington, D.C. 20590
Tel. 202--426--0714

Federal Water Pollution Control Administration
now
Air and Water Programs Office
Environmental Protection Agency
Office of Public Affairs
Communications Services Division
401 M Street SW.
Washington, D.C. 20460
Tel. 202–755–0707

Food and Drug Administration
U.S. Public Health Service
200 C Street SW.
Washington, D.C. 20204
Tel. 202--962–6637

Foreign Affiars Documentation Center
Bureau of Intelligence and Research
U.S. Department of State
2201 C Street NW.
Washington, D.C. 20520
Tel. 202–632–1342

Foreign Agricultural Service
U.S. Department of Agriculture
Washington, D.C. 20250
Tel. 202--447–3448

Foreign Service Institute
Bureau of Intelligence and Research
U.S. Department of State
2201 C Street NW
Washington, D.C. 20520
Tel. 202--632–1342

Forest Products Laboratory
U.S. Forest Service
P.O. Box 5130
Madison, Wisconsin 53705
Tel. 608--257–2211

Forest Service
Twelfth Street and Independence Avenue
Washington, D.C. 20250
Tel. 202–447–6957

202--447--3957

Geological Survey
U.S. Department of the Interior
12201 Sunrise Valley Drive
Reston, Va. 22092
Tel. 703-860--7444

Health Manpower Education Bureau
Health Resources Administration
5600 Fishers Lane
Rockville, Md. 20852
Tel. 301-496-2251

Health Resources Administration
U.S. Public Health Service
5600 Fishers Lane
Rockville, Md. 20852
Tel. 301-443-2106

Health Services Administration
U.S. Public Health Service
5600 Fishers Lane
Rockville, Md. 20852
Tel. 301-443-2016

Health Services and Mental Health Administration
functions have been divided among Center for Disease
Control, the Health Resources Administration, and
the Health Services Administration.

Housing and Urban Development Department
451 Seventh Street SW.
Washington, D.C. 20410
Tel. 202--655-4000

Indian Affairs Bureau
U.S. Department of the Interior
1951 Constitution Avenue
Washington, D.C. 20245
Tel. 202-343-2460

Indian Arts and Crafts Board
1951 Constitution Avenue
Washington, D.C. 20240

Tel. 202–343–2773

Interior Department
Eighteenth and C Streets NW.
Washington, D.C. 20240
Tel. 202–343–3171

Interior Department
Library Services Office
Eighteenth and C Streets NW.
Washington, D.C. 20240
Tel. 202–343–5815

Intermountain Forest and Range Experiment Station
U.S. Forest Service
507 Twenty–fifth Street
Ogden, Utah 84401
Tel. 801–399–6011

International Commerce Bureau
now
Domestic and International Business Administration
Washington, D.C. 20230
Tel. 202–967–3808

Justice Department
Constitution Avenue and Tenth St. NW.
Washington, D.C. 20530
Tel. 202–739–2014

Labor Department
Fourteenth Street and Constitution Avenue
Washington, D.C. 20210
Tel. 202–393–2420

Labor Statistics Bureau
Office of Publications
Department of Labor
441 G Street NW.
Washington, D.C. 20212
Tel. 202–961–2913

Law Enforcement Assistance Administration
U.S. Department of Justice
Washington, D.C. 20530

280

Tel. 202--963--5244

Library of Congress
Information Office
10 First Street SE.
Washington, D.C. 20540
Tel. 202--426--5108
    (See also individual divisions and offices)

Manpower Intelligence Division
   now
Bureau of Health Manpower Education
Health Resources Administration
5600 Fishers Lane
Rockville, Md. 20852

Marine Corps
U.S. Department of the Navy
Washington, D.C. 20380
Tel. 202--694--2500

Maritime Administration
U.S. Department of Commerce
Washington, D.C. 20230
Tel. 202--967--2746

Maternal and Child Health Service
Health Services Administration
5600 Fishers Lane
Rockville, Md. 20852
Tel. 301--443--2300

Military Academy
U.S. Army
West Point, New York

Military History Office
U.S. Department of the Army
Tempo C Building
Second and T Streets SW.
Washington, D.C. 20315

Mines Bureau
Division of Production and Distribution
4800 Forbes Avenue

Pittsburg, Pa. 15213
Tel. 412–621–4500

Minority Business Enterprise Office
U.S. Department of Commerce
Washington, D.C. 20230
Tel. 202–967–5542

Narcotics and Dangerous Drugs Bureau
now
Drug Enforcement Administration
1405 I Street NW.
Washington, D.C. 20005
Tel. 202–382–5706

National Agriculutral Library
U.S. Department of Agriculture
Beltsville, Md. 20705
Tel. 301–344–3761 (Interlibrary Loan Office)

National Air Pollution Control Administration
now
Air and Water Programs Office
Environmental Protection Agency
Office of Public Affairs
Communications Services Division
410 M Street NW.
Washington, D.C. 20460
Tel. 202–755–0707

National Bureau of Standards
U.S. Department of Commerce
Washington, D.C. 20234
Tel. 301–921–1000

National Cancer Institute
National Institutes of Health
Bethesda, Md. 20014
Tel. 301–496–7776

National Center for Health Services Research and
       Development
Health Resources Administration
5600 Fishers Lane
Rockville, Md. 20852

Tel. 301–443–2800

National Center for Health Statistics
Health Resources Administration
5600 Fishers Lane
Rockville, Md. 20852
Tel. 301–443–1200

National Clearinghouse for Drug Abuse Prevention
now
Special Action Office for Drug Abuse Prevention
712 Jackson Place NW.
Washington, D.C. 20506
Tel. 202–382–8715

National Climatic Center
Environmental Data Service
National Oceanic Atmospheric Administration
Federal Building
Asheville, N.C. 28801

National Health and Lung Institute
National Institutes of Health
Bethesda, Md. 20014
Tel. 301–496–4236

National Institute of Allergy and Infectious Disease
National Institutes of Health
Bethesda, Md. 20014
Tel. 301–496–5717

National Institute of Arthritis, Metabolism, and Digestive
Diseases
National Institutes of Health
Bethesda, Md. 20014
Tel. 301–496–6158

National Institute of Mental Health
National Institutes of Health
Bethesda, Md. 20014
Tel. 301–656–4000

National Institute of Neurological Disease and Stroke
National Institutes of Health
Bethesda, Md. 20014

Tel. 301–496–5751

National Highway Safety Bureau
Federal Highway Administration
Department of Transportation
400 Seventh Street SW.
Washington, D.C. 20590
Tel. 202–426–0714

National Highway Traffic Safety Administration
Department of Transportation
400 Seventh Street SW.
Washington, D.C. 20590
Tel. 202–426–1810

National Labor Relations Board
1717 Pennsylvania Avenue
Washington, D.C. 20570
Tel. 202–254–9033

National Marine Fisheries Service
National Oceanic Atmospheric Administration
Washington, D.C. 20235
Tel. 202–243–4007

National Oceanic Atmospheric Administration
Washington Science Center
Bldg. 5
6010 Executive Blvd.
Rockville, Md. 20852
Tel. 201–656–4060

National Technical Information Service
U.S. Department of Commerce
Springfield, Va. 22151
Tel. 703–321–8500

National Transportation Safety Board
U.S. Department of Transportation
Publications Section
Washington, D.C. 20591
Tel. 202–426–8169

Naval Oceanographic Office
Office of the Oceanographer of the Navy

Hoffman Bldg. II
200 Stoval Street
Alexandria, Va. 22332
Tel. 202–352–9275

Naval Personnel Bureau
U.S. Department of the Navy
Washington, D.C. 20370
Tel. 202–694–1271

Naval Research Office
U.S. Department of the Navy
Ballston Tower no. 1
800 N. Quincy Street
Arlington, Va. 22217
Tel. 202–692–4259

Navy Department
The Pentagon
Washington, D.C. 20350
Tel. 202–697–7391

North Central Forest Experiment Station
U.S. Forest Service
Folwell Avenue
St. Paul, Minn. 55101
Tel. 612–645–0841

Outdoor Recreation Bureau
U.S. Department of the Interior
Nineteenth and C Streets NW.
Washington, D.C. 20240
Tel. 202–343–5726

Pacific Air Forces
CINC PACAF (DPSR)/ Director
PACAF Libraries
APO
San Francisco, Calif. 96553

Pacific Northwest Forest and Range Experiment Station
U.S. Forest Service
P.O. Box 3141
Portland, Oregon 97208
Tel. 503–234–3361

Pacific Southwest Forest and Range Experiment Station
U.S. Forest Service
P.O. Box 245
Berkley, Calif. 94701
Tel. 415–841–5121

President
see
U.S. President

Processing Department
Library of Congress
10 First Street SE.
Washington, D.C. 20540

Public Health Service
5600 Fishers Lane
Rockville, Md. 20852

Radiological Health Bureau
Food and Drug Administration
U.S. Public Health Service
5600 Fishers Lane
Rockville, Md. 20852
Tel. 301--443–3434

Reclamation Bureau
Department of the Interior
P.O. Box 25007
Denver Federal Center
Denver, Colo. 80225
Tel. 303--234–3022

Regional Medical Programs Service
Health Resources Administration
5600 Fishers Lane
Rockville, Md. 20852
Tel. 301–443--1620

Rocy Mountain Forest and Range Experiment Station
U.S. Forest Service
240 West Prospect Street
Fort Collins, Colo. 80521
Tel. 303--482–7332

Rural Electrification Administration
U.S. Department of Agriculture
Washington, D.C. 20250
Tel. 202--447--5606

Saline Water Office
U.S. Department of the Interior
Eighteenth and C Streets NW.
Washington, D.C. 20240
Tel. 202--343--6992

Small Business Administration
1441 L Street NW
Washington, D.C. 20416
Tel. 202--382--1891

Smithsonian Institution
Reading is Fundamental
A & I Bldg.
Room 2407
Washington, D.C. 20560

Social and Rehabilitation Service Administration
330 C Street SW.
Washington, D.C. 20201
Tel. 202--962--2102

Social Security Administration
6401 Security Blvd.
Baltimore, Md. 21235
Tel. 301--594--1234

Solid Waste Management Office
Office of Public Affairs
Environmental Protection Agency
401 M Street SW.
Washington, D.C. 20460
Tel. 202--755--0707

Southeastern Forest Experiment Station
U.S. Forest Service
P.O. Box 2570
Asheville, N.C. 28802
Tel. 704--254--0961

Southern Forest Experiment Station
U.S. Forest Service
Federal Building
701 Loyola Avenue
New Orleans, La. 70113
Tel. 504--589--6787

Sport Fisheries and Wildlife Bureau
U.S. Department of the Interior
Eighteenth and C Streets NW
Washington, D.C. 20240
Tel. 202--343--4717

State Department
Bureau of Public Affairs
2201 C Street NW.
Washington, D.C. 20520
Tel. 202--632--1152
    202--632--1153

Tennessee Valley Authority
Fertilizer Center
Muscle Shoals, Alabama 35660
Tel. 205--383--4631

Tennessee Valley Authority
Technical Library
Knoxville, Tenn. 37902
Tel. 615--637--0101

Transportation Department
400 Seventh Street SW
Washington, D.C. 20590
Tel. 202--426--4000

Unemployment Insurance Service
Manpower Administration
U.S. Department of Labor
Fourteenth Street and Constitution Avenue NW
Washington, D.C. 20210
Tel. 202--961--2822

Congress
House Committee on Education and Labor
Suite 2181
Longworth House Office Bldg.

Washington, D.C. 20515

U.S. Congress. House
Committee on Science and Astronautics
Suite 2321
Longworth House Office Bldg.
Washington, D.C. 20515

U.S. Congress
Joint Economic Committee
Room G--133
Dirksen Senate Office Building
Washington, D.C. 20510

U.S. Congress. Senate
Committee on Government Operations
Suite 3308
Dirksen Senate Office Bldg.
Washington, D.C. 20510

U.S. Congress. Senate
Committee on Interior and Insular Affairs
Suite 3106
Dirksen Senate Office Bldg.
Washington, D.C. 20510

U.S. Congress. Senate
Committee on the Judiciary
Suite 2226
Dirksen Senate Office Bldg.
Washington, D.C. 20510

U.S. Congress. Senate
Special Committee on Aging
Room G–225
Dirksen Senate Office Bldg.
Washington, D.C. 20510

U.S. Interagency Racial Data Committee
Morton Skiar, Chairman
School of Law
Catholic University
Washington, D.C. 20017

U.S. President
Executive Office
1600 Pennsylvania Avenue NW.
Washington, D.C. 20500
Tel. 202–456–1414

U.S. President's Committee on Employment of the Handi-
 capped
7131 Department of Labor Bldg.
Fourteenth and Constitution Avenue NW.
Washington, D.C. 20210
Tel. 202--961--3401

Veterans' Administration
810 Vermont Avenue NW.
Washington, D.C. 20420
Tel. 202–389--2678

Water Programs Office
 now
Air and Water Programs Office
Environmental Protection Agency
Office of Public Affairs
Communication Services Division
401 M Street SW.
Washington, D.C. 20460
Tel. 202--755–0707

Water Programs Office
 now
Water Resources Research Office
Eighteenth and C Streets NW.
Washington, D.C. 20240
Tel. 202--755–0707

Water Resources Scientific Information Center
Office of Water Resources Research
Eighteenth and C Streets NW.
Washington, D.C. 20240
Tel. 202--343--5975

World Data Center A
Environmental Data Service
National Climatic Center
Federal Building

Asheville, N.C. 28801
Tel. 704–254–0961

Youth Development and Delinquency Prevention Administration
U.S. Social and Rehabilitation Service.
330 C Street SW.
Washington, D.C. 20201
Tel. 202–962–2102

Ordering from the National Technical Information Service

National Technical Information Service (NTIS) publications should be paid with check, postal money order, or express order or charged against a personal or institutional NTIS account. Prices (October 1974) for microfiche publications are $2.25; paper copy prices vary.

Order from:
National Technical Information Service
U.S. Department of Commerce
P.O. Box 1553
Springfield, Virginia 22151
Tel. 703–321–8500

Index

This is primarily a subject index with selected distinctive titles appearing in all upper case letters.

A

Alcoholism, 715 *see also* Drugs and drug abuse
ALCOHOLISM TREATMENT AND REHABILITATION, 665
Alcott, Louisa May, CENTENNIAL FOR LITTLE WOMEN, 554
Alienation, SOCIAL ASPECTS OF ALIENATION, 795
Alpha–particles, 1023--1026
ALTIMETRY, LITERATURE REVIEW AND BIBLIOGRAPHY, 993
Aluminum industry, air pollutant source, 334
Ambulance service, 679
AMERICAN DOCTORAL DISSERTATIONS ON THE ARAB
    WORLD, 1883--1968, 896
American Indian *see* Indian, North American
AMERICAN IVORY--BILLED WOODPECKER, 1014
American Revolution *see* History, U.S.
Amphetamines, 669 *see also* Drugs and drug abuse
Anatidae, 1013
Anatomy, 752
Anesthetics, methylpentynol, 589
Anga, 80
Animal neoplasia, PARTIAL BIBLIOGRAPHY ON TYPE–B AND
    TYPE–C VIRUSES IN RELATION TO ANIMAL NEOPLASIA,
    745
Animals, farm, 25, 267
ANTARCTIC BIBLIOGRAPHY, 431--434
Anthropology, 78, 80
ANTI--DEPRESSANT DRUG STUDIES, 1955--1966, 666
APPAREL AND ACCESSORIES FOR WOMEN, MISSES, AND
    CHILDREN, 206
Apparel, SOURCES OF STATISTICAL DATA, TEXTILE AND
    APPAREL, 124
Archeology, SALVAGE ARCHEOLOGY IN THE UNITED STATES,
    436
Architecture:
    architecture, 287, 294, 296
    ARCHITECTURE, BUILDING AND ENGINEERING, 289--290
    WEATHER AND ARCHITECTURE, 449
Archives, ADMINISTRATION OF MODERN ARCHIVES, 512
Arid lands, remote sensing, 418 *see also* Deserts
Armed Forces: *see also* specific branches
    Armed Forces, 907–923
    COLLEGE GRADUATE AND NATIONAL SECURITY:
        UTILIZATION OF MANPOWER BY THE ARMED
        SERVICES, 146
    military affairs, 907--923
    MILITARY JUSTICE, 915

ATOMIC TRANSITION PROBABILITIES, 1142
Atomic waste disposal, 1112
Atoms, ION--MOLECULE REACTION RATES, 1038
Audio--visuals: *see also* Motion pictures
    Agriculture Department, 1,2
    BOOKS ON MAGNETIC TAPE, 546
    BOOKS ON OPEN--REEL TAPE, 547
    CASSETTE BOOKS, 548
    health scientists, audio--visuals for, 650
    State Department, 846
    TALKING BOOKS TO PROFIT BY, 549
    URBAN OUTLOOK, SELECTED BIBLIOGRAPHY OF FILMS,
        FILMSTRIPS, SLIDES, AND AUDIOTAPES, 305
Australasia, 897--898
Australia, 899
Authorities, government, 828
AUTOMATED MULTIPHASIC HEALTH TESTING, 681
AUTOMATION OF FISH PROCESSING AND HANDLING, 595
AUTOMATION FOR SMALL OFFICES, 114
Aviation:
    civil, 1206
    Civil Aeronautics Board publications, 1198
    Federal Aviation Administration publications, 1204
    SOVIET LITERATURE ON AVIATION, ALPINE AND SPACE
        BIOLOGY AND MEDICINE, 996
AVIATION MEDICINE TRANSLATIONS, 711--714

B

Bangladesh, 879
Barbiturates, 669
Bartlett, John Henry, 819
Bartsch, Paul, BIBLIOGRAPHY AND ZOOLOGICAL TAXA OF
    PAUL BARTSCH, 616
Basutoland, official publications, 852
Batteries, SECONDARY AEROSPACE BATTERIES AND BATTERY
    MATERIALS, 1036
Beach Erosion Board publications, 1075
Beach erosion control, 1078
Beautification, 322
BEAUTY FOR AMERICA, 288
Bechuanaland, official publications, 852
Behavioral sciences:
    BEHAVIOR MODIFICATION IN CHILD AND SCHOOL MENTAL
        HEALTH, 799
    behavioral science, 984--985
    COPING AND ADAPTION, 805
    fatigue, 627

Boilers, air pollutant, 327
Book catalogs:
LIBRARY OF CONGRESS CATALOGS IN BOOK FORM, 542
MONTHLY CATALOG OF UNITED STATES GOVERNMENT
PUBLICATIONS, 539
Book selection, *see* Library selection aids, Literature, and specific
subject
BOOKSTORES, 207
Botany, LINNEA IN THE COLLECTION OF THE NATIONAL
AGRICULTURAL LIBRARY, 57
Botswana, official publications, 852
BRAIN DEATH, 637
Brewer, Mark Spencer, 819
Brine effluents, disposal of, 366
Briquettes, UTILIZATION OF WOOD RESIDUES, 66
British Togoland, 853
Budworms, 42
Building, 289–291, 294, 295a–b
Buildings and structures, 295a, 1215
BUILDINGS BIBLIOGRAPHY, 295b
BUILT ENVIRONMENT, THE, 292
Burma, 875
Business: *see also* Retail business, Small business, and specific
type of business
business and industry, 107–238
BUSINESS SERVICE CHECKLIST, 108
international business, 117a
inventory management, 211
library reference sources, 115
minority business, 109
mortgage finance, 134
PUBLICATIONS FOR BUSINESS, 107
SOURCES OF INFORMATION ON AMERICAN FIRMS FOR
INTERNATIONAL BUYERS, 118
BUSINESS AND OFFICE EDUCATION, INSTRUCTIONAL
MATERIALS, 268

C

Cable television, 1059
CADMIUM IN WATER, 382
CALIFORNIA CONDOR (GYMNOGYPS CALIFORNIANUS), 1015
Campbell, Thomas Edward, 819
Cameras *see* Photographic equipment

301

Ecology, 262, 311–324 *see also* Environment
Ecology, TERRESTRIAL, FRESHWATER, AND MARINE
RADIATION ECOLOGY, 1121
Economics:
ECONOMIC DEVELOPMENT OF AMERICAN INDIANS
AND ESKIMOS, 81
Economic Research Service publications, 4
ECONOMICS OF AGRICULTURE, 5
ECONOMICS OF SWEETNER MARKETING, 17
national economy, 135
U.S. Joint Economic Committee publications, 826
Ecosystems, PINYON–JUNIPER ECOSYSTEMS, 43
Edgerton, Alfred Peck, 819
Education: *see also* Vocational education and specific subject
ADULT BASIC EDUCATION, 258
adult education, 256–259
agricultural education, 267, 273, 280
American Indian, 96–97
business, 268, 274, 281
compensatory education, 243
distributive, 268, 274, 281
EARLY CHILDHOOD EDUCATION, 240
education, 239–285
EDUCATION, LITERATURE OF THE PROFESSION, 245–
245a
Education Office publications, 250
educational statistics, 253
EDUCATIONAL TECHNOLOGY AND TEACHING–LEARNING
PROCESS, 632b
elementary and secondary education, 260–265
ELEMENTARY AND SECONDARY EDUCATION ACT OF
1965, 260
ENVIRONMENTAL–ECOLOGICAL EDUCATION, 262
ERIC PRODUCTS, 244
health occupations, 275
international education, 246, 255
language development research, 246, 261
media selection aids, 242–242a
Mexican Americans, 248
migrant education, 248
OUTDOOR EDUCATION, 251–252
RESEARCH IN EDUCATION, 241
RURAL EDUCATION AND SMALL SCHOOLS, 263–264
social studies, 260
Eelgrass, 594
Eggs, 13

Electrical engineering, 984--985, 1057
Electricity:
   AIR POLLUTION ASPECTS OF EMISSION SOURCES:
      ELECTRIC POWER PRODUCTION, 329
   ENVIRONMENTAL EFFECTS OF PRODUCING ELECTRIC
      POWER,
Electronics:
   COMPUTER--AIDED CIRCUIT ANALYSIS AND DESIGN, 1061
   ELECTRONIC COMPOSITION, 1053
   electronics, 976, 984--985, 1054--1055, 1057, 1060
   equipment, 976
   MEASUREMENT OF CARRIER LIFETIME, IN SEMI--
      CONDUCTORS, 1068
   MEASUREMENT OF INHOMOGENEITIES IN SEMI--
      CONDUCTORS, 1065
   microelectronic interconnections, 1073
   WIRE--BOND ELECTRICAL CONNECTIONS, 1073
Electromagnetic wave propogation, 1058
Elements, ANALYSES OF OPTICAL ATOMIC SPECTRA, 1136--
   1139
Ellsworth, Harris, 819
EMERGENCY HEALTH SERVICES, 678--679, 687
Employees: *see also* Labor, Occupations, Personnel management,
      Government employees
   absenteeism, 170
   compensation, 232
   EMPLOYEE BENEFITS AND SERVICES, 234--235
   EMPLOYEE--MANAGEMENT RELATIONS IN PUBLIC
      SERVICE, 163
   performance, 165
   psychological testing, 170--171
Employment: *see also* Manpower
   equal employment opportunity, 128--131
   PUBLICATIONS OF THE BUREAU OF LABOR STATISTICS,
      1886--1971, 155
   statistics, 142
ENDOCARDITIS, 724
ENDOCRINOLOGY INDEX, 749
Energy:
   energy and energy resources, 458--465, 976
   energy conversion (non--propulsive), 984--985
   NSF--RANN ENERGY RESEARCH ABSTRACTS, 458
Engineering: *see also* specific type of engineering
   engineering, 962--963, 1094
   NASA PATENT ABSTRACTS, 975
   reference sources, 1134
Engineers, 145 *see also* specific type of engineer

311

Engineers, Corps of, publications, 1075, 1079, 1081
Environment: *see also* Ecology, special subjects
    ENVIRONMENT: A BIBLIOGRAPHY OF SOCIAL SCIENCE
        AND RELATED LITERATURE, 316
    ENVIRONMENT AND COMMUNITY, 299
    ENVIRONMENTAL BIBLIOGRAPHY, 317
    ENVIRONMENTAL--ECOLOGICAL EDUCATION, 262
    ENVIRONMENTAL POLLUTION, 324, 322
    ENVIRONMENTAL PROTECTION AGNECY RESEARCH
        AND DEVELOPMENT OFFICE REPORTS, 314
    ENVIRONMENTAL QUALITY AS IT RELATES TO HEALTH,
        768
    ENVIRONMENTAL RESEARCH PUBLICATIONS, 318
    ENVIRONMENTAL SERVICES, 319
    EPA REPORTS BIBLIOGRAPHY, 315
    MAN, HIS WORK AND THE ENVIRONMENT, 627
    mercury contamination, 312
    THE QUEST FOR ENVIRONMENTAL QUALITY, 306
    research, 314, 962--963
    socio--physical technology, 304
    studies of the environment,
        Iraq, 309a
        Israel, 310
        Jordan, 309a
        Poland, 309
        Syria, 309a
Environmental design, 289--291, 294, 296--299
Environmental Science Services Administration publications, 452
Epilepsy:
    BLOOD LEVEL DETERMINATIONS OF ANTIEPILEPTIC
        DRUGS, CLINICAL VALUE AND METHODS, 758
    EPILEPSY ABSTRACTS, 760
    EPILEPSY BIBLIOGRAPHY, 1900--50, 761
Epidemiology, 765
EPIDEMIOLOGY OF MENTAL DISORDERS, 801
Equal employment opportunity, 128--130
EQUAL OPPORTUNITY, BIBLIOGRAPHY OF RESEARCH ON
    EQUAL OPPORTUNITY IN HOUSING, 286
EQUILIBRIUM CRITICAL PHENOMENA IN FLUIDS AND
    MIXTURES, 1046
Eskimos:
    art, 522
    economic development, 81
    folktales, 528
Espionage, 913--914

Israel: *see also* East, Middle
ACCESSIONS LIST, 561
ARAB–ISRAELI CONFLICT, 890
environment, 310

J

Japan:
foreign relations with U.S., 863
JAPAN: ANALYSTICAL BIBLIOGRAPHY WITH
SUPPLEMENTARY RESEARCH AIDS AND SELECTED
DATA ON OKINAWA, REPUBLIC OF CHINA (TAIWAN),
REPUBLIC OF KOREA, 878
JAPAN AND OKINAWA, 870
labor, 156
Jobs *see* Manpower, Occupations
Johnson, James E., 819
Johnston, George Doherty, 819
Jones, Roger Warren, 819
Jordon, environment, 309a *see also* East, Middle
Justice, administration of, 823
Juvenile delinquency:
delinquency prevention, 1159
JUVENILE AND FAMILY COURTS, LEGAL BIBLIOGRAPHY,
837–839a
juvenile delinquency, 1159–1162, 1164–1172
YOUTH DEVELOPMENT AND DELINQUENCY PREVENTION
ADMINISTRATION PUBLICATIONS, 1172

K

Kidney research, 747
KOREA, 872–873
Korea, COMMUNIST NORTH KOREA, 877
Kraft pulping industry, 354
KuKuKuKu, 80

L

Labor:
bargaining, 163
foreign labor, Japan, 156
Labor Department acquisitions, 160
Labor Management Relations Act, 184–186
LABOR MANAGEMENT RELATIONS IN THE PUBLIC

Leadership, 194
Learning, 781
Lebanon, environmental studies, 309a *see also* East, Middle
LEGAL ASPECTS OF WATER POLLUTION IN NEW ENGLAND, 389
LEGAL BIBLIOGRAPHY FOR JUVENILE AND FAMILY COURTS, 837--839
Lesotho, official publications, 852
Libraries:
federal libraries, 1224
Library of Congress, 1218
Library of Congress publications, 542--543
Library selection aids, 115, 530--536, 539 *see also* specific subject
Life science, 962--963 *see also* specific subject
Lightning, 445
Limnology, 398--400
Linguistics *see* Language
LINNEA IN THE COLLECTION OF THE NATIONAL AGRICULTURAL LIBRARY, 57
Liquids, critical phenomena in, 1046
Literature: *see also* Reading Guides
BLACK LITERATURE, 530
FICTION MEN READ, 531
CHILDREN'S BOOKS, 550
CHILDREN'S LITERATURE, 551
FOLKLORE OF NORTH AMERICAN INDIANS, 552
LITERATURE FOR DISADVANTAGED CHILDREN, 247
NON--FICTION MEN READ, 532
Livestock marketing, 204a
Lobster, 586
Logging, effects on fish, 597
LONGLEAF PINE, 46
LUBRICATION, CORROSION AND WEAR, 1090
LUNAR AND PLANETARY RESEARCH, 987
Lunar studies, 976, 995
LUNAR SURFACE STUDIES, 1004
Lyman, Charles, 819

M

McIlhenny, John Avery, 819
Machine elements and processes, 976
MACHINE SHOPS – JOB TYPE, 212
McMillin, Lucille Foster, 819
Macy, John Williams, jr., 819
Mail order selling, 116

Meat and meat products:
  marketing, 204a
  processing, 16
Mechanical engineering, 984--985
Medical care: *see also* Health care and service, Medicine, Public health
  comprehensive care for all U.S. citizens, 670
  IMPACT OF MEDICARE, 701
  MEDICARE, 702, 1147
  REGIONAL MEDICAL PROGRAMS, 699--700
Medical instruments, 685
Medical specialities, 148
Medical research: *see also* specific subject
  ABRIDGED INDEX MEDICUS, 638, 642–644
  aerospace medicine, 716--717
  ARTIFICIAL KIDNEY BIBLIOGRAPHY, 747
  AVIATION MEDICINE TRANSLATIONS, 711--714
  BIOMEDICAL AND ENVIRONMENTAL RESEARCH, 708
  cerebrovascular studies, 759
  chelating agents, 764
  CIRCADIAN RHYTHMS, 710
  epidemiology, 765
  epilepsy, 760--761
  INDEX MEDICUS, 646
  INFORMATION SOURCES IN MEDICAL RESEARCH, 770
  LIST OF JOURNALS INDEXED IN INDEX MEDICUS, 648
  kidney research, 747
  medical research, 703--772, 984--985
  MEDICAL RESEARCH AND DEVELOPMENT ARTICLES,
    709
  MEDICAL USES OF TECHNETIUM–99m, 1965–1971, 703
  MONTHLY BIBLIOGRAPHY OF MEDICAL REVIEWS, 766
  NUCLEAR MEDICINE, 705--707
  Parkison's disease, 762--763
  Soviet studies on space medicine, 996
  transplantation of human tissue, 791--792
Medicine:
  CHINESE SOURCES ON MEDICINE AND PUBLIC HEALTH
    IN THE PEOPLE'S REPUBLIC OF CHINA, 1960--1970,
    633
  FILM REFERENCE GUIDE FOR MEDICINE AND ALLIED
    SCIENCES, 645
  films, 626
  history, 639--641a
  MEDICOLEGAL SERIALS (1736–1967), 647

SOVIET MEDICINE, BIBLIOGRAPHY OF
BIBLIOGRAPHIES, 634
Melanesia, 900
MEN'S AND BOYS' WEAR STORES, 214
Mental health:
community centers, 789
consultation, 790, 797
EARLY CHILDHOOD PSYCHOSIS: INFANTILE AUTISM,
CHILDHOOD SCHIZOPHRENIA AND RELATED
DISORDERS, ANNOTATED BIBLIOGRAPHY 1964--69,
806
EPIDEMIOLOGY OF MENTAL DISORDERS, 801--802
MENTAL HEALTH AND SOCIAL CHANGE, 807
MENTAL HEALTH IN THE SCHOOLS, 798
PLANNING FOR CREATIVE CHANGE IN MENTAL HEALTH
SERVICES, 809--811
SELECTED SOURCES OF INEXPENSIVE MENTAL HEALTH
MATERIALS, 794
staff training, 784--786
VOLUNTEER SERVICES IN MENTAL HEALTH, 796
Mental retardation:
brain death, 637
mental retardation, 773--779
READING SUGGESTIONS FOR PARENTS OF MENTALLY
RETARDED, 774
MERCURY AND AIR POLLUTION, 346
MERCURY CONTAMINATION IN THE NATURAL ENVIRONMENT,
312
Metals:
activation analysis, 1045
BIOLOGICAL EFFECTS OF METALS IN THE AQUATIC
ENVIRONMENTS, 401
GEOCHEMISTRY OF GOLD, 478
Meterology:
DROUGHT BIBLIOGRAPHY, 455
meteorology, 453--454, 976
METEOROLOGY, CLIMATOLOGY, AND PHYSICAL
CHEMICAL OCEANOGRAPHY OF THE CARIBBEAN AND
ADJACENT REGIONS, 621
sea--salt cycle, 448
Meteoritics, 479
Methane, thermophysical properties of, 1041
METHAQUALONE, 663
Methylpentynol, 589
Metrics, 983--983a

Mexican Americans, 98, 100–102, 248
Mexico, GUIDE TO THE LAW AND LEGAL LITERATURE OF
    MEXICO, 862
Microbiology, 984–985, 1017
Micronesia, 900
MICRONESIA, POLYNESIA, AND AUSTRALASIA, 897, 898
Microwaves, REGULATIONS, STANDARDS, AND GUIDES FOR
    MICROWAVES, ULTRAVIOLET RADIATION FROM
    LASERS AND TELEVISION RECEIVERS, 938
Middle East see East, Middle and Near
MIGRANT EDUCATION, 249
Military, the: see also Armed forces, individual branches of the
    military
    military history, 496–505, 527
    military installations, FORT LEAVENWORTH, 499–500
    MILITARY JUSTICE, 915
    military sciences, 984–985
    STRATEGY AND TACTICS, 1000A.D. -- 1970, 918
Milk, 675
Millimeter waves, 1058
Milling timber, 70, 74
Mineralogy: see also specific minerals, subjects
    minerals, 465
    Mines Bureau publications, 411–415
    rare earths and scandium, 470
    remote sensing, 481
Mines and mining, 411–415, 465
Minority groups: see also individual minority group
    minorities, 98–99, 102
    minorities in the military, 99, 917
    MINORITY BUSINESS ENTERPRISE, 109
    minority group relations, 106
    MINORITY GROUPS IN MEDICINE, 139
Mitchell, Harry B., 819
Mitchell, James Matlack, 819
Missiles, 984–985, 995
MOBILE HOMES AND PARKS, 215
Molecules, ION--MOLECULE REACTION RATES, 1135
Mollusks:
    BIBLIOGRAPHY AND ZOOLOGICAL TAXA OF PAUL
        BARTSCH, 616
    NEOGENE MARINE MOLLUSKS OF THE PACIFIC COAST
        OF NORTH AMERICA, 598
    TERTIARY MARINE MOLLUSKS OF ALASKA, 599
Money management, 126–127

Mongolism, 741
MONTHLY CATALOG OF UNITED STATES GOVERNMENT
PUBLICATIONS, 539
Monuments, national, 1219
Moon *see* Lunar
Moore, George Mansfield, 819
Morrison, Martin Andrew, 819
MORTGAGE FINANCE, 134
MOTELS, 216
Motion picture guides: *see also* Audio--visuals
air pollution, 353
children, 1158
dentistry and dental health, 626, 977
environment, 977
Forest Service, 26
medicine and related areas, 626, 645, 650
National Bureau of Standards, 977
oceanography, 623
reproduction and development, 631
safety, 977
weights and measures, 977
Youth Development and Delinquency Prevention, 1172
Motor vehicles:
RELATIONSHIP BETWEEN DEFECTS IN MOTOR VEHICLES
AND CRASHES, 954
safety, 953
traffic safety, 945--953, 955
MULTI--ETHNIC LITERATURE IN HIGH SCHOOL, 808
MULTIPHASIC HEALTH TESTING SYSTEMS, 695
MUNICIPAL INCINERATION, 347

N

Natick Laboratories publications, 961
National Aeronautics and Space Administration:
NASA, 995
NASA PATENT ABSTRACTS BIBLIOGRAPHY, 975
SCIENTIFIC AND TECHNICAL AEROSPACE REPORTS, 976
NATIONAL ARCHIVES AND RECORDS SERVICE SELECTED
PUBLICATIONS LIST, 514
National Bureau of Standards:
films, 977
publications, 978–982
NATIONAL CENTER FOR EDUCATIONAL STATISTICS
PUBLICATIONS, 253

National Center for Health Services Research publications, 697a--698
National growth policy, 824
National Highway Traffic Safety Administration research reports, 955
National Highway Safety Bureau reports, 946
National Institute for Occupational Safety and Health publications, 630
National Institutes of Health publications, 742
NATIONAL LIBRARY OF MEDICINE CURRENT CATALOG, 649
NATIONAL MEDICAL AUDIOVISUAL CENTER 1973 MOTION PICTURE AND VIDEOTAPE CATALOG, 650
National Museum publications, 1222, 1226
National Oceanic Atmospheric Administration publications, 456
NATIONAL PARKS, HISTORIC SITES, NATIONAL MONUMENTS, 1219
NATIONAL TRANSPORTATION SAFETY BOARD LIST OF PUBLICATIONS, 956
NATIVE AMERICAN ARTS AND CRAFTS OF THE UNITED STATES, 523
NATURAL ENVIRONMENTAL RADIOACTIVITY, 307
Natural gas, 460
NATURAL RESOURCES IN FOREIGN COUNTRIES, CONTRI-- BUTION TOWARD A BIBLIOGRAPHY OF BIBLIOGRAPHIES, 468
Naturalization, 832
Naval Oceanographic Office publications, 437, 578
Navigation, 437, 578, 984--985
Navy:
    advancement study, 181
    history, 505
    NAVAL GUNFIRE SUPPORT, 922
    NAVY, MARINE CORPS AND COAST GUARD, 921
    reading list for officers, 537
    research aboard Navy Pool (T--AGOR) ships, 620
    training manuals, 181
Near East *see* East, Middle and Near
THE NEGRO IN THE UNITED STATES, 103
NEIGHBORHOOD CONSERVATION AND PROPERTY REHABILITATION, 302
NEMATODES OF SOYBEANS, 50
NEOGENE MARINE MOLLUSKS OF THE PACIFIC COAST OF NORTH AMERICA, 598
Nepal, ACCESSIONS LIST, 563
Neurology:
    BRAIN DEATH, 637

MATERNAL NUTRITION, 688
nutrition, 14, 18, 20, 671
NUTRITION OF RICE, 21
protein of cereal grains, 15
NURSERY BUSINESS, 217
Nursing, 632a--632d
Nuts, production and marketing research, 202

O

Oberly, John H., 819
Occupational safety and health, 161, 234--235, 675
Occupations: *see also* Manpower, specific occupation or profession
FEDERAL CAREER LITERATURE, 143
health, 270, 275, 282
job descriptions, 147
office occupations, 268, 277, 284
technical, 270, 278, 285
trade and industrial, 272, 279
training programs, 162, 172
semi--professionals in human service jobs, 1189
Oceana, THE FUTURE, 844
Oceanography:
COOPERATIVE INVESTIGATION OF THE CARIBBEAN
AND ADJACENT REGIONS, 615, 617, 621
films, 622
MARINE SCIENCE NEWSLETTERS, 576
Naval Oceanographic Office publications, 437, 578
OCEAN SCIENCE AND TECHNOLOGY DIVISION REPORT
AVAILABILITY NOTICE, 580
oceanography, 580--581, 617--625, 984--985
OCEANOGRAPHY, BIBLIOGRAPHY OF SELECTED
ACTIVATION ANALYSIS LITERATURE, 574
physical oceanography, 617--625
remote sensing, 481
RESEARCH ABOARD NAVY POOL (T--AGOR) SHIPS,
1963--69, 620
SEA--GRANT PUBLICATIONS INDEX, 577
SELECTED READINGS IN THE MARINE SCIENCES, 579
Soviet publications, 619
technical literature guide, 623
World Data Center A accessions, 618
ODORS AND AIR POLLUTION, 348
Office machines, 114
Oil pollution:
BIOLOGICAL EFFECTS OF OIL POLLUTION, 320

Plastics, 1031–1033
PLOWSHARE, SELECTED ANNOTATED BIBLIOGRAPHY OF
CIVIL, INDUSTRIAL, AND SCIENTIFIC USES OF NUCLEAR
EXPLOSIVES, 1107
Plutonium–238, 1133
Poetry, CHILDREN AND POETRY, 541
Poison *see* Toxicity
Poland, environmental studies, 309
Polar regions, 417 *see also* Cold regions
Police, 1164–1170
POLITICAL SCIENCE. GOVERNMENT, CRIME, DISTRICT OF
COLUMBIA, 834
Pollution *see* specific type of pollution
POLLUTION ANALYSIS, 1049
pollution control, 314–319
Polonium–210, 1133
Polychlorinated biphenyls, 390
Polymers:
LITERATURE SURVEY ON THERMAL DEGRADATION,
THERMAL OXIDATION, AND THERMAL ANALYSIS OF
HIGH POLYMERS, 1029–1030
PYRRONE AND BBB PUBLICATIONS, 1034
Polynesia, 897–898, 900
POPULAR NAMES OF U.S. GOVERNMENT REPORTS, 835
POPULAR PUBLICATIONS FOR FARMER, SUBURBANITE,
HOMEMAKER, CONSUMER, 1215
Population:
THE MALTHUSIAN SPECTRE, 1173
population planning, 1185, 1186
POPULATION SCIENCES, 752
research, 740
PORT INFORMATION SOURCES, 1212
Ports, 1213
Portugal, 556
Postal Service, 1210
POSTERS AND CHARTS, 1220
Potato diseases, 52
Poultry:
poultry, 25
processing, 16
research, 13
Poverty:
MARKETING AND THE LOW INCOME CONSUMER, 122
THE POOR, 1188
POOR PEOPLE AT WORK, 1189

338

1148

Public health: *see also* Health care and services, Medical care, Medicine

CHINESE SOURCES ON MEDICINE AND PUBLIC HEALTH IN THE PEOPLE'S REPUBLIC OF CHINA, 1960--1970, 633

PUBLIC HEALTH ENGINEERING ABSTRACTS, 675

PUBLIC LANDS BIBLIOGRAPHY, 831

PUBLIC LAW 480, 120

Public opinion surveys, 933

Public service strikes, 166

Pulp and paper industry, air pollution source, 337

PULSARS, 1108--1111

Pyrometry, 1039

Pyrrone, 1034

Q

QUESTIONNAIRES FOR RESEARCH, 933

R

Raccoon, 1012

Race relations:
    Federal Racial/Ethnic Data Center, 104
    race relations, 99, 917, 104--106
    racism, 105

Radar, 1060

Radiation:
    EFFECTS OF HUMAN EXPOSURE TO RADIATION, 704
    ionizing radiation, 1102--1103
    LOW AND VERY LOW DOSE INFLUENCES OF IONIZING RADIATIONS ON CELLS AND ORGANISMS, INCLUDING MAN, 729
    radiation source technology, 962--963
    RADIO--ACTIVE OCCURRENCES IN THE U.S., 1122
    REGULATIONS, STANDARDS, AND GUIDES FOR MICRO--WAVES, ULTRAVIOLET RADITION AND RADIATION FROM LASERS AND T.V. RECEIVERS, 938
    REGULATIONS, STANDARDS, AND GUIDES PERTAINING TO MEDICAL AND DENTAL RADIATION PROTECTION, 939

RADIO AND ELECTRICITY, ELECTRONICS, RADAR, AND COMMUNICATIONS, 1060

RADIOACTIVE WASTE MANAGEMENT, 364

RADIOACTIVE WASTE PROCESSING AND DISPOSAL, 1112

341

CHEMICAL WASTEWATER TREATMENT, 410
deep well injection, 377, 406
industrial wastes, 675
LIVESTOCK WASTE MANAGEMENT, 368
SANITARY LANDFILLS, 367, 378
sewerage, 368--375, 675
SOLID WASTE MANAGEMENT, 365, 368--375
waste treatment, 315, 368--375
Sonic boom, 992
South Asia *see* Asia
Southeast Asia *see* Asia
Soviet Union:
foreign relations, 883--889
THE FUTURE, 844
invasion of Czeckoslovakia, 886
literature, 566
periodicals, 568, 570
SINO--SOVIET CONFLICT, 885
social science research, 888
SOVIET INTELLIGENCE AND SECURITY SERVICES, 1964--
70, 883a
SOVIET LITERATURE ACCESSIONS IN THE ATMOSPHERIC
SCIENCES LIBRARY AND THE GEOPHYSICAL
SCIENCES LIBRARY, 451
SOVIET MEDICINE, 634
Soviet serial publications, 568, 570
USSR STRATEGIC SURVEY, 887
Soybeans, nematodes, 50
Space science:
EFFECT OF THE SPACE ENVIRONMENT ON MAN'S
RESPONSE TO INFECTION, 1003
Orbiting Geophysical Observatory, 1005--1006
outer space, 988, 997
SPACE, MISSILES, THE MOON, NASA, AND SATELLITES,
995
space sciences, 976
space technology, 984--985
Space vehicles, 976
Spain, 556
SPANISH--LANGUAGE HEALTH COMMUNICATIONS TEACHING
AIDS, 680
SPANISH--SPEAKING AFRICA, GUIDE TO OFFICIAL PUBLI--
CATIONS, 854
SPANISH SPEAKING IN THE UNITED STATES, 98
Spectra, atomic, 1140

Spectroscopy, mass, 1020, 1098
Speech:
BIBLIOGRAPHY ON SPEECH, HEARING, AND LANGUAGE IN
IN RELATION TO MENTAL RETARDATION, 1900--
1968, 776
NEUROANATOMY OF SPEECH, 754
SPINAL CORD INJURY, 772
SPORT FISHERY ABSTRACTS, 582
SPRINKLER IRRIGATION, 1084
Spruce:
Sitka, 39
western, 42
white spruce regeneration, 38
Standards, scientific, 971, 978--982
Stark broadening, 1141
STATE, COUNTY AND MUNICIPAL PERSONNEL PUBLICATIONS,
174
State Department publications and audiovisuals, 846
STATE WATER--RIGHTS LAWS AND RELATED SUBJECTS, 829
STATES AND TERRITORIES OF THE UNITED STATES AND
THEIR RESOURCES, INCLUDING BEAUTIFICATION,
PUBLIC BUILDINGS, AND LANDS, AND RECREATIONAL
RESOURCES, 1223
STATES AND URBAN CRISIS, 830
States, publications of, 565
Statistical procedures, 739
Statistical publications, foreign, 1214
Statistical services, 110--111
STATISTICS AND MAPS FOR NATIONAL MARKET ANALYSIS,
205
Steel mills, air pollutant, 330
Sterility, 646, 752
Stores see particular type of store
Strategic Arms Limitation Talks, 908
STRATEGIC TRIAD, 908
STRATEGY AND TACTICS, 1000 A.D. -- 1970, 918
Streams, reaeration, 319
Streptococcal infections, 726--728
Strikes see Labor
Stress, COPING AND ADAPTATION, 805
Structural mechanics, 976
SUB--SAHARAN AFRICA: A GUIDE TO SERIALS, 555
SUBSURFACE WASTE DISPOSAL BY MEANS OF WELLS, 377
SUBSURFACE WATER POLLUTION, 406--408
SUBURBAN SHOPPING CENTERS, 225

SUDDEN INFANT DEATH SYNDROME, 753
Sugar, marketing, 17
SUICIDE AND SUICIDE PREVENTION, 788, 803
Sulfur, hydrides and oxides, 1043
Sulfuric acid manufacturing, air pollutant, 338
SUNFLOWER, LITERATURE SURVEY, JANUARY 1960–JUNE
1967, 58
SUPERCONDUCTING DEVICES AND MATERIALS, 1072
SUPERSONIC TRANSPORTS, 1200
Surgery, *see* specific subject
Surveying, 1089
Sweetner market, 117
SYSTEMS APPROACH TO MANAGEMENT, 183a
Syria, environment of, 309a
Swaziland, official publications, 852

T

Taiwan, 868–869, 878
TALKING BOOKS TO PROFIT BY, 549
TARIFF AND TAXATION, 1221
Tautogolabrus adspersus, 602
Taxation, 1221
Technetium--99m, medical uses, 703
Technology: *see also* specific subjects
data sources, 1134
SCIENCE AND SOCIETY, 964–965
studies in technology, 149
TECHNOLOGY ASSESSMENT, 966
TECHNOLOGY TRANSFER, 1063
Television:
broadcasting via satellite, 1062
microwave and radiation regulations, standards, and guides,
938
TECHNICAL REQUIREMENTS FOR BROADBAND CABLE
TELESERVICES, 1059
TELEVISION AND SOCIAL BEHAVIOR, 812
TELEVISION IN EDUCATION, 239
Temperature properties and measurement, 1039--1040
Tennessee Valley Authority:
program, 1227
publications, 1228
Termites, 1019
TERRESTRIAL AND FRESHWATER RADIOECOLOGY, 1124--
1127
TERRESTRIAL IMPACT STRUCTURES, BIBLIOGRAPHY 1965--

68, 479
Territories of the United States, 900, 1223
TERTIARY MARINE MOLLUSKS OF ALASKA, 599
Textiles, statistical sources, 124
Thailand, 864, 875
Thailand, climatology, 447
THERMAL DEGRADATION, THERMAL OXIDATION, AND
    THERMAL ANALYSIS OF HIGH POLYMERS, 1029–1030
Thermodynamics:
    air, 1040
    fluids, 1046
    general, 976
    HIGH TEMPERATURE CHEMISTRY AND PHYSICS OF
        MATERIALS, 1042
    methane, 1041
    mixtures, 1046
Thoman, Leroy Delano, 819
Thompson, Hugh Smith, 819
Thrombolysis, 746
Thyroid studies, 749
Tillage, 22
Traction, 22
Timber: *see also* Forests and forestry, Wood technology
    MEASUREMENT PROBLEMS IN THE DOUGLAS--FIR
        REGION, 75
    MILLING AND UTILIZATION OF TIMBER PRODUCTS, 70
TIME AND FREQUENCY, 1145
Toxicology:
    DRUG INTERACTIONS, 816
    lead, 814–815
    TOXICITY BIBLIOGRAPHY, 817
    TOXICITY OF HERBICIDES TO MAMMALS, AQUATIC LIFE,
        SOIL, MICROORGANISMS, BENEFICIAL INSECTS,
        AND CULTIVATED PLANTS, 1950--65, 10c
Trace elements, 477, 1037
Trademarks, 113
Traffic safety research, 955, 956
Trailer parks, 215
Training: *see also* Management, Personnel management
    salesmen, 192--193
    training methodology --
        audiovisuals, 190
        instruction, 189
        planning, 188
        theory, 187

Transplants:
    kidney, 747
    PSYCHOLOGICAL AND SOCIAL ASPECTS OF HUMAN
        TISSUE TRANSPLANTATION, 791–792
Transportation:
    high speed transportation, 1195–1196
    transportation, 1197
    TRANSPORTATION FOR THE HANDICAPPED, 1193
    TRANSPORTATION, HIGHWAYS, ROADS, AND POSTAL
        SERVICE, 1210
    URBAN MASS TRANSPORTATION, 1194
Transportation Department readings, 1192
TRANSPLUTONIUM ELEMENTS, 1128–1131
Trees *see* Forests and forestry, specific tree
Trenholm, William Lee, 819
TRIAD, 908
Tritium disposal, 363
Tuna, 612
TUNNEL GEOLOGY BIBLIOGRAPHY, 466

U

UFOS AND RELATED SUBJECTS, 988
Ultraviolet radiation *see* Radiation
Union of Soviet Socialist Republics *see* Soviet Union
Unions *see* Labor
UNITED STATES AND JAPAN, 863
UNITED STATES AND THE UNITED NATIONS, 843
United States future, 844
UNITED STATES IN THE CARIBBEAN, 855
UNITED STATES NAVAL HISTORY, 505
USE OF NATURALLY IMPAIRED WATER, 396
USSR AND EASTERN EUROPE, PERIODICALS IN WESTERN
    LANGUAGES, 570
Urbanology: *see also* Cities and towns
    URBAN CRISIS, BEHAVIORAL, PSYCHOLOGICAL, AND
        SOCIOLOGICAL ASPECTS OF URBAN CRISIS, 305a
    urban development, 296--305a
    URBAN MASS TRANSPORTATION, 1194
    URBAN OUTLOOK, SELECTED BIBLIOGRAPHY OF FILMS,
        FILMSTRIPS, SLIDES, AND AUDIOTAPES, 305
    urban renewal, 302
    URBAN TRANSPORTATION BIBLIOGRAPHY, 1197
    URBAN WATER PLANNING, 395
URBAN STORM WATER RUNOFF, 409a

UTILIZATION OF HEALTH SERVICES, 697
UTILIZATION OF WOOD RESIDUES, 66

V

Van der Walls broadening, 1141
Vanadium, geology and resources, 473
VARIETY STORES, 227
Vascular disease, 759
Vegetation:
    moisture loss, 53
    natural plant communities, 54
Veneer, 970
Venereal disease, 732–733
Veterans' affairs, 920
Veterinary medicine, CHAGAS' DISEASE (1909--69), 1011
Vietnam, 865, 875, 880
Viruses, Type--B and Type--C, 745
Vital and health statistics, 628, 697a--698a, 715
Vocational education:
    agriculture, 267, 273, 280
    cooperative education, 269
    distributive education, 269, 274, 281
    health occupations, 270, 275, 282
    home economics, 271, 276, 283
    office occupations, 268, 277, 284
    technical education, 278, 285
    trade and industrial education, 272, 279
    vocational education, 266--285
VOLUNTEER FORCE, ZERO DRAFT, AND SELECTIVE
    SERVICE, 909--910
VOLUNTEER SERVICES IN MENTAL HEALTH, 796

W

Wages and earnings:
    area wage surveys, 229–231
    federal workers, 236--237
    industry wage surveys, 233
    private industry, 236--237
    wages and earnings, 232
Workman's Compensation, 161
Wales, George Russell, 819
Walnut, 31
Walrus, 588
War: